PSYCHOANALYSIS
AT THE
LIMIT

PSYCHOANALYSIS

AT THE LIMIT

*Epistemology, Mind, and
the Question of Science*

EDITED BY

JON MILLS

STATE UNIVERSITY OF NEW YORK PRESS

Published by
STATE UNIVERSITY OF NEW YORK PRESS, ALBANY

© 2004 State University of New York

For information, address the State University of New York Press,
90 State Street, Suite 700, Albany, NY 12207

Production, Laurie Searl
Marketing, Michael Campochiaro

Library of Congress Cataloging-in-Publication Data

Psychoanalysis at the limit : epistemology, mind, and the question of science / [edited by]
Jon Mills.
   p. cm.
   Includes bibliographical references and index.
   ISBN 0-7914-6065-7 (alk. paper)
   1. Psychoanalysis—Philosophy. I. Mills, Jon, 1964–

BF173.P7753 2004
150.19'5—dc21   2003052605

10 9 8 7 6 5 4 3 2 1

For my mother Rachel:

Yet mothers can ponder many things in their hearts which their lips cannot express.

—*Alfred North Whitehead*

CONTENTS

PREFACE

We are approaching a Freud renaissance within the ivory tower: psycho-analysis is unequivocally in vogue in academe and has become a cardinal focus of contemporary European and North American intellectual life. We may especially observe a resurgence of interest in Freud studies as represented by the humanities and social sciences including philosophy, literature, politi-cal theory, sociology, anthropology, psychobiology, neurocognitive science, theory of culture, history, religion, feminist thought, art and film studies, and the history of ideas. Nevertheless, despite burgeoning interest in psychoana-lytic thought, psychoanalysis today is facing a crisis. Confronted with meth-odological, discursive, epistemological, and empirical challenges to theory and practice, not to mention waning public interest in psychoanalytic treat-ment, psychoanalysis continues to find itself displaced from mainstream scientific and therapeutic approaches within the behavioral sciences. Not only is psychoanalysis questioned on its scientific credibility and therapeutic efficacy from other disciplines, it is even disputed within contemporary psy-choanalysis itself.[1] Criticized for its problematic epistemology, theory of mind, and scientific merit, psychoanalysis is at the limit.

Historically within philosophy, psychoanalysis has been labeled "my-thology" by Wittgenstein, "unintelligible" by James, "illegitimate" by MacIntyre, "unscientific" by Grünbaum, and, more recently, "pseudoscience" by Cioffi.[2] Some have even gone so far as to deny the existence of the unconscious altogether,[3] thus making the whole theory and practice of psy-choanalysis a dubious enterprise to begin with. Adding to this controversy, proponents of empirical psychology claim that psychoanalysis as a discipline is withering on the vine mainly due to its lack of empirical and scientific critique, its marginalization among the fields of contemporary psychology and psychiatry, and its tendency toward self-destruction due to mismanage-ment by its adherents. Within psychoanalytic psychology, Bornstein advo-cates that only rigorous scientific and research-based interventions can resuscitate the psychoanalytic corpse.[4] In the end, both analytic philosophy and scientific psychology clamor for reform on the grounds that psychoanalysis fails as a legitimate form of science.

The conception of psychoanalysis as a science was as much a criticism of Freud's time as it is today.[5] Popper and Grünbaum argue that psychoanalysis simply fails as a natural science because it is too private, not open to clinical testing or falsification, and not modeled after physics,[6] while Sulloway and Webster decry that it must forgo the status of a serious science because it does not conform to Darwinian biology.[7] In a recent defense of psychoanalysis, Marcus Bowman argues that outdated and misapplied notions of science and positivism erroneously serve as the main resistance against accepting the value of psychoanalysis as a rational inquiry into the conditions of internal human conflict.[8] He claims that critics of psychoanalysis hold onto the illusory hope that human science should be modeled on physical science and/or evolutionary biology when these propositions themselves may be interpreted as category mistakes, distort the real practice of scientific observation that is based on consensus and agreement, and generally reflect an exaggeration of the authority of science as a touchstone to truth. Even Freud himself recognized the limits to the so-called scientific method: "We have often heard it maintained that sciences should be built up on clear and sharply defined basic concepts. In actual fact no science, not even the most exact, begins with such definitions."[9] For anyone actually working in empirical research, we all know how easy it is to statistically manipulate data: 'scientific' reports are primarily based on the theoretical beliefs of the researcher who is attempting to advocate a specific line of argument under the rubric of 'objectivity.' Freud saw through this game: "Cases which are devoted from the first to scientific purposes and treated accordingly suffer in their outcome; while the most successful cases are those in which one proceeds, as it were, without any purpose in view, allows oneself to be taken by surprise by any new turn in them, and always meets them with an open mind, free from any presuppositions."[10] But it is precisely the question of psychoanalysis *as* science that psychoanalysis itself attempts to defend. At the end of his life, Freud confirmed that psychoanalysis, like "psychology, too, is a natural science."[11]

The organization of this volume attempts to situate psychoanalysis within the philosophical context of examining its relation to science, epistemology, unconscious experience, and contemporary theories of mind. The contributors assembled here are from diverse interdisciplinary backgrounds in psychoanalysis, philosophy, and psychology and offer competing accounts—both favorable and critical—of psychoanalytic theory and practice from Freud through contemporary revisionist philosophical perspectives interfacing with variegated conceptions of mind, phenomenology, metaphysics, and the scientific status of psychoanalysis today.

Psychoanalytic phenomenology and its relation to unconscious ontology is becoming increasingly appreciated in the psychoanalytic literature. In chapter 1, M. Guy Thompson reviews specific philosophical problems inherent in Freud's conceptualization of the unconscious including unresolved aspects of his topographic and structural models as well as his thesis concerning two principles of mental functioning. Situating Sartre's phenomenological theory of consciousness, Heidegger's existential ontology, and Laing's conception of experience within psychoanalysis, Thompson offers a phenomenology of unconscious experience that is compatible with Freud's ontological commitments on unconscious processes.

In chapter 2, Roger Frie elaborates the revisionist accounts of unconscious experience developed by Binswanger and Sullivan in relation to Freud. Examining the contrast between intrapsychic and interpersonal dimensions to unconscious experience, Frie demonstrates the ways in which the unconscious remains a pivotal theoretical and clinical issue that affects our understanding of the structures of subjectivity.

In the next chapter, Marcia Cavell examines the notion of objectivity within the context of contemporary psychoanalytic conceptions of intersubjectivity and the therapeutic encounter. Arguing for an objectivist position that challenges the radical subjectivity championed by leading psychoanalytic theorists, Cavell asserts that while the epistemological process of truth and subjective reality may change, objective reality does not—truth is objective and independent from the subjective mind and the triangular, intersubjective matrix regardless of the beliefs and constructed meaning that condition our subjective experience of reality.

Leading theorists in the philosophy of mind privilege the ontology of consciousness over unconscious mental states. In chapter 4, David Livingstone Smith contrasts Freud and Searle on the ontology of unconscious activity. Smith shows that while Searle largely views unconscious processes as dispositional states of the nervous system that can only be regarded as mental because of their dispositional powers to produce conscious mental states, Freud came to prefer a theory of occurrent unconscious mental events. Smith claims that Searle's argument involves a confusion between supervenience and causation; and through the use of what he calls the continuity argument, demonstrates how Freud is able to refute dispositionalism.

In chapter 5, I examine the epistemology of paranoiac knowledge situated in Lacan's three contexts of being. Developmentally, knowledge is paranoiac because it is acquired through our imaginary relation to the other as a primordial misidentification or illusory self-recognition of autonomy, control, and mastery, thus leading to persecutory anxiety and self-alienation. Secondarily, through the symbolic structures of language and speech, desire is foisted upon us as a foreboding demand threatening to invade and destroy our uniquely subjective inner experiences. And finally, the process of knowing itself is paranoiac because it horrifically confronts the real, namely, the unknown. Through an examination of a clinical case study, paranoiac knowledge manifests itself as the desire not to know.

Among Anglo-American analytic philosophy, the question and status of psychoanalysis as a legitimate science has been a grave source of controversy. In chapter 6, James C. Edwards explores Wittgenstein's critique of Freud as allegedly inventing a new mythology rather than a new science. By examining the uncanny character of both the phenomena of dreams and neuroses, as well as the kinds of interpretation Freud offers to explain such phenomena, Edwards shows that the force of Wittgenstein's argument is that Freud's mystique is wedded in how beautifully he matches the uncanniness of the phenomena to be explained with the uncanniness of the explanation itself. For Wittgenstein, Freud's ideas are dangerous because he posits a metaphysics of true explanation rather than a description of psychic events.

In the next chapter, Adolf Grünbaum argues for a scientific conception of psychoanalysis through a scathing criticism of the hermeneutic critique characterized by many European continental philosophers. Grünbaum convincingly shows that Freud envisioned psychoanalysis as a science rather than as a theory of meaning, but in Grünbaum's signature way, he goes on to challenge the psychoanalytic conception of science and the epistemologically problematic causal inferences Freud himself purports. Through examining examples from Freud's case studies on dreams, symptoms, and transference, he argues that a hermeneutic account of psychoanalysis does little to explain unconscious motivations and etiologic inferences, accounts for which Grünbaum thinks are illegitimate claims that psychoanalysis makes in the first place.

In chapter 8, Joseph Margolis contrasts the essentially biological nature of the unconscious in Freud's system with the Lacanian notion of the unconscious as a cultural medium. Challenging traditional criticisms and materialist accounts that psychoanalysis is not science, Margolis advocates for a viable theory of science that appropriates our folk-theoretic descriptions and explanations of human experience. Juxtaposed to the paradox of the Lacanian subject that is subverted through language and culturally determined, Margolis reinforces the Freudian implication that all modes of inquiry into objective determinations are already infused with unconscious subjective dynamics informing such determinations.

In our final chapter, Donald Levy examines the question of incompleteness and experimental untestability in psychoanalysis. Drawing on Freud's own words about the limitations of psychoanalysis, Levy addresses what many analytic philosophers consider to be the single most important criticism of psychoanalysis: namely, the charge that psychoanalytic claims consistently fail when subjected to experimental testing, and that this failure properly discredits psychoanalysis as a science. By revisiting the assent criterion and its relation to the problem of psychoanalytic interpretation, Levy argues that the 'failure' of interpretation is not because of a lack of empirical verifiablity, rather, what is revealed by that 'failure' is the inapplicability of experimental testing and the inescapability of the assent criterion.

Taken together, this volume offers an important and impelling reexamination of the question of science, epistemology, and lived unconscious experience in psychoanalytic theory and practice. One aspiration Freud harbored was that psychoanalysis, which he ultimately defined as "the science of unconscious mental processes," would inspire appreciation among the disparate fields that psychoanalysis itself attempts to explain. In the end, Freud was humble: "Something will become of . . . my life's labours . . . in the future, though I cannot myself tell whether it will be much or little. I can, however, express a hope that I have opened up a pathway for an important advance in our knowledge."[12]

NOTES

1. Contemporary relational and intersubjective approaches to psychoanalysis have largely displaced classical psychoanalytic theory and practice, instead emphasizing the domain of consciousness over the unconscious, the interpersonal present versus the intrapsychic past, and the primacy on affective relatedness rather than on insight in psychoanalytic cure. For a critique, see J. Mills, ed., *Relational and Intersubjective Perspectives in Psychoanalysis* (Northvale, NJ: Aronson, 2004).

2. Cf. Ludwig Wittgenstein, *The Blue and Brown Books* (Oxford: Blackwell, 1958) [First dictated in 1933–1934]; "Conversations on Freud." In C. Barrett, ed., *Lectures and Conversations on Aesthetics, Psychology and Religious Belief* (Berkeley: University of California Press, 1966); William James, *The Principles of Psychology*, 2 Vols. (New York: Dover, 1890/1950); Alasdair MacIntyre, *The Unconscious: A Conceptual Study* (London: Routledge, 1958); Adolf Grünbaum, *The Foundations of Psychoanalysis* (Berkeley: University of California Press, 1984); and Frank Cioffi, *Freud and the Question of Pseudoscience* (Chicago: Open Court, 1998).

3. See Richard Webster, *Why Freud Was Wrong: Sin, Science, and Psychoanalysis* (New York, Basic Books, 1995); also see Sartre's existential critique in *Being and Nothingness*, H. Barnes, trans. (New York: Washington Square Press, 1943/1956), and T. R. Miles, *Eliminating the Unconscious* (Oxford: Pergamon Press, 1966).

4. See Robert F. Bornstein, The Impending Death of Psychoanalysis, *Psychoanalytic Psychology*, 18, no. 1 (2001): 3–20. Also see my critique of Bornstein: J. Mills, Reexamining the Psychoanalytic Corpse: From Scientific Psychology to Philosophy, *Psychoanalytic Psychology*, 19, no. 3 (2002): 552–558.

5. Freud states: "I have always felt it a gross injustice that people have refused to treat psychoanalysis like any other science" *Standard Edition*, Vol. 20, 1925, 58.

6. See Popper, *Conjectures and Refutation* (London: Routledge, 1972); Grünbaum, *The Foundations of Psychoanalysis* (Berkeley: University of California Press, 1984).

7. Cf. Frank Sulloway, *Freud: Biologist of the Mind* (London: Harper Collins, 1979); Richard Webster, *Why Freud Was Wrong* (New York: Basic Books, 1995).

8. Cf. Marcus Bowman, *The Last Resistance: The Concept of Science as a Defense Against Psychoanalysis* (Albany: State University of New York Press, 2002).

9. "Instincts and their Vicissitudes," *Standard Edition*, Vol. 14, 1915, 117.

10. S. Freud, "Recommendations to Physicians Practising Psycho-Analysis," *Standard Edition*, Vol. 12, 1912, 114.

11. See "Some Elementary Lessons in Psycho-Analysis," *Standard Edition*, Vol. 23, 1940, 282.

12. Freud, "An Autobiographical Study," *Standard Edition*, 1925, Vol. 20, 70.

ACKNOWLEDGMENTS

I wish to sincerely thank Andrew MacRae and the Research Institute at Lakeridge Health for providing me with a research grant for this project. I am also appreciative of the critiques and constructive suggestions that were offered from the anonymous reviewers who evaluated this volume. The following essays have been published in previous forms, and I wish to thank the publishers for permission to reproduce them here: Chapter 1, "Is the Unconscious Really all that Unconscious?: The Role of Being and Experience in the Psychoanalytic Encounter." *Contemporary Psychoanalysis,* (2001) 37 (4), 571–612; Chapter 3, "Triangulation, Objectivity, and One's Own Mind." *International Journal of Psycho-Analysis,* (1998), 79, 449–469; Chapter 5, "Lacan on Paranoiac Knowledge." *Psychoanalytic Psychology,* (2003), 20(1), 30–51; and Chapter 7, "The Hermeneutic Versus the Scientific Conception of Psychoanalysis: An Unsuccessful Effort to Chart a *Via Media* For the Human Sciences." In D. Aerts et al., (Eds), *The White Book of Einstein Meets Magritte* (Dordrecht: Kluwer Academic Publishers, 1999, 219–239). Most important, I am deeply grateful to Jane Bunker, Senior Acquisitions Editor, and Laurie Searl, Senior Production Editor, State University of New York Press, for their continued support, encouragement, and interest in my work.

Every science is based on observations and experiences arrived at through the medium of our psychical apparatus.

—Freud

ONE

THE ROLE OF BEING AND EXPERIENCE IN FREUD'S UNCONSCIOUS ONTOLOGY

M. GUY THOMPSON

THERE IS LITTLE QUESTION in the minds of every psychoanalytic practitioner that Freud's conception of the unconscious is the pivot around which psychoanalysis orbits, even if the particulars as to what the unconscious comprises has been debated by every psychoanalytic school that has followed in his wake.[1] Yet despite the controversial nature of this concept, there is a pervasive agreement among analysts that whatever the unconscious is, it is certainly not a form of *consciousness*. That being said, this is precisely the dilemma that philosophers have found most troubling about the psychoanalytic conception of the unconscious and the reason why so many have questioned its efficacy. In a recent book, Grotstein[2] addressed a fundamental and as yet unresolved difficulty in prevailing conceptions of the unconscious, which follows when we attempt to assign the very core of our being to a hypothesized unconscious agent that we can never know directly, and whose existence we must infer and, hence, *believe* to be so, as an article of faith. Grotstein concluded that we are still, after one hundred years of trying, unable to account for this persistent yet obstinate contradiction: that the unconscious knows all, but is "known" by no one.

Like many, I have been haunted by this anomaly over the course of my analytic career. For the purposes of this chapter, however, my concern is not a theoretical one but one of approaching the problem phenomenologically—that is, from the perspective of the psychoanalyst's *lived experience*, what has

1

been depicted by the interpersonal school as an experience-near paradigm. Therefore, I do not intend to offer a new theory about the nature of the unconscious but rather to explore the relationship between the alleged existence of the unconscious and one's experience of it. In the course of my exploration of this problem I address a number of critical questions: Does it make sense, for example, to speak in terms of one's capacity to "experience" the unconscious if the very concept of the unconscious refers to that which is beyond experience? Moreover, does it make sense to talk in terms of suffering "unconscious experiences" if one is not *aware* of the experiences one is presumed to be suffering? And finally, allowing that experience is, at its margins, tentative and ambiguous, how does one account for those phenomena on the periphery of experience, whether such phenomena are characterized as unconscious (Freud), ambiguous (Merleau-Ponty), mysterious (Heidegger), unformulated (Sullivan), or simply hidden?

I do not claim to have found the answers to these questions or even to advance a preliminary step in that direction. Instead, I merely seek to explore some of the problematics that the psychoanalytic conception of the unconscious has obliged us to live with ever since Freud formulated it one century ago. First, I review Freud's depiction of the unconscious in relation to his conception of psychical reality, and then turn to some of the philosophical problems that derive from his characterization of the "two types" of mental functioning, primary and secondary thought processes. Finally, I review some of the implications that derive from the psychoanalytic conception of the unconscious by employing a phenomenological critique of its presuppositions, and exploring the role of Being and experience in Freud's conception of the psychoanalytic encounter. Though my concern is strictly theoretical, it is nonetheless philosophical because the questions raised are of a philosophical nature. While I am aware of the fact that numerous psychoanalysts since Freud have endeavored to situate his conception of the unconscious in the light of subsequent theoretical developments, my purpose is not to assess these developments with a view to contrasting them with Freud's. Instead, I review the problematics of Freud's thesis in the light of those philosophers whose perspective is at odds with the very notion of an "unconscious" portion of the mind and who endeavor to situate the phenomena that Freud deemed unconscious in the context of consciousness itself, or in the case of Heidegger one that dispenses with the conscious-unconscious controversy altogether. To this end I will propose that the Freudian unconscious is a form of sentient, nascent "consciousness" (implied in Freud's own depiction of it) but a form of consciousness that is unavailable to *experience*. Hence I characterize the purpose of the psychoanalytic endeavor as one of bringing those aspects of consciousness that lie on the periphery of experience to experience, to the degree that is feasible in each case.

FREUD'S CONCEPTION OF PSYCHIC REALITY

Freud's first topography for demarcating the distinction between conscious and unconscious aspects of the mind concerned the nature of fantasy and the role it plays in the life of the neurotic. As a consequence of his experiments with hypnotism Freud surmised that every individual is driven by two kinds of fantasies: one of which one is aware and the other of which one is unaware. Freud opted to term those of which one is unaware "unconscious" because we have no conscious experience of them, but are nonetheless capable of discerning their existence when hypnotized. Such so-called unconscious fantasies have been repressed, but because they reside "in" the unconscious they engender psychic conflict, the manifestation of which accounts for psychopathology, dream formation, and parapraxes.

Thus Freud's first, topographical model of the unconscious was relatively simple: one portion of the mind is conscious and the thoughts it contains are in the forefront of awareness (or *conscious experience*), whereas another portion of the mind is unconscious and is composed of fantasies that have suffered repression (or more primitive defense mechanisms). Freud also included a third element in this topography, the "preconscious," which contains thoughts and memories that, though not immediately conscious, are nonetheless available to consciousness in principle. Freud's earlier topography is essentially an outline of the vicissitudes of the individual's psychic life, what Freud termed psychic reality. Freud's depiction of psychic reality is not, however, predicated on the kind of factual reality that is investigated by the empirical sciences, because it is a kind of "reality" that one *experiences* in the form of fantasy, delusion, or hallucination. Quoting Freud: "What lie behind the sense of guilt of neurotics [for example] are always *psychical* realities and never *factual* ones. What characterizes neurotics is that they prefer psychical to factual reality and react just as seriously to thoughts as normal people do to realities."[3] Yet in what sense can one treat such fantasies as "realities" when they are not *real?* Freud recognized that fantasies can be experienced as real in the same way that objective reality, which is to say, that which is not our invention, is typically experienced. In other words, fantasies, though not literal depictions of the past, nevertheless convey meaning, and such meanings are capable of telling us more about our patients than the so-called facts of their history. By interpreting both fantasies and symptoms as meaningful, Freud was able to obtain truths about his patients that were otherwise hidden. His opposition between "psychic" and "external" realities served to juxtapose an inherently personal reality with a more literal one. This isn't to say that literal, or objective, reality is necessarily false, but it was Freud's genius to see that the truth about one's history can be derived from the communication of otherwise innocuous musings, by interpreting a patient's fantasies as disguised messages. The recognition that fantasies could be conceived as messages suggested there was something "hidden" in them that the patient neither recognized nor appreciated.

Hence, fantasies serve a purpose: they disclose the intentional structure of the individual's deepest longings and aspirations. But Freud lacked a conception of intentionality that could explain how his patients were able to convey truths they didn't "know" in a disguised and indirect manner. In other words, his patients *unconsciously intended* their symptoms and the attendant fantasies that explained them; they weren't "caused" by their unconscious. Freud nevertheless suspected the existence of an unconscious form of subjectivity that was capable of intending symptoms when he coined the term *counter-will* in one of his earliest papers. Leavy brought attention to Freud's difficulty in grappling with the notion of an "unconscious subject" in a study of the development of Freud's psychoanalytic theories:

> One of Freud's earliest ways of presenting the idea of unconscious motivation was as "counter-will" (Gegenwille), a word that is worth keeping in mind whenever we say "the unconscious." Will, so rich in philosophical overtones, has been played down by psychoanalysis. Being a verb as well as a noun, the word will always implies a subject. When I do something that I claim I didn't want to do . . . it does no good to plead that blind, impersonal, unconscious forces "did" the act: *they* are *me*.[4] (emphases added)

Leavy's use of the term *will* is not, of course, limited to the conventional usage of *conscious* will, any more than Freud's expression *counter-will* is. The term will refers to an intentional act that often alludes to *pre-reflective* (or "unconscious") sources of motivation. Freud first used the term counter-will in a paper on hypnotism in which he referred to an idea that the patient is unaware of, but was brought to conscious awareness under hypnosis.[5] Freud continued to use the term in a variety of contexts for some twenty years. The last time he apparently used it was in a paper on love and sexual impotence that was published in 1912. Leavy notes that the term seems to have disappeared thereafter. According to Leavy, "Probably the generalization fell apart into concepts like resistance, repression, unconscious conflict, and ultimately, drive. But the gain in specificity was accompanied by the loss of the implication of a personal 'will.' "[6]

As Freud pursued his project of establishing the empirical "causes" of symptoms, his earlier notion of the unconscious as a subtle agent, or anonymous ego, or counter-will, receded into the background. Yet the tendency to depersonalize the unconscious into impersonal drives and forces has not met with universal acceptance, even in psychoanalytic circles. The term "drive" was scarcely used before 1905, though the concept was there under other guises. Yet expressions like "affective ideas" and "wishful impulses" clearly convey more subjective nuances than the terms *drive* or *excitations*, for example. With all the current debate over Strachey's translation of Freud into English, especially the translation of *Trieb* into either "drive" or "instinct," neither the use of *Trieb* or drive alters Freud's understanding of the concept.

Whichever term one prefers, whether drive or instinct, psychoanalysts, with few exceptions, find it agreeable to use a term in which the impersonal aspect of the unconscious predominates. One of those exceptions, in addition to Leavy, was Hans Loewald, who took considerable care to explain how his use of the term *instinct* was intended to convey a human quality. According to Loewald: "When I speak of instinctual forces and of instincts or instinctual drives, I define them as motivational, i.e., both motivated and motivating. . . . [For me] instincts remain relational phenomena, rather than being considered energies within a closed system."[7]

Terms such as *motive* and *relational* lend a clearly personal nuance to the term *instinct*, and even the word *phenomena* sounds more personal than *forces*. If Freud's shift from counter-will to drive lent credence to his claim that psychoanalysis, at least in appearance, deserved the status of a science, it is nevertheless a science more similar to that of academic psychologists who "study" rats or physicists who "measure" energies. However much some analysts may strive to measure the psychoanalytic experience in specifically scientific terms, the legitimacy of one's fantasy life can only be grasped metaphorically and experientially, in terms that remain personal in nature.[8]

FREUD'S FORMULATION OF TWO TYPES OF MENTAL FUNCTIONING

After Freud formulated his theory of the structural model in 1923, his earlier allusions to the unconscious as a "second subject" that behaved as a "counter-will" gradually disappeared. The precedent for this revision was predetermined even earlier by Freud's distinction between primary and secondary thought processes. Indeed, the publication of Freud's "Formulations on the Two Principles of Mental Functioning" in 1911[9] roughly coincided with his final reference to the unconscious as "counter-will" in 1912.

In this formulation Freud conceived the primary thought processes as essentially "unconscious." Hence they were deemed to account for such psychic phenomena as displacement, condensation, the ability to symbolize and apprehend time and syntax, as well as dreaming. Since the primary thought processes are supposed to be governed by the pleasure principle they are responsible for that portion of the mind that "strives toward gaining pleasure" and withdraws from "any event that might arouse [pain]."[10] More to the point, Freud held that unconscious processes were "the older, primary processes [and] the residues of a phase of development in which they were the only kind of mental process" that was available to the infant.[11] Thus, whatever the infant wished for, says Freud, "was simply presented in a hallucinatory manner, just as still happens today with our dream-thoughts each night."[12]

However primitive the primary thought processes may seem, they are nonetheless perfectly capable of sensing that when the infant's hallucinatory anticipation of pleasure fails to materialize, another means of obtaining gratification must be substituted in its place. Moreover, the primary thought processes are also presumed to be capable of "experiencing" disappointment, leading to the necessity for another means of engaging the world. Quoting Freud:

> It was . . . the non-occurrence of the expected satisfaction, the disappointment *experienced*, that led to the abandonment of this attempt at satisfaction by means of hallucination. Instead of it, the psychical apparatus *had to decide* to form a conception of the real circumstances in the external world and to endeavor to make a real alteration in them. A new principle of mental functioning was thus introduced; what was presented in the mind was no longer what was agreeable but what was real, even if it happened to be disagreeable, [thus paving the way for] setting up the reality principle.[13] (emphases added)

Freud's conception of the unconscious is based more or less entirely on the distinction between these two principles of thinking. Now the secondary thought processes, governed by the reality principle, assume responsibility for the individual's relationship with the social world, including the capacity for rationality, logic, grammar, and verbalization. It doesn't take much reflection to see that there is something unwieldy, even contradictory, about the way Freud unceremoniously divides facets of the mind between these two principles of mental functioning. For example, if the primary thought processes are only capable of striving toward pleasure and avoiding unpleasure, and the secondary thought processes are in turn responsible for delaying gratification while formulating plans in pursuit of one's goals, to *what* or *whom* is Freud referring when he suggests that it is the "psychical apparatus" that "decides to form a conception of the real circumstances" encountered, and then "endeavors to make a real alteration in them"?[14] Is the so-called "psychical apparatus" (*Seele* in German, or "soul") the primary, or the secondary, thought processes?

We can presumably eliminate the secondary thought processes from this logical conundrum since Freud just explained that the *psychical apparatus* (whatever that is) was obliged to bring these very processes *into being* in the first place. On the other hand, we can also eliminate the primary thought processes from contention since Freud proposes the need for a more realistic mode of thinking than already existed, precisely because the primary processes are, by definition, incapable of executing them.

Many of the questions that Grotstein raises in response to Freud's formulation of the two types of mental functioning are devoted to the need to find a resolution to this problem, and there has been no shortage of subsequent analysts who have raised this point. For example, Charles Rycroft questioned Freud's conception of the "two types" of thinking in his 1962 paper, "Beyond the Reality Principle."[15] There he questions whether it makes sense to insist that the primary thought processes necessarily precede the secondary ones. Rycroft notes that even Freud doubted it, since according to a footnote in his paper on the "Two Principles of Mental Functioning," Freud himself admitted that

> It will rightly be objected that an organization which was a slave to the pleasure-principle and neglected the reality of the external world could not maintain itself alive for the shortest time, so that it could not come into existence at all. The employment of a fiction like this is, however, justified when one considers that the infant—provided that one includes with it the care it receives from its mother—does almost realize a psychical system of this kind.[16]

Freud might have added to this "fiction" the notion that the infant is as helpless as Freud suggests before it elicits the "protection" of its developing ego. Rycroft observes, "Freud's notion that the primary processes precede the secondary in individual development was dependent on . . . the helplessness of the infant and his having therefore assumed that the mother-infant relationship . . . was one in which the mother was in touch with reality while the infant only had wishes."[17] Again, we cannot help being struck by the notion that the infant needs somebody else (in this case, the mother or, later, an ego) to grapple with the social world *on its behalf.* Rycroft concurs with the view of many child analysts that infants aren't as helpless as Freud supposed. According to Rycroft:

> If one starts from the assumption that the mother is the infant's external reality and that the mother–infant relationship is from the very beginning a process of mental adaptation, to which the infant contributes by actions such as crying, clinging, and sucking, which evoke maternal responses in the mother, one is forced to conclude that the infant engages in realistic and adaptive behavior [from the very start].[18]

Rycroft concludes that the secondary thought processes probably operate earlier than Freud suspected and that they even coincide with primary process thinking. Even if Freud was right in proposing that infants are indeed ruled by primary thought processes, what if those processes happen to include those very qualities he attributed to the secondary, such as rationality, judgment, and decision making, even an acute grasp of reality? Wouldn't such a scenario, in turn, negate the utility of the ego's so-called synthetic powers? If Freud's *original* formulation of the ego is retained—that it is essentially defensive in nature—then the so-called unconscious id that is governed by the primary thought processes could be conceived as *a form of consciousness*. Freud's wish to distinguish between two types of thinking could be retained, but only after remodeling their capacities and functions. Paradoxically, what I am proposing would in many ways reverse Freud's schema. The primary thought processes, which I propose are "conscious" but prereflective and, hence, not *experienced*, enjoy a spontaneous relationship with the social world, while the secondary thought processes—those employing the tasks of reflective consciousness—determine the individual's relationship with him- or herself.

The nature of subjectivity has always puzzled philosophers and psychologists alike. Freud's depiction of an "unconscious" agency whose designs need to be interpreted to be understood was his singular contribution to our age. But his theories could never explain what his intuition was capable of perceiving. Freud hypothesized some sort of self, or agency, prior to the formation of the ego. This was supported by his theory of primary thought processes and, in another context, by his conception of primary narcissism. We know that the id is capable of thought because, after all, it decided to form an extension of itself—the ego—to insulate itself against the anxiety of being in the world.

In practical terms, the division between the id and the ego is a false one. As Freud himself acknowledged, the ego is merely an "outer layer" of the id; it was never conceived as a separate entity. If we expect to be consistent with the ego's origins, then that ego—following even Freud's reasoning—is nothing more than a "reservoir" of anxiety; in fact, our experience of anxiety itself.

SARTRE'S CRITIQUE OF THE UNCONSCIOUS

Given all the attendant problems that Freud's conception of the unconscious has elicited, it is surprising that there is little, if any, attention paid to the prevailing conception of consciousness it presupposes. Whereas Freud depicted psychoanalysis as essentially a science of the unconscious, it is impossible to escape the observation that it is also a science, if we can call it that, that is preoccupied with consciousness itself, if only implicitly. Terms like truth, epistemology, knowledge, understanding, and comprehension pervade virtually every psychoanalytic paper that is devoted to the unconscious as a concept. But isn't our fascination about the unconscious and our failure to resolve questions about its nature a consequence of our obsession with "consciousness" and the epistemological bias it engenders?

These are among the questions that phenomenologists such as Jean-Paul Sartre, Maurice Merleau-Ponty, Martin Heidegger, and Paul Ricoeur devoted the bulk of their philosophical writings to: what is the importance of knowledge and what role does it serve in our everyday lives? Of all the phenomenologists, it was perhaps Sartre who took psychoanalysis the most seriously, even conceiving his own brand of "existential psychoanalysis."[19] Fascinated with Freud the man as well as his project, Sartre was also a Frenchman and, like all French philosophers, was preoccupied with the nature of rationality, a legacy of Descartes. Yet Sartre's fascination with Freud alerted him at a very early stage of his intellectual development to the problems I have summarized earlier.

Sartre[20, 21] rejected Freud's topographical model for reasons similar to Freud's. In Freud's earlier topographical model the only thing separating the system-conscious from the system-unconscious is the so-called censor that serves to regulate what is permitted into consciousness and, contrariwise, what is repressed into the unconscious. Hence the censor is aware of everything, what is conscious and unconscious alike. Yet because the ego is unaware of the censor, this model posits a "second consciousness" (the censor) that is both unknown and unknowable to the ego in principle. Sartre's problem with this model is obvious: the so-called censor is the de facto "person" who is being analyzed and who disclaims knowledge of all the shannanigans he employs to disguise what he is up to, "bad faith" in its essence. As we saw earlier, Freud also had problems with the implications of a "second thinking subject," and decided to discard this model for a more ambiguous one that contained only one subject that *knows*, the conscious portion of the ego, and not one but *three* subjects (i.e., "agencies") that do not know: the id, the superego, and that portion of the ego that is responsible for defense mechanisms (although, it must be added, the individual is arguably aware of some aspects of the superego, the id, and even defensive maneuvers).

Freud's subsequent revision of his earlier model, however, fares little better in Sartre's opinion. The topographical model is replaced with one that is less concerned with demarcating conscious and unconscious portions of the psyche than with determining the complex nature of psychic agency, or subjectivity. Although the two models are not completely complementary, it is easy to recognize those elements of the second model that were intended to remedy the problems engendered by the first. Now the id more or less assumes the role of the system-unconscious, whereas the ego more or less assumes the tasks of the system-conscious. Ironically, the system-preconscious does not enjoy a direct parallel with the third agency in Freud's new apparatus, the superego; instead, the superego adopts some of the functions of the now-abandoned censor, due to its ability to prohibit those wishes and desires it deems unacceptable. Sartre's principal complaint with the new model is that it still fails to resolve the problem of bad faith, the problem of a "lie without a liar." If anything, the new model gets even further away from Sartre's efforts to personalize the unconscious, by instituting three psychic agencies that protect the conscious ego from any responsibility for its actions. How would Sartre propose to remedy this situation, to account for those actions that Freud claimed the "conscious" patient is "unconscious" of devising, while holding the conscious patient responsible for performing them?

Sartre accomplishes this by introducing two sets of critical distinctions into the prevailing psychoanalytic vocabulary. The first is a distinction between *pre-reflective* consciousness and *reflective* consciousness, and the second is between *consciousness* and *knowledge*. Sartre summarizes the basic dilemma in Freud's conception of the unconscious, contained in both the topographical and structural models, with the following questions: How can the subject (a divided "subject" notwithstanding) not know that she is possessed of a feeling or sentiment that she is in possession of? And if, indeed, the unconscious is just another word for consciousness (Sartre's position), how can the subject, even by Sartre's reckoning, not know what she is "conscious" of? Sartre's thesis of "pre-reflective" consciousness, probably derived from Brentano, is his effort to solve this riddle. Following Husserl's thesis, Sartre saw consciousness as *intentional,* which means it is always conscious *of something.* Hence there is no such thing as "empty" consciousness; nor is there such a thing as a "container" or "receptacle" that houses consciousness, a formulation that rejects not only Freud's thesis but Melanie Klein's "part-objects" hypothesis as well. Rather, consciousness is always "outside" itself and "in" the things that constitute it *as* consciousness-of something. In Sartre's words: "Intentionality is not the way in which a subject tries to make "contact" with an object that exists beside it. *Intentionality is what makes up the very subjectivity of subjects.*"[22] In other words, the concept of intentionality renders subjectivity as already and in its essence a *theory of intersubjectivity,* since to be a subject is, by necessity, to be engaged with some thing "other" than one's self, even if this other something is just an idea (including the act of self-awareness). Sartre elaborates how this thesis would be applied to the social world specifically:

> When I run after a streetcar, when I look at the time, when I am absorbed in contemplating a portrait, there is no *I* (or "ego"). There is [only] consciousness *of the streetcar-having-to-be-overtaken,* etc. . . . In fact, I am then plunged into the world of objects; it is *they* which constitute the unity of my consciousness; it is *they* which present themselves with values, with attractive and repellent qualities—but *me*—I have disappeared; I have annihilated myself [in the moment of conscious apprehension].[23]

Thus, when I experience a rock, a tree, a feeling of sadness, or the object of my desire in the bedroom, I experience them just where they are: beside a hill, in the meadow, in my heart, in relation to myself and my beloved. Consciousness and the object-of-consciousness are given at one stroke. These things constitute my consciousness of them just as I constitute their existence *as* things through the act in which I perceive them and give them a name. And because naming things is a purely human activity, these things, says Sartre, do not exist as rocks, trees, or emotions in the absence of a human consciousness that is capable of apprehending them through the constitutive power of language.

However, such acts of apprehension do not necessarily imply "knowledge" of what I am conscious of. Sartre makes a distinction between the pre-reflective apprehension of an object and our reflective "witnessing" of the act. Ordinarily when I am pre-reflectively conscious of a feeling, for example, I intuit the feeling of sadness and, in turn, reflectively acknowledge this feeling *as* sadness: I feel sad and experience myself as a sad individual more or less simultaneously. But I am also capable of feeling sadness, or anger, or envy without *knowing* I am sad, or angry, or envious, as such. When such a state is pointed out to me by my analyst I am surprised to be alerted to this observation. Of course, I may resist the analyst's intervention and reject it, but I may also admit it because, on being alerted to this possibility, I am also capable of recognizing this feeling *as mine*. Sartre argues that I would be incapable of recognizing thoughts or ideas that I claim no awareness of *unless I had been conscious of these feelings in the first place on a pre-reflective level.*

In other words, what Freud labels consciousness Sartre designates "reflective consciousness" (i.e., knowing *that* I am conscious of it) and what Freud labels the unconscious (or preconscious) Sartre designates as that moment of pre-reflective consciousness that, due to resistance, has not yielded to reflective awareness and, hence, to "knowledge" of it, after the fact. This is why I can be conscious of something that I have no immediate knowledge of, and why I can become knowledgeable about something that I am, so to speak, "unconscious" of, but am subsequently able to recognize as mine when a timely interpretation alerts me to it. Thus, I can only *experience* something I have knowledge of, not what I am merely "conscious" of. The power of analysis, according to Sartre, lies in its capacity to "arrest" time for the patient, by allowing the neurotic (or psychotic) the opportunity to slow the pace of his anxiety-ridden experience to ponder what his experience is, in its immediacy.

Of course, the decisive difference between Sartre's and Freud's respective formulations isn't that it merely substitutes Freud's terminology with Sartre's; on a more radical level it eliminates a need for the notion of a "second thinking subject" *behind* or *beneath* consciousness, and ultimately offers a means for personalizing the unconscious in a manner that Freud was unable to. There are still problems, however, even with Sartre's formulation. Because Sartre shared with Freud an obsession with the nature of consciousness, he went even further than Freud and eliminated the need for an "unconscious" altogether, replacing Freud's formulation with a model that was rooted solely in a theory of consciousness, a solution that was even more rationalistic than Freud's. Sartre even acknowledged late in life that his earlier project had been too indebted to Descartes and suffered from being infused with rationalism, as though "comprehension" is the final arbiter to psychic liberation.

Ironically, despite Freud's preoccupation with epistemology, he moved away from his earlier bent toward intellectualism and subsequently adopted the more skeptical position that knowledge, per se, plays a limited role in the psychoanalytic experience. The move away from interpretative schemes toward transference (and, more recently, relational) conceptualizations of psychoanalysis reflect the growing influence of phenomenology, skepticism, and hermeneutics on psychoanalytic practice. If we want to find a philosophical model that can integrate all these influences, however, we will not find it in Sartre but in someone who was a mentor to him in the earliest days of his intellectual development: Martin Heidegger. I will now review those elements of Heidegger's philosophy that appear to solve the problem of the unconscious that neither Freud or Sartre were able to.

HEIDEGGER'S CONCEPTION OF BEING AND EXPERIENCE

Although he was never all that interested in psychoanalysis and what little he knew of it dismayed him, there are many aspects of Heidegger's philosophy that are sympathetic with it. Unlike Sartre and Freud, Heidegger was not interested in the nature of consciousness, per se, because he thought it tended to psycholigize our conception of human experience instead of getting to its roots. Heidegger's reasons for taking this position were complex, but at the heart of them was a conviction that epistemology is not a viable means for getting to the bottom of what our suffering is about. Of all the phenomenologists of his generation, Heidegger was alone in conceiving philosophy as a therapy whose purpose is to heal the human soul. This made Heidegger unpopular with academic philosophers but a valuable resource to a group of European psychiatrists and psychoanalysts who saw in his work a humanistic alternative to Freud's penchant for theory. Ironically, many of them, including Medard Boss, Ludwig Binswanger, Eugene Minkowski, and Viktor Frankl, threw out the baby with the bathwater in their haste to separate themselves from the psychoanalytic *Zeitgeist* by replacing it with Heidegger as the basis for their clinical theories. This culminated in the impoverishment of both traditions, and only a handful of psychoanalysts (e.g., Hans Loewald, Stanley Leavy, Paul Federn, and R. D. Laing) sought to integrate elements of Heidegger's philosophy into Freud's conception of psychoanalysis.

Heidegger is probably most famous for his decision to root his philosophy in ontology, the study of Being, instead of epistemology, the study of knowledge. This is irritating to philosophers and psychologists alike because it discards epistemological questions in favor of a fundamental critique of what human existence is about. This is a topic that most people would prefer to leave alone, for why question the "why" of our existence when it is patently obvious that we, in fact, exist? But Heidegger was not simply interested in why we exist but how, and to what end. For example, when I pause to take stock of myself by asking, "Who am I?" I am asking the question about the *meaning of Being*. In fact, we submit to Being all the time, but without knowing it. Whenever we are engaged in writing a paper, painting a picture, driving a car, or riding a bicycle, we "let go" of our rational and conscious control of the world and in that letting-go we submit to Being, an experience that, by its nature, we cannot think our way through. Arguably the most radical critic of Descartes's rationalistic constitution of subjectivity, Heidegger countered that we live our lives in an everyday sort of way *without* thinking about what we are doing and, more important, without having to think our way through our activities as a matter of course. The place he assigned to reason is, in effect, an after-the-fact operation that is not primary to our engagement with the world, but secondary; it is only when our involvement with the world breaks down that we take the time to divorce ourselves from it for the purpose of pondering what has happened and why.

Contrary to both Husserl and Sartre who believed it is possible to employ the conscious portion of the mind to fathom the bedrock of who I am in tandem with the choices that determine my subjectivity, Heidegger countered that it is impossible to ever get "behind" our constitutive acts in such a way that we can determine the acts we intend to embark on *before* committing them. Whereas Sartre argued that I "choose" the person that I am and can always change who I am by choosing to be someone else, Heidegger observed that my ability to comprehend the choices I make necessarily occurs *after* the fact, so that I am always endeavoring to "discover" (or disclose) the acts I have already made in a world that is not my construction but always "other" to my intent or volition. This is because I am always embedded in a situation that is imbued with moods and feelings that conspire to influence my choices before I am ever conscious of having made them. Thus, my experience of myself is one of having been "thrown" into the situation I find myself in, and then collecting myself to fathom how I got here and what my motives have been, afterward.

Hence, more primary for Heidegger than the comprehension of the world (Descartes), the search for pleasure (Freud), or relief from anxiety (Melanie Klein) is the *need to orient* ourselves at every moment in time, by asking ourselves: Where are we, what are we doing here, to what do we belong? It is my sense of "who" I am to ask this question that constitutes me in my existence. Although the question of who-ness is the foundation of Heidegger's philosophy, it is important to understand that this is not a psychological question of identity, as per Erikson, but an ontological question of Being, because it is bigger than the psyche or the self. At bottom, this question is presupposed when we query the role of the unconscious, but it replaces Freud's psychologization of this question with an existential one. If one removes these questions from a strictly philosophical context and inserts them into one that is specifically clinical, one readily recognizes that Heidegger is raising the same questions that our analytic patients are struggling with, only they lack the the means with which to consider them.

Because Heidegger rejected epistemology, his philosophy is inherently sceptical,[24] not in the sense of doubting that I can know anything but because knowledge doesn't get to the heart of what my life is about. Moreover, this attitude is easily adapted for the purposes of psychoanalytic inquiry, as any number of contemporary psychoanalysts have recognized. The novelty of this perspective has also insinuated its way into the thinking of many disparate (including "classical" as well as contemporary) psychoanalytic practitioners, some by virtue of their acquaintance with Heidegger's philosophy (Leavy,[25, 26] Laing[27, 28]), some by virtue of Sullivan's interpersonal theory (Levenson,[29, 30, 31] Stern,[32] Bromberg,[33] Langan[34]), and others through the influence of classical psychoanalysts such as Hans Loewald,[35] a self-identified Freudian analyst who studied with Heidegger in his youth. What holds such disparate theoretical outlooks together is their respective conceptions of experience. Heidegger's movement from epistemology toward ontology led to his abandoning concepts like consciousness and even intentionality (as it was conceived by Husserl) in favor of a critique of our relationship with Being and the manner it is disclosed to us in the immediacy of everyday experience.

How, then, does Heidegger conceive of experience and why is this an ontological question instead of an epistemological or strictly psychological one? From a strictly Heideggerian perspective, psychoanalysis is already concerned with our manner of Being and has been from the start. People go into analysis because they are not satisfied with the manner of Being they are in and want to change it. But in order to determine what our manner of Being is about we have to give ourselves to it, through our experience of it. In its essence, psychoanalysis gives us the opportunity to give thought to our experience by taking the time that is needed to ponder it. Heidegger would have agreed with Freud that there are indeed "two types" of thinking that we typically employ, though he wouldn't formulate them in the way that either Freud or Sartre proposed. Heidegger not only rejected Freud's conception of the unconscious but also avoided employing the term consciousness in the convoluted manner that Sartre did, opting instead to focus his attention on two types of "thinking": calculative and meditative. Basically, Heidegger believed that the nature of consciousness is so inherently mysterious that it is misleading to equate it with synonyms like "awareness" or "knowledge." We have seen from the thicket of contradictions that both Freud and Sartre entertained about the distinction between a conscious and unconscious portion of the mind that such a distinction ultimately dissolves into a well of confusion.

Whereas analysts are abundantly familiar with the observation that their patients frequently resist thinking about certain topics because they are distressing and would prefer to think about those topics that are more pleasing or interesting to them, Heidegger observed that one manner of thinking (whatever the topic may be) is inherently comforting while the other is more liable to elicit anxiety or dread (*angst*). We tend to avoid thinking the thoughts that make us anxious and abandon ourselves to thoughts, speculations, and fantasies that are soporific. The prospect of enduring the kind of anxiety that genuine thought entails is distressing and the tactics we employ to avoid it are universal. The task of analysis is to nudge our thinking into those areas we typically avoid so that we can access a region of our existence we loathe to explore, but which lies at the heart of our humanity. This is effected by *experiencing what our suffering is about*, and allowing such experiences to change us; not by virtue of knowing more than we already do about ourselves, but by helping us accommodate a dimension of our experience that we avoid at every turn. When we succumb to such experiences we are thrown into a different manner of experiencing ourselves and what we, as "selves," are about.

For this to make any sense we must understand why Heidegger insists on depicting the manner of Being he is concerned with with a capital B, a distinction that Heidegger calls "the ontological difference." The word "being" (with a little b) is an "entity" and, as such, is the object of scientific investigation as well as our everyday ordinary perceptions: trees, houses, tables, feelings, and so on. In other words, it refers to things as they seem at first blush. Heidegger, however, transforms these "things" (beings or entities) into Being by recognizing their temporal dimension, that "beings" necessarily exist *in time*, in a temporal flux of past-present-future: what we ordinarily call "now." This temporalization of beings into Being, however, can only be achieved by a human being who is privy to a relationship with objects of reflection by virtue of the capacity to think about them and interpret what they mean. Hence, our relationship with time reveals what the Being of "beings" share in common: the world as it is disclosed or "illuminated" *to a person* by virtue of his or her capacity to experience the object in question. In other words, beings (things, objects, perceptions) are transformed into Being when they are experienced by virtue of my capacity to interpret their significance for *me*. This observation sheds light on what psychoanalysts have already been doing whenever they employ interpretations to help their patients realize that everything they experience is unique to them alone, because everything they are capable of experiencing contains an historical component. Where Heidegger parts company with most analysts however, is that such realizations are not intended to merely help patients "understand" themselves better but to *experience* who and what they are, fundamentally. Like Heidegger, the analyst "temporalizes" the patient's experience by interpreting its historical antecedents, and in that act of temporalization helps the patient's world come alive. This is what Heidegger calls doing "fundamental ontology."

THOUGHT—AND THE *EXPERIENCE* OF THINKING

As noted earlier, in Heidegger's later thought he emphasized a form of thinking he characterized as meditative, a kind of thought that is usually dismissed
as irrelevant by scientists and academics who employ a manner of thinking
that Heidegger depicts as calculative. But what kind of thought does meditative thinking entail? J. Glenn Gray suggests it is helpful first to understand
what Heidegger does not mean by meditative thinking.

> Thinking is, in the first place, not what we call having an opinion
> or a notion. Second, it is not representing or having an idea
> (*Vorstellen*) about something or a state of affairs. . . . Third, thinking
> is not ratiocination, developing a chain of premises which lead to
> a valid conclusion. . . . [Meditative] thinking is not so much an act
> as a way of living or dwelling—as we in America would put it, a way
> of life.[36]

Offering a different perspective on this enigmatic proposition, Macquarrie
proposes that: " 'Meditation ' suggests a kind of thought in which the mind
is docile and receptive to whatever it is thinking about. Such thought may
be contrasted [for example] with the active investigative thought of the
natural sciences."[37] In comparison, Heidegger characterizes calculative thinking as the conventional norm and a by-product of the technological age in
which we live. Though its roots go all the way back to Plato, its impact on
culture was not fully formed until the scientific revolution that was inspired
by Descartes in the seventeenth century. The tendency to perceive the world
in the abstract and conceptual manner that calculative thinking entails took
an even sharper turn in the twentieth century with the birth of the computer
era and the amazing gains that technology has enjoyed over the past century,
evidenced in the development of housing, transportation, medicine, and so
on. The question of technology is a complicated one and remained the focus
of Heidegger's attention throughout his lifetime. Though it would be extreme to say that Heidegger was opposed to science, there is little doubt that
he believed science has overtaken our lives to such a degree that we have
now forgotten how to think in a nonscientific manner. One of Heidegger's
most infamous statements about the status of science is that "science does
not *think*" and that the thinking science employs is an impoverished varia-
tion of it, epitomized by the credence given to scientific "research" and the
like, which Heidegger dismisses as thought-less and thought-poor.

Indeed, one of the consequences of the technological age is what has
recently been depicted as the "postmodern condition," the ultimate expression of our contemporary obsession with technology and the technology
culture it has spawned. This is a culture that, from Heidegger's perspective,

is fundamentally ill in the sense of being "ill at ease" with itself, a product of the pervasive emptiness that characterizes the twentieth-century neurosis. Heidegger saw psychoanalysis as the inevitable response to the malaise in which postmodern man is imprisoned, because once we created this dire situation it was necessary that we fashion a cure for it. What, in Heidegger's opinion, is the cure for such malaise? To simply remember how to think in the manner that we have forgotten. In fact, this is the kind of thinking that Freud, despite his penchant for science, stumbled upon on his own, not by engaging in scientific research but by examining his own condition.[38] As we know, his efforts culminated in the radical treatment scheme that lies at the heart of the psychoanalytic endeavor, epitomized by the free association method and its complement, the mode of "free-floating attentiveness" (neutrality) that he counseled his followers to adopt.

Whereas in Heidegger's earlier period he emphasized the region of our everyday activities that we perform as a matter of course without recourse to having to think our way through them, the period of his development in which he distinguished between calculative and meditative thinking entailed a "turn" in his thinking that focused on the kind of experience we are capable of obtaining once we are cured of our obsession for knowledge. Though Heidegger abandoned terms such as intentionality and consciousness in his later period, he emphasized to an even greater degree than before the importance of *attending to experience* and argued that the only means we have of "touching Being" is by pondering what our experience tells us from this novel perspective. Thus, for Heidegger experience, proper speaking, is ontological, that is, one does not experience with one's feelings or one's mind, but with one's *Being*; hence one cannot feel or think one's way to experience because, by its nature, one must *submit* to it.

To summarize, whereas Sartre distinguishes between pre-reflective and reflective modes of consciousness, Heidegger distinguishes between a region of our existence that is unavailable to experience and the capacity we have to access this region by giving ourselves to it. Whereas Freud's conception of the unconscious conceives it as an "underworld" of hidden aims, intentions, and conspiracies that shadow the world we are conscious of (i.e., the world in which we live), Heidegger reverses this thesis in favor of one that dispenses with the psychoanalytic notion of the unconscious altogether. Instead, Heidegger sees a cleavage between the acts we commit without thinking (i.e., that we have no knowledge of when we commit them) and the acts that become available to experience by giving them thought. Conversely, it is the world I inhabit *without* thinking where I reside, not the one (as per Freud) I am conscious of. Indeed, this is the world I bring to awareness in analysis, but a world that I will never, no matter how much I try, be fully conscious of—at least not in the obsessive way that the neurotic would have it.

R. D. LAING'S CRITIQUE OF 'UNCONSCIOUS EXPERIENCE'

Much of this, I imagine, is probably familiar to you, not because you have studied Heidegger but because, with enough experience of your own, you have already adopted a phenomenological perspective, but without "knowing" it. This is one of the virtues of phenomenology: since we are only capable of grasping it intuitively, many people stumble on it on their own, as Freud did, without formal instruction. In many respects, despite his protestations to the contrary, Freud was a closet phenomenologist, and many of his ideas about psychoanalysis, including the bulk of his technical recommendations, were faithful to the phenomenological perspective. In fact, Heidegger recognized that Freud's conception of free association and the analyst's endeavor to effect a state of free-floating attentiveness was compatible with the kind of meditative thinking Heidegger was advocating.[39]

Given the parallels between Heidegger's and Freud's respective conceptions of meditative thinking and the analytic attitude (i.e., free association, neutrality),[40] it is all the more surprising that Heidegger's influence has not been more evident in psychoanalytic circles. Despite his influence on a generation of continental psychiatrists following the Second World War, there has been little effort among psychoanalysts to critique Freud's conception of the unconscious from a Heideggerian perspective. A singular exception is the work of R. D. Laing who studied Heidegger before he trained as a psychoanalyst and published his first, Heideggerian-inspired, book during his analytic training (1960). Laing's first two books, *The Divided Self*[41] and *Self and Others*,[42] were inspired attempts to apply some of Heidegger's insights to the psychoanalytic conception of the unconscious and the relation it bears on what is given to experience.[43]

In Laing's *Self and Others*, he confronts some of the problems with Freud's conception of the unconscious (noted earlier) in a critique of a paper by Susan Isaacs, a follower of Melanie Klein. Though Isaacs's paper is mostly related to Klein's technical vocabulary, one of the themes in Isaacs's study that caught Laing's attention originated with Freud and has been adopted by virtually every psychoanalyst since: the notion of "unconscious experience," a contradiction in terms for the reasons we reviewed earlier. Indeed, Laing avers: "It is a contradiction in terms to speak of 'unconscious experience,' [because] a person's experience comprises anything that 'he' or 'any part of him' is aware of, whether 'he' or every part of him is aware of every level of his awareness or not."[44]

Laing's thesis is that the psychoanalytic notion of unconscious experience alludes to a more fundamental contradiction that Freud's conception of the unconscious begins with: that there is such a thing as an unconscious portion of the mind that one is capable of experiencing. Indeed, Freud's decision to conceive a separate portion of the mind that the (conscious) mind has no awareness of sets up a series of false theoretical dualities between inner experience and outer reality that land one, in the words of Juliet Mitchell, "in a welter of contradictions such as the notion that 'mind' is a reality outside experience—yet is the 'place' from which experience comes."[45] Mitchell observes that "This problem is peculiar to psychoanalysis . . . because the 'object' of the science . . . *experiences* the investigation of the scientists."[46]

The heart of Laing's argument revolves around the difficulty that every psychoanalyst faces if he or she believes that the psychoanalyst is in a position to know more about the patient's experience (conscious or unconscious) than the patient does:

> My impression is that most adult Europeans and North Americans would subscribe to the following: the other person's experience is not directly experienced by self. For the present it does not matter whether this is necessarily so, is so elsewhere on the planet, or has always been the case. But if we agree that you do not experience my experience, [then] we agree that we rely on our communications to give us our clues as to how or what we are thinking, feeling, imagining, dreaming, and so forth. Things are going to be difficult if you tell me that I am *experiencing* something which I am not experiencing. If that is what I think you mean by unconscious experience.[47]

Even when one allows that the psychoanalyst is investigating the experience of the analysand, the analyst must remember that he has no direct access to the patient's experience other than what the patient tells him, whether the patient's account of her experience is reliable and to what degree. Yet it seems that the analyst is not content with the limitations of the situation that is imposed on him and prefers to engage in wild speculations and inferences as to what he "supposes" is going on in the patient's mind, of which the patient is presumed to be unaware:

> Beyond the mere attribution of agency, motive, intention, experiences that the patient disclaims, there is an extraordinary exfoliation of forces, energies, dynamics, economics, processes, structures to explain the 'unconscious.' Psychoanalytic concepts of this doubly chimerical order include concepts of mental structures, economics, dynamisms, death and life instincts, internal objects, etc. They are postulated as principles of regularity, governing or underlying forces, governing or underlying experience that Jack thinks Jill has, but does not know she has, as inferred by Jack from Jack's experience of Jill's behavior. In the meantime, what *is* Jack's experience of Jill, Jill's experience of herself, or Jill's experience of Jack?[48]

Indeed, the subtle interplay of how one's experience of other affects one and, in turn, how one's reaction to this effect elicits behavior that affects other's experience as well was a major theme in Laing's writings throughout his career. The book in which Laing's critique of Isaacs's paper appeared was a full-scale examination of the effect that human beings have on each other in the etiology of severe psychological disturbance, fueled by the acts of deception and self-deception that characterize our most seemingly innocent exchanges with one another. Heidegger's influence on Laing's clinical outlook was explicitly acknowledged by Laing when citing Heidegger's essay, "On the Essence of Truth"[49] in that work. Noting Heidegger's adoption of the pre-Socratic term for truth, *aletheia* (which conceives truth as that which emerges from concealment), Laing put his own twist on Heidegger's thesis by emphasizing the interdependency between candor and secrecy in the way that one's personal truth emerges and recedes in every conversation with others, an innovation that owes just as much to Sartre and Freud as to Heidegger's ontological preoccupations.

Many of the terms that Laing introduced in that book for the first time (e.g., collusion, mystification, attribution, injunction, untenable positions) were coined for the purpose of providing a conceptual vocabulary that could help explain how human beings, in their everyday interactions with each other, are able to distort the truth so effectively that they are able to affect each other's reality, and hence their sanity as well. It was just this vocabulary that Laing suggested was missing in Freud's psychoanalytic nomenclature. In the language of psychic conflict, Laing agreed with Freud that people who suffer conflicts are essentially of *two minds:* they struggle against the intrusion of a reality that is too painful to accept, on the one hand, and harbor a fantasy that is incapable of being acknowledged on the other. Consequently, their lives are held in abeyance until they are able to speak of their experience to someone who is willing to hear it with benign acceptance, without a vested interest in what one's experience ought to be.

Like Heidegger, Laing avoided employing terms such as consciousness and unconscious and situated his thinking instead in the language of experience and how experience determines our perception of the world and ourselves. Instead of characterizing what we do not know as that which has been repressed into one's "unconscious," Laing was more apt to depict such phenomena descriptively, as that which I am unconscious *of;* or better, as that which is not available, or given, to experience, even if in the depths of my Being I intuitively sense I am harboring a truth that is too painful or elusive to grasp. Laing also adhered to Heidegger's thesis that my experience of the world is dependent on what I interpret the world to be, so that if I want to change my experience of the world I have to reconsider my interpretation of it.[50]

It should be remembered that these words were written forty years ago, long before the subsequent development of hermeneutic, relational, constructivist, and intersubjective schools of psychoanalysis, that have in turn noted some of the same problems that Laing presaged but rarely gets credit for. One possible explanation for this oversight is that Laing's commentary is *still*, forty years hence, radical in comparison with contemporary treatments of this theme; indeed, virtually all the schools previously listed continue to embrace the notion of "unconscious experience"! Space does not permit me to compare and contrast Laing's contribution to this discussion with more contemporary versions of it; my concern is limited to that of assessing Freud's conception of the unconscious and some of the problems that inhere from its presuppositions. I include Laing in this discussion because of the emphasis that he, more than any other psychoanalyst, has reserved for the place of experience in the psychoanalytic encounter and the problems that derive from it. That being said, there are aspects of Freud's conception of experience that are surprisingly consistent with Heidegger's and are compatible with the ontological dimension of human experience.

FREUD'S AND HEIDEGGER'S RESPECTIVE CONCEPTIONS OF EXPERIENCE

I will now review those aspects of Freud's conception of the unconscious that are compatible with Heidegger's philosophy and the respective importance that each assigns to the role of experience in our lives. Over the past two centuries the German language has offered perhaps the richest and most subtle variations on the kinds of experience that English subsumes under one term. It should not be surprising, therefore, that German philosophers have dominated the nineteenth- and twentieth-century investigations into the nature of experience that subsequently spilled over to other European countries, including France, Great Britain, and Spain. I am thinking of Hegel, Schopenhauer, Dilthey, Nietzsche, Husserl, and Heidegger specifically, each of whom elaborated on the notion of experience in their respective philosophies, granting the concept a central role in both phenomenology and existential philosophy. Before exploring their impact on phenomenology, however, I will say a few words about the German conception of experience and the etymology from which the terms they employ are derived.

The first is the German *Erfahrung*, which contains the word *Fahrt*, meaning "journey." Hence, *Erfahrung* suggests the notion of temporal duration, such as, for example, when one accumulates experience over time, including the accruing of wisdom that comes with old age. The other German term for experience is *Erlebnis*, which derives from the word *Leben*, meaning "life." Hence, the use of the word *Erlebnis* connotes a vital immediacy in contrast to the more historical perspective of *Erfahrung*. When invoking *Erlebnis*, the speaker is emphasizing a primitive unity that precedes intellectual reflection.[51] In the scientific community the notion of experience suggests the accumulation of empirical knowledge through the use of experimentation, a supposedly objective endeavor. On the other hand, experience may also suggest something that happens to us when in a passive state and vulnerable to stimuli, such as what occurs in a movie theater. It may also suggest the process whereby we submit to education, entailing the accumulation and memorization of knowledge over a considerable period of time. Finally, the term may also be used to connote a journey I have taken while traveling to a foreign country, perhaps in wartime when I am faced with obstacles and danger, the experience of which may have expedited my journey into manhood.

You can see from these distinctions between the two types of experience we are capable of having that, even while offering tantalizing hints as to what the term means, there remains something ineffable about the concept itself. This presents us with a paradox, because the word is often employed, according to Martin Jay, "to gesture towards precisely that which exceeds concepts and even language itself."[52] In fact, the word experience has frequently been used as a marker for what is ineffable and so private or personal that it cannot be rendered in words. One's experience of love, for example, is an experience that many insist is impossible to express or grasp in words alone, precisely because it is experienced long before it is understood, if then. As Laing observed earlier, even when I try to communicate what I experience to others, only I can know what my experience is. Hence, our efforts to convey our experience are imperfect because it cannot be reduced to words. This observation has enormous consequences for the experience of psychoanalysis for both patient and analyst who rely almost entirely on the passage of words between them.

So what does the essential nature of experience entail? Is experience antithetical to our capacity to reason, as some have claimed, or is our ability to reason dependent on our capacity to experience the very thoughts that our words endeavor to convey? As we know, many of the last century's philosophers and academics sought to reduce human activity to language, suggesting that one's capacity to experience is mediated through words and, hence, is secondary to the power that words possess. This view implies that pre-verbal experience is inconceivable, so that even the experience of pain relies on one's "knowledge" of what pain entails. Many of the features of structuralism, deconstructionism, poststructuralism, and the postmodernist perspective argue that the very notion of a conscious, sentient, self that is capable of determining its own truth is an antiquated idea that should be replaced with a schema that views the subject, not in terms of an experiencing agent, but as an effect, or "construct," of hidden forces.

To appreciate the contribution of phenomenology to our conception of experience it is important to note that, historically, empiricist philosophers such as Hume separated experience from rationality by consigning to experience sensual data alone. Hence, modern scientific methodology, which endeavors to combine the experience we derive from our senses with our capacity to think about and reflect on the nature of such experience, is unable to account for the experience of ideas, thoughts, and imagination. In other words, philosophers have traditionally "split" human Being in half, assigning one portion of the human project to rationality, the mind, and the other portion to sense experience, the body.

The singular contribution of Husserl at the turn of the century was to reconcile the split between sense experience and rationality by suggesting that experience is already inherently thoughtful, because the nature of consciousness, according to Husserl, is intentional, so that the act of consciousness and its object are given at one stroke. One isn't "related" (as per object relations theory) to the other because each is irrevocably dependent on the other, so that neither is capable of standing alone. As some Buddhists have argued, the presumed split to which Western thought has been devoted is illusory, because the two are actually One. Heidegger concluded that there are levels of experience—just as there are levels of awareness or consciousness—depending on my capacity to interpret *to the depths* what my experience discloses to me.

This thesis is especially relevant to the psychoanalyst who endeavors to direct the patient's attention to his or her experience by interpreting its meaning. Viewed from this angle, a good interpretation is never intended to explain one's experience, but to deepen it, in the phenomenological sense. Alternately, *what the patient experiences and how reveal to the analyst the person that the patient happens to be*. Thus, as Laing noted earlier, patient and analyst alike are interested not only in their own experience of the situation they share together, but in what each takes the other's experience to be, however imperfect the ability to understand the other's experience may be.

This is why Heidegger sees experience as the "revealing" of Being; because experience discloses who I am as well as the world I inhabit, the two are inextricably connected. I am neither strictly constituted by the world, nor is the world I inhabit my invention: the two are interdependent because each serves to constitute the other. Thus, the distinctive feature of experience from a Heideggerian perspective is its capacity to shock the world I inhabit at the roots, because experience does not only reveal things that are hidden, it is also capable of changing, by virtue of such revelations, *who* I am. Hence, "When we talk of 'undergoing' an experience, we mean specifically that the experience is not of our own making, [so that *in order* to undergo experience] we [must] endure it, suffer it, [and] receive it as it strikes us, and [finally] submit to it."[53] By anticipating my experiences with a specific purpose in mind I can make use of them to gain insight into the person I am. Moreover, there are degrees to experience; it isn't all or nothing. This is why I am also capable of resisting experience, avoiding it, and even forgetting experiences that (due to repression) are too painful to bear. In turn, the degree to which I am able to experience anything—a piece of music, the paper you are now reading, even psychoanalysis—is determined by how willing I am to give myself to the experience in question.

What, then, does the ontological structure of experience have to do with the unconscious? Some would argue, nothing. After all, psychoanalysis is concerned with exploring the unconscious whereas Heidegger's conception of phenomenology is devoted to the revelation of Being through the critique of one's experience. Despite what Freud said about the ego "no longer being the master of its own house," experience nevertheless plays a vital role in Freud's conception of analysis and the conflicts that patients typically suffer. Basically, Freud believed that our capacity to bear painful experience (*Erlebnis*) as children goes a long way in determining whether we will develop neurotic symptoms, or worse, when we grow up. This is actually a Heideggerian conception of experience, though Freud never knew this. According to Freud, if a child is faced with an experience that is too painful to bear, the child simply represses it from consciousness, making the child's experience of frustration disappear. As Freud realized, it isn't the actual experience of frustration that is repressed but the *knowledge* (or as Heidegger would say, the "interpretation" of what one takes the case to be) of the incident that elicited the experience in the first place; hence, after this piece of knowledge (i.e., interpretation) is suppressed, the individual continues to experience moments of sadness or anxiety, for example, but has forgotten why. The only problem with this solution is that the repressed memory finds an alternate means of expression that transforms it into a symptom, which the adult subsequently suffers and complains about, though the individual hasn't a clue what caused the symptom or what purpose it serves.

For Freud, the purpose of pathogenic symptoms is to shield the individual from experiencing a disappointment of traumatic proportions that the person who suffers the symptom (that replaced the original trauma) wants desperately to suppress. Since the disappointment in question was repressed (or disavowed, projected, etc.) but not entirely eradicated, the individual instinctively *avoids experiencing similar disappointments and anything that may serve to remind him of it in the future.* Analytic patients are loathe to risk disappointment because to really *be* disappointed is not only transformative, but necessarily painful. But such disappointments are transformative only and to the degree to which they are finally experienced at the heart of one's being, in the give-and-take of the treatment situation.

Just because one has a fleeting thought, idea, or intuition, for example, doesn't guarantee that one will have a full-throttle *experience* of it. The phenomenologist accounts for this phenomenon by suggesting that Freud's unconscious is nothing more than a *mode of thinking* (consciousness) that the patient is unaware of thinking. In other words, the patient has no experience of thinking the thoughts attributed to her because she failed to *hear* herself thinking the thoughts in question. At the moment such thoughts occurred, her mind was "somewhere else." The psychoanalyst says she was unconscious of what she was thinking, but the phenomenologist would say she simply failed to listen to, and hence experience, the thoughts in question, as they occurred to her.

Based on this hypothesis, psychoanalytic treatment is nothing more than an investigation into the patient's experience, suffered over the entirety of one's life. Hence, analysts seek to learn about the experiences (*Erfahrung*) that patients remember over the course of their history, just as they seek to understand the patient's experience of the analytic situation (*Erlebnis*) that is, the patient's *experience of his or her relationship with the analyst:* the so-called transference phenomena. But analysts are also interested in eliciting what may be characterized as "lost" experience (what Heidegger would call potential experience) through the patient's free associations. Change comes about through the patient's ability to speak of his experience instead of concealing it, as he has in the past. In other words, giving voice to experience deepens it, but only if the experience elicited plunges the patient to the depths of his suffering.

CONCLUDING UNSCIENTIFIC POSTSCRIPT

What does Heidegger's emphasis on the ontological dimension of experience tell us about the psychoanalytic conception of the unconscious? Does it do away with it entirely or does it offer another way of conceiving it? How, in turn, does it relate to Sartre's distinction between reflective and pre-reflective consciousness? Are Heidegger's and Sartre's respective views compatible or are they hopelessly irreconcilable? And finally, is it possible to be "conscious" of something that one has no experience of, or is it necessary to experience something to know it, even "pre-reflectively"? Or contrariwise, is there a dimension to experience that one is not *aware* of experiencing, or is it essential to be conscious of experience to construe it as experience, as such, whether one is referring to *Erlebnis* or *Erfahrung*?

Recall that Sartre makes a distinction between *pre*-reflective consciousness and *reflective* consciousness (i.e., that which we ordinarily term *conscious awareness*). Even while Sartre is indecisive on this point, for Heidegger, Sartre's notion of pre-reflective consciousness only makes sense if it is conceived as a form of nascent awareness that is not immediately available to experience, properly speaking. Only when I *reflect on* my pre-reflective acts of consciousness am I capable of experiencing them and, hence, *be* with them. Thus, from a Heideggerian perspective, there is no such thing as "unconscious experience," despite the views of Melanie Klein, Wilfried Bion, Harry Stack Sullivan, and so on. If Sartre's conception of pre-reflective consciousness is simply another term for what Freud calls primary process thinking, then *the unconscious should be conceived as a form of consciousness that is not yet available to experience;* in other words, that which is un-available to experience is un-conscious.

As we saw earlier, Heidegger lost interest in exploring the distinctions between consciousness, awareness, and intentionality because he felt they were inadequate concepts for describing the nature of thought and why it is available to experience in some situations but not others. Thus, the capacity to experience is the final arbiter for what it means to inhabit the world and to be-in-the-world authentically, as the person I genuinely am, because experience, whatever form it assumes, is irrevocably my *own.* Heidegger finally rejected the primacy of consciousness because he was concerned with how one comes to *be* who one is and the weight of guilt and anxiety that being oneself inevitably entails.

If Freud's conception of the unconscious is finally a scientific one, it is nevertheless imbued with ontological overtones that are evident, for example, when he characterizes the way we stumble on it in our dreams, parapraxes, and symptoms. From this perspective, the unconscious is nothing more than an algebraic "x" that serves to explain that which is not immediately given to experience. Moreover, one can discern parallels between Freud's and Sartre's (as well as Heidegger's) respective depictions of "two types of thinking" that, when treated phenomenologically, betray ontological connotations to Freud's intuitions, if not his theoretical conceptualizations. Thus, what Freud depicts as primary thought processes may be conceived as a version of Sartre's notion of pre-reflective consciousness, and what Freud depicts as secondary thought processes are editions of what Sartre terms reflective consciousness. Seen from this angle, the primary thought processes are a form of consciousness, but lack the *reflective* capacities that the ego is only capable of obtaining after the acquisition of language. Another way of understanding the distinction between *Erlebnis* and *Erhfarung* is to conceive the former as a form of pre-verbal experience (i.e., the experience of the infant) whereas the latter pertains to the child's (and later, the adult's) capacity to reflect on his or her experience after having acquired the capacity for language. The child's ability to learn from experience will evolve and develop, just as the *capacity to experience* will also evolve, from the most primitive aspects of *Erlebnis* to the more sophisticated editions of *Erfahrung*. Thus, Freud's topographical and structural models are indeed scientific but only to the degree that psychoanalysis is a theoretical science that presumes to explain that which is inaccessible to experience. As a theoretical construct it may be accurate or not. We do not know, nor can we, whether and to what degree they are accurate, which probably explains why the history of psychoanalysis is littered with a seemingly endless array of alternative formulations to Freud's, each of which is just as feasible (or not) as the next. Whomever's theory one opts for (whether Klein's, Sullivan's, Bion's, or Lacan's, for example), however compelling or attractive or elegant it may be, it is still just as theoretical, abstract, and impossible to prove (or disprove) as Freud's.

From Heidegger's ontological perspective, the unconscious is not a theoretical construct, nor is it "in" my head, but "out" *there*, in the world, a dimension of Being. Hence it is my abode, my past, and my destiny converged, so that "I," the one for whom the unconscious comes into Being, am simply the experience of this tripartite intersection. We apprehend it as an enigma, a dimension of our existence that lies hidden one moment, then slips into view the next, only to disappear again, in perpetuity. If our only access to it is through the vehicle of interpretation, it is not the interpretation (i.e., "translation") of this or that psychoanalytic theory into a language of the consensus, but the kind of interpretation we render each moment of our lives, by virtue of giving things a name and a significance. This is because everything we are capable of experiencing conveys meaning, and the only way to understand what something means is to determine what it means for *me*, when it is experienced and how.

Consequently, the unconscious is never unconscious for me, but a living presence in my world. This is why the purpose of analysis is not to simply "know" the unconscious, but to return the analytic patient to the ground of an experience that was lost, in order to finally claim it, as his or her own.

NOTES

1. An earlier version of this chapter was presented as the Presidential Address at the Eleventh Annual Interdisciplinary Conference of the International Federation for Psychoanalytic Education, Chicago Illinois, November 4, 2000.

2. J. Grotstein. *Who Is the Dreamer Who Dreams the Dream?* (Hillsdale, NJ: The Analytic Press, 2000).

3. S. Freud. *Totem and Taboo.* S.E., 13:1–161 (London: Hogarth Press, 1958), 159.

4. S. Leavy. *In The Image of God: A Psychoanalyst's View* (New Haven: Yale University Press, 1988), 8.

5. S. Freud. Case of a Successful Treatment by Hypnosis. S.E., 1:115–128 (London: Hogarth Press, 1966).

6. Leavy, op. cit., 12n.

7. H. W. Hoewald. *Papers on Psychoanalysis* (New Haven: Yale University Press, 1980), 152–153.

8. For a more thorough treatment of Freud's conception of psychic reality see Thompson, 1994, 1–50.

9. S. Freud. Formulations on the Two Principles of Mental Functioning. S.E., 12:215–226 (London: Hogarth Press, 1958).

10. Ibid., 219.

11. Ibid.

12. Ibid.

13. Ibid.

14. Ibid.

15. C. Rycroft. *Imagination and Reality* (New York: International Universities Press, 1968), 102–113.

16. Quoted in Rycroft, ibid., 102–103.

17. Ibid., 103.

18. Ibid.

19. J.-P. Sartre. *Existential Psychoanalysis* Hazel Barnes, trans. (Washington, D. C.: Regnary Gatewaym 1981).

20. J.-P. Sartre. *Sketch for a Theory of the Emotions* Philip Mairet, trans. (London: Methuen and Co., 1962), 48–55.

21. J.-P. Sartre. *Existential Psychoanalysis*, op. cit., 153–171.

22. J.-P. Sartre. *The Transcendence of the Ego.* Forest Williams and Robert Kirkpatrick, trans. (New York: Noonday Press, 1957), 48–49.

23. Ibid.

24. See Thompson, 2000b, for a discussion on the skeptical dimension to Heidegger's and Freud's respective conceptions of the human condition.

25. S. Leavy. *The Psychoanalytic Dialogue* (New Haven: Yale University Press, 1980).

26. S. Leavy, 1988, op. cit.

27. R. D. Laing. *The Divided Self* (New York: Pantheon Books, 1960).

28. R. D. Laing. *Self and Others*, 2nd rev. ed. (New York: Pantheon Books, 1969).

29. E. Levenson. *The Fallacy of Understanding: An Inquiry into the Changing Structure of Psychoanalysis* (New York and London: Basic Books, 1972).

30. E. Levenson. *The Ambiguity of Change: An Inquiry into the Nature of Psychoanalytic Reality* (New York: Basic Books, 1983).

31. E. Levenson. *The Purloined Self: Interpersonal Perspectives in Psychoanalysis* (New York: Contemporary Psychoanalysis Books, 1991).

32. D. B. Stern. *Unformulated Experience: From Dissociation to Imagination in Psychoanalysis* (Hillsdale, NJ and London: The Analytic Press, 1997).

33. P. Bromberg. *Standing in the Spaces: Essays on Clinical Process, Trauma, and Dissociation* (Hillsdale, NJ and London: The Analytic Press, 1998).

34. R. Langan. The Depth of the Field, *Contemporary Psychoanalysis* 29, No. 4 (October 1993).

35. H. W. Loewald. *Papers on Psychoanalysis* (New Haven: Yale University Press, 1980).

36. J. G. Gray. Introduction to *What Is Called Thinking?* by Martin Heidegger (San Francisco: Harper and Row, 1968), x–xi.

37. J. Macquarrie. *Heidegger and Christianity* (New York: Continuum Publishing Company, 1994), 77–78.

38. See Thompson, 1998 and 2000b, for a more detailed exploration of how Freud developed the principles of free association and neutrality.

39. See Medard Boss's account of Heidegger's take on Freud in Boss, 1988, 9–10.

40. See Thompson, 1996a, 1996b, and 2000b for a more detailed exploration of Freud's conception of free association and neutrality in light of the sceptic and phenomenological traditions.

41. R. D. Laing. (1960), op. cit.

42. R. D. Laing. (1969[1961]), op. cit.

43. The theme of experience preoccupied Laing throughout his lifetime. Two of his other books, *The Politics of Experience* (1967) and *The Voice of Experience* (1982), even contain the word experience in their titles. (See more on the history of experience in Western culture in Thompson, 2000a.)

44. R. D. Laing. (1969[1961]), op. cit., 8.

45. J. Mitchell. *Psychoanalysis and Feminism* (New York: Pantheon Books, 1964), 254.

46. Ibid.

47. R. D. Laing. (1969[1961]), op. cit., 12–13.

48. Ibid., 14–15.

49. M. Heidegger. (1977) On the Essence of Truth. In *Basic Writings*, David Farrell Krell, ed. (New York and London: Harper and Row, 1977), 113–142.

50. R. D. Laing, H. Phillipson, and A. R. Lee, A. R. *Interpersonal Perception: A Theory and a Method of Research* (London: Tavistock Publications, 1966), 10–11.

51. Whereas Sartre would imply that pre-reflective consciousness is a form of experience (*Erlebnis*), Heidegger would argue that in order for knowledge to be available to experience it must be *thought*; hence, for Heidegger pre-reflective consciousness is not *experienced*, per se. For this reason Heidegger disputed the notion of *Erlebnis* as a feature of experience, properly speaking, although he would have no problem with employing this term so long as it connotes an act that is *reflectively* conscious to the person at the moment it is experienced. For more on this see Heidegger, 1970.

52. M. Jay. The Crisis of Experience in a Post-Subjective Age. Public Lecture, University of California, Berkeley, CA, November 14, 1998.

53. M. Heidegger. *On the Way to Language*, Peter D. Hertz, trans. (San Francisco: Harper and Row 1971), 57.

REFERENCES

Boss, M. (1988). Martin Heidegger's Zollikon Seminars. In K. Hoeller, ed., pp. 7–20, *Heidegger and Psychology*, a special issue of the *Review of Existential Psychology and Psychiatry*, Seattle, WA, 1988.

Bromberg, P. (1998). *Standing in the Spaces: Essays on Clinical Process, Trauma, and Dissociation*. Hillsdale, NJ and London: The Analytic Press.

Freud, S. (1892). Case of a Successful Treatment by Hypnosis. *S.E.*, 1:115–128. London: Hogarth Press, 1966.

Freud, S. (1911). Formulations on the Two Principles of Mental Functioning. *S.E.*, 12:215–226. London: Hogarth Press, 1958.

Freud, S. (1912). On the Universal Tendency to Debasement in the Sphere of Love. *S.E.*, 11:177–190. London: Hogarth Press, 1957.

Freud, S. (1913). *Totem and Taboo. S.E.*, 13:1–161. London: Hogarth Press, 1958.

Gray, J. G. (1968). Introduction to *What Is Called Thinking?*, by Martin Heidegger. San Francisco: Harper and Row, 1968.

Grotstein, J. (1999). *Who Is The Dreamer That Dreams The Dream?* London: Karnac Books.

Heidegger, M. (1968). *What Is Called Thinking?* Trans. J. Glenn Gray. San Francisco: Harper and Row.

Heidegger, M. (1970). *Hegel's Concept of Experience*. New York and London: Harper and Row.

Heidegger, M. (1971). *On the Way to Language*. Trans. Peter D. Hertz. San Francisco: Harper and Row.

Heidegger, M. (1977). On the Essence of Truth. In *Basic Writings*, David Farrell Krell, ed. New York and London: Harper and Row, 1977, 113–142.

Jay, M. (1998). The Crisis of Experience in a Post-Subjective Age. Public Lecture, University of California, Berkeley, CA, November 14, 1998.

Laing, R. D. (1960). *The Divided Self*. New York: Pantheon Books.

Laing, R. D. (1969[1961]). *Self and Others* (2nd rev. ed.). New York: Pantheon Books.

Laing, R. D. (1982). *The Voice of Experience*. New York: Pantheon Books.

Laing, R. D., Phillipson, H., and Lee, A. R. (1966). *Interpersonal Perception: A Theory and a Method of Research*. London: Tavistock Publications.

Langan, R. (1993). The Depth of the Field. *Contemporary Psychoanalysis*, 29, No. 4 (October 1993).

Leavy, S. (1980). *The Psychoanalytic Dialogue*. New Haven: Yale University Press.

Leavy, S. (1988). *In The Image of God: A Psychoanalyst's View*. New Haven: Yale University Press.

Levenson, E. (1972). *The Fallacy of Understanding: An Inquiry into the Changing Structure of Psychoanalysis*. New York and London: Basic Books.

Levenson, E. (1983). *The Ambiguity of Change: An Inquiry into the Nature of Psychoanalytic Reality*. New York: Basic Books.

Levenson, E. (1991). *The Purloined Self: Interpersonal Perspectives in Psychoanalysis*. New York: Contemporary Psychoanalysis Books.

Loewald, H. W. (1980). *Papers on Psychoanalysis*. New Haven: Yale University Press.

Macquarrie, J. (1994). *Heidegger and Christianity*. New York: Continuum Publishing Company.

Mitchell, J. (1974). *Psychoanalysis and Feminism*. New York: Pantheon Books.

Rycroft, C. (1968). *Imagination and Reality*. New York: International Universities Press.

Sartre, J.-P. (1957). *The Transcendence of the Ego*. Trans. Forest Williams and Robert Kirkpatrick. New York: Noonday Press.

Sartre, J.-P. (1962). *Sketch for a Theory of the Emotions*. Trans. Philip Mairet. London: Methuen and Co.

Sartre, J.-P. (1981). *Existential Psychoanalysis*. Trans. Hazel Barnes. Washington, D. C.: Regnary Gateway.

Stern, D. B. (1997). *Unformulated Experience: From Dissociation to Imagination in Psychoanalysis*. Hillsdale, NJ and London: The Analytic Press.

Thompson, M. G. (1994). *The Truth About Freud's Technique: The Encounter with the Real*. New York and London: New York University Press.

Thompson, M. G. (1996a). The Rule of Neutrality. *Psychoanalysis and Contemporary Thought* 19, No. 1 (1996).

Thompson, M. G. (1996b). Freud's Conception of Neutrality. *Contemporary Psychoanalysis*, 32, No. 1 (January 1996).

Thompson, M. G. (1998). Manifestations of Transference: Love, Friendship, Rapport. *Contemporary Psychoanalysis* 34, No. 1 (October 1998).

Thompson, M. G. (2000a). The Crisis of Experience in Contemporary Psychoanalysis. *Contemporary Psychoanalysis* 36, No. 1 (January 2000).

Thompson, M. G. (2000b). The Sceptic Dimension to Psychoanalysis: Toward an Ethic of Experience. *Contemporary Psychoanalysis* 36, No. 3 (July 2000).

Thompson, M. G. (2000c). Logos and Psychoanalysis: The Role of Truth and Creativity in Heidegger's Conception of Language. *Psychologist Psychoanalyst* 20, No. 4 (Fall 2000).

TWO

FORMULATING UNCONSCIOUS EXPERIENCE: FROM FREUD TO BINSWANGER AND SULLIVAN

ROGER FRIE

THE QUESTION OF what constitutes unconscious experience is crucial to the psychoanalytic cannon. It is also what distinguishes Freud's project from revisionist accounts of psychoanalysis. Debate about the unconscious began early on and was central to the relationship between Freud and his philosophically inclined colleague, the Swiss psychiatrist and psychoanalyst Ludwig Binswanger. The two men first met in 1907, when a young Binswanger accompanied C. G. Jung to visit Freud in Vienna. Even though Binswanger and Freud disagreed on central tenets of psychoanalytic theory, the two men remained in close contact until the latter's death in 1939. Indeed, Binswanger was one of the few serious critics of psychoanalysis with whom Freud did not break off relations.

Freud's tolerance of his younger colleague's divergent philosophical perspective had its limits, however. In recounting their thirty-year friendship, Binswanger tells us that in 1917, when he first presented Freud with his phenomenological perspective on the mind, Freud replied: "What are you going to do without the unconscious, or rather, how will you manage without the unconscious? Has the philosophical devil got you in its claws after all? Reassure me."[1] Although critical of psychoanalysis, Binswanger was always respectful of Freud, whom he saw both as a teacher and a colleague. As if in reply to Freud, Binswanger tells us: "Needless to say, I have never 'managed without the unconscious.' . . . But after I turned to phenomenology and Daseinsanalysis, I conceived of the unconscious in a different way. The problems it presented became broader and deeper, as it became less and less defined as merely the opposite of the 'conscious.' "[2]

Binswanger's remarks shed light on an important chapter of psychoanalytic history that remains relatively unknown. By combining insights from psychoanalysis with the work of existential-phenomenological philosophers, Binswanger developed a unique clinical and theoretical perspective, known as Daseinsanalysis. Binswanger's critique of the unconscious and development of this alternative conception of unconscious experience raise a number of important issues, which will be the focus of this chapter: how is it possible to formulate unconscious experience once Freud's theory of the unconscious is placed in question? Does the application of existential-phenomenological philosophy to the problem of unconscious experience clarify or complicate this project? Is the attempt to formulate unconscious experience more consistent with an intrapsychic or an interpersonal psychoanalytic perspective? And finally, how can we understand the relationship between unconscious experience and individual subjectivity?

To begin answering these questions, it will be useful to examine the background to Binswanger's Daseinsanalysis. Binswanger's theoretical divergence from Freud will be elaborated within the context of his own philosophical development. To elucidate Binswanger's perspective on unconscious experience, parallels will be drawn to the work of another psychoanalytic revisionist and critic, Harry Stack Sullivan. Like Binswanger, Sullivan seeks to account for the nature of unconscious experience. While Sullivan emphasizes the interpersonal dimension of this experience, however, Binswanger is interested in its individual meaning. This contrast between the interpersonal and the individual provides a useful backdrop for thinking about the relation of unconscious experience to individual subjectivity. Ultimately this chapter seeks to demonstrate the ways in which the unconscious remains a relevant theoretical and clinical issue, albeit one that is conceptualized differently from Freud's initial intent.

PSYCHOANALYTIC AND PHILOSOPHICAL BEGINNINGS

Freud's relationship to philosophy was always tenuous. His interest in establishing the validity of his explanations as science led him to distinguish sharply between psychoanalysis and philosophy. He separated the findings of psychoanalysis from pronouncements of a similar nature in philosophy. Thus, while Freud recognized the way in which the philosophies of Schopenhauer and Nietzsche coincided with the theories of psychoanalysis, he made the dubious claim not to have read either. Freud's project of creating a science while maintaining a bulwark against what he referred to as "speculative metaphysics" had a lasting effect on the discipline of psychoanalysis. Today's clinicians often know little of contemporary philosophical thinking, yet alone Descartes and classical philosophy. As the issue of psychoanalysis as science begins to recede, however, there is room for renewed consideration of the connections between psychoanalytic and philosophical inquiry.

Against this backdrop, the relationship between Freud and Binswanger provides us with the opportunity to examine the way in which philosophical thinking impacted early psychoanalytic revisionism. But who was Binswanger? Certainly little is known about him and his work today. During the late 1950s and 1960s, Binswanger attained a measured popularity. Binswanger's work was first introduced to English-speaking audiences by Rollo May and his colleagues in *Existence: A New Dimension in Psychiatry and Psychology* (1958).[3] Very little of Binswanger's writings were ever translated, however, resulting in a situation in which he became identified chiefly by rather arbitrarily selected essays and case studies. Before examining Binswanger's perspective on unconscious experience, it will therefore be useful to provide some background to the clinician and philosopher.

Binswanger bridged the divide between psychiatry, psychoanalysis, and philosophy with relative ease. Early in his career he worked closely together with Freud and Eugen Bleuler. As his interest in philosophy grew, he initiated personal contact and entered into a substantial correspondence with Edmund Husserl, Martin Heidegger, and Martin Buber. Each would have a direct impact on the development of Binswanger's ideas. Yet Binswanger never became a follower of a particular thinker or school of thought. Instead, he drew connections between different ways of thinking and thus developed his philosophical approach to psychiatry, Daseinsanalysis.

Binswanger belonged to a continental European tradition of intellectual thought that freely combined insights from philosophy and clinical practice. He was born in Kreuzlingen, Switzerland, in 1881, into a family of prominent psychiatrists. Binswanger attended the universities of Lausanne, Heidelberg, and Zurich, and received his medical degree from Zurich in 1907. He trained as a psychiatrist under Bleuler and Jung at the Bürgholzli Hospital in Zurich. There he became acquainted with the burgeoning field of psychoanalysis and, in 1907, met Freud for the first time. Binswanger developed a friendship with Freud that continued through personal visits and a large correspondence until Freud's death in 1939.[4] From 1910 to 1956, Binswanger was director of his family's Bellevue Sanatorium in Kreuzlingen and dedicated much of his time to the integration of theoretical and clinical insights from philosophy, psychoanalysis, and psychiatry.

Binswanger's early association with Freud had a significant impact on his theoretical and clinical pursuits. Binswanger was initially attracted to psychoanalysis because of the insights it provided into human behavior. In 1909, while working at the University of Jena, Binswanger published the first psychoanalytic case study at a German university psychiatric clinic. In 1910, he was president of the Zurich Psychoanalytic Society. Even in this early period, however, Binswanger had reservations about Freud's ideas. Binswanger cautioned Freud against scientific reductionism and was critical of the proto-physiological basis on which Freud's drive theory and models of the mind were based. Nor did he think that psychoanalysis sufficiently accounted for the role of other people in the development of personality. In a later recollection of his friendship with Freud, Binswanger remarked that his entire scientific development, in both positive as well as negative respects, was determined by his effort to formulate a philosophical as well as a scientific basis for psychoanalysis.[5]

Although Binswanger never questioned the explanatory potential of natural science, he sought above all to develop an account of human nature that was not reductionistic. This project culminated in his first book, *Introduction to the Problems of General Psychology* (1922).[6] Although the book was dedicated to "my teachers, Bleuler and Freud," it also marked the turn toward philosophy in Binswanger's work. Binswanger argued that the object of investigation must always be seen in its full phenomenal reality. His purpose was to understand and explain human beings in the totality of their existence, not simply as natural objects constructed from various parts. Husserl's phenomenology provided Binswanger with a method to explain the "visual reality" of his patients. It was, however, Heidegger's move beyond Husserl in *Being and Time* (1927), that influenced Binswanger's thinking most directly.[7] Heidegger's fundamental ontology, particularly the notion of being-in-the-world, enabled Binswanger to develop a philosophically oriented approach to psychiatry that sought to account for the human being's "total existence."

HEIDEGGER AND DASEINSANALYSIS

Binswanger recognized early on the contributions that Heidegger's philosophy could make to psychiatry. In the early 1940s, following Heidegger's example, Binswanger adopted the term Daseinsanalysis—translated by Rollo May in *Existence* as "existential analysis"—to describe his clinical approach. According to Binswanger, Heidegger's fundamental ontology provided an analysis of the primary structures of human existence, and constituted a necessary foundation for the human sciences. Binswanger was primarily interested in Heidegger's analysis of existence, which is oriented toward an ontological end. In *Being and Time*, Heidegger calls for the return to the meaning of Being as such. Heidegger refers to the human being that questions the meaning of Being as "Dasein." Heidegger argues that Dasein is neither autonomous nor self-contained, but always already situated in the world. Thus, Dasein exists as "being-in-the-world."

As interpreted by Binswanger, the notion of being-in-the-world signified that we are not isolated, encapsulated egos, but rather, beings who are always in relation to other humans and the world around us. This implies that there is neither a subject-object dichotomy nor a division between subjective and objective experience. According to Binswanger, therefore, Heidegger's conception of world—the matrix of relations in which Dasein exists and discovers meaning—provides the clinician with a key conceptual tool for understanding and describing human experience.[8]

Binswanger enlarged Heidegger's ontological conception of world to include the horizon in which human beings live and through which they understand themselves. At the same time, Binswanger recognized three simultaneous modes of being-in-the-world: the *Umwelt*, constituting the environment within which a person exists; the *Mitwelt*, or world of social relations; and the *Eigenwelt*, the private world of self. According to Binswanger, the three modes together constitute a person's world-design—the general context of meaning within which a person exists. In the first of his existential analytic studies, *Dream and Existence* (1930), Binswanger described dreams in terms of the dreamer's world-designs, rather than psychic processes.[9] Similarly, in his studies on mania (1933) and schizophrenia (1957), Binswanger used the notion of world-designs of patients to elaborate the nature of manic experience and the spatial, temporal, and verbal structures of schizophrenic existence.[10]

Binswanger argued that the main goal of psychopathology was to achieve knowledge and scientific description of world-designs: that is, to see how patients relate to the people and social environment around them and thus to examine the way in which patients structure the world in which they exist. Since from Binswanger's perspective person and world are one, the aim is to understand and explain the human being in the totality of one's existence, which always includes one's relationship to others.

Indeed, for Binswanger the human being could never be understood separately, apart from others. In this sense, his position is surprisingly close to that of Harry Stack Sullivan and interpersonal psychoanalysis.[11] This is not entirely fortuitous, as Binswanger and Sullivan both develop a dialogical perspective, via the work of Martin Buber and George Herbert Mead respectively. Thus, in his chief theoretical work, *Basic Forms and Knowledge of Human Existence* (1942), Binswanger draws on Buber to elaborate a theory of dialogical interaction.[12] Similarly, Sullivan draws on Mead to emphasize the role of the other in human development. For Binswanger and Sullivan alike, the self always exists in relationship to others. And, as we will see shortly, there is a similar commonality in their elaboration of unconscious experience.

FREUD: APPRECIATION AND CRITIQUE

The development of a Daseinsanalytical perspective allowed Binswanger to elaborate his early reservations about the psychoanalytic theory of mind. Indeed, the intellectual distance traveled by Binswanger between his presidency of the Zurich Psychoanalytic Society in 1910 and his criticisms of

Freud during the 1930s are noteworthy. After adapting the notion of being-in-the-world to his clinical work, Binswanger essentially rejected the whole Freudian mental apparatus. Nor was he hesitant about informing his teacher and colleague of his disagreements.

In a public tribute, given in 1936 in celebration of Freud's eightieth birthday, Binswanger criticizes Freud for his avowed "naturalism." Binswanger argued that although Freud enlarged and deepened our insight into human nature, he achieved these insights in a scientific-theoretical garb that was not suited to the task. The result, for Binswanger, was a reductive and deterministic theory of mind. Although Freud was unable to attend the celebration in his honor, his written response to Binswanger is ironic and to the point:

> Dear friend. Your lecture was a pleasant surprise! Those who heard it and told me about it were obviously unimpressed; it must have been too difficult for them. As I read it I was delighted with your beautiful language, your erudition, the vastness of your horizon, your tactfulness in contradicting me. As is well known, one can put up with immense quantities of praise. Naturally you have failed to convince me![13]

Binswanger's arguments obviously did not sway Freud or his followers. Yet this fact does not detract from the importance of what Binswanger had to say about the psychoanalytic theory of mind and the unconscious. Rather, it suggests the need for closer analysis, but with one proviso. My objective is not to enter into a discussion about the validity of each of Binswanger claims against Freud, but simply to show the ways in which his critique made possible the development of a new and different perspective on unconscious experience.

Binswanger was chiefly concerned with what he referred to as the "reductionism" implicit in psychoanalytic theory. In criticizing Freud's structural account of the psyche, for example, Binswanger argues "when the self is objectified, isolated and theorized into an ego, or into an id, ego and superego, it is driven out of its authentic sphere of being, namely existence."[14] Binswanger was particularly opposed to the concept of causality that Freud derived from his model of mental functions: namely, the idea that human behavior is causally determined by the instinctual energy of the id. In a particularly significant passage, Binswanger states:

> Human existence never becomes apparent exclusively as mind or exclusively as drive; it is always both, drive and mind. Only theoretically and abstractly can "the mind and the drives" be differentiated. . . . If Nietzsche and psychoanalysis have shown that drives, especially in the form of sexuality, reach up to the highest pinnacle of human consciousness, I have tried to show the degree

to which consciousness extends its reach down to the deepest ground of "vitality." In other words, religious, moral, and aesthetic life must be acknowledged where the human being until now appeared to be dominated entirely by the vital or instinctual spheres. . . . One speaks of religion, morality and aesthetics not only where the human being has achieved in a clear self-awareness, a permanent sense of self, but everywhere where there is a self—though not always a permanent or constant self—intending an object. As is readily apparent, this is concerned with the positive clarification of the term, an "unconscious" mind.[15]

For Binswanger, the psychoanalytic conception of an unconscious, as the source of psychic energy and center of repressed mental processes, was not compatible with the notion of being-in-the-world. That Binswanger would take this position is hardly surprising. It is difficult to conceive of the place of the Freudian unconscious in Heidegger's analytic of Dasein.[16] The two systems of thought are in certain fundamental ways opposed to one another.

The aim of Heidegger's fundamental ontology is to overcome all forms of the subjectification of being. Heidegger seeks to undercut the Cartesian notion of an isolated, autonomous subject that exists in a world of separate objects by arguing that Dasein comes to be through its interactions with the world in which it exists. Because Dasein, according to Heidegger, is a prepersonal and pre-egological form of existence, it bears no relation to Cartesian subjectivism. On the one hand, Freud's notion of the unconscious also challenges the autonomy and mastery of the Cartesian mind. By positing the unconscious as a center of repressed drives, Freud calls into question the sovereignty of our thinking nature. On the other hand, however, his insistence on an "internalized" or "repressed" level of consciousness remains at base Cartesian and, as such, is incompatible with Dasein as being-in-the-world.

Following Heidegger, Binswanger conceives of Dasein as coming-to-be in the world. Dasein's experience of itself must always be understood in the context of its world. For Binswanger, the purpose of Daseinsanalysis is to elaborate the structure of an individual's world as it appears to, and is experienced by, that individual. It is on this point that Binswanger also sets himself apart from Heidegger. In his fundamental ontology, Heidegger insists that Dasein refers a presubjective form of being. Binswanger in essence concretizes this concept of Dasein to account for the psychological realities of human experience. In the process he allows for a subjective level of experiencing that is ostensibly excluded from Heidegger's analysis.

This step away from Heidegger is crucial since it enables Binswanger to conjecture about the role of an unconscious in human behavior. Binswanger allows that the unconscious may refer to a part of the human mind. Yet it cannot be understood to exist in a world of its own, nor relate to itself through a world. According to Binswanger:

An unconscious id is not the world in the sense of existence (Dasein), for being-in-the-world always means to be in the world as I-myself, He-himself, We-ourselves, or anonymous oneself; and least of all does the id know anything of "home," as is true of the dual We, of the I and Thou. The id is a scientific construct which objectifies existence—a "reservoir of instinctual energy."[17]

According to Binswanger, Freud's approach to the unconscious is akin to construing "behind the conscious personality an 'unconscious' second person."[18] Binswanger makes his point most sharply when he argues that Freud betrays his most profound insight by making the unconscious into an 'it' (the literal translation of *Es*). Binswanger states:

> It was after all precisely Freud who taught us that the "I-cannot" of patients must always be understood as an "I will not," in other words, that the "I-not-I" relationship must be understood as an "I-I myself" relationship. . . . Psychoanalysis in general has its existential justification only insofar as this translation is possible or at least meaningful. Yet Freud transforms, with a literally suicidal intention, the "*I will* not" to an "*it can* not."[19]

On this basis, Binswanger takes issue with the notions of causality and determinism implicit in Freud's theory of mind. Given the radicality of this critique, it must be noted that Binswanger, like Sartre after him, tends to view Freud's unconscious in terms of the his early work, in which a split is made between the unconscious and the conscious mind. As a result, Freud's modifications in his mature model of the mind are not sufficiently taken into account. Nevertheless, Binswanger's objective is not to develop a new and different theory of the mind, but to demonstrate the flaws inherent in a deterministic theory. Thus, insofar as the unconscious represents a part of human Dasein, he argues that it is Dasein that relates to the unconscious, and determines it, at least as much as Dasein finds itself determined by the unconscious.

Binswanger's contention that a part of the subject cannot determine the whole is more fully developed in Jean-Paul Sartre's *Being and Nothingness* (1943). According to Sartre, the idea of unconscious energy determining conscious behavior is seriously flawed. Using the example of "bad faith," he contends that for repression and resistance to be possible, the subject must be conscious of the impulses it wants to repress. As Sartre argues:

> How can we conceive of a knowledge which is ignorant of itself? . . . All knowing is consciousness of knowing. Thus the resistance of the patient implies on the level of the censor an awareness of the thing repressed as such, a comprehension of the end toward which the questions of the psychoanalyst are leading, and an act of synthetic

connection by which it compares the truth of the repressed complex to the psychoanalytic hypothesis which aims at it.[20]

Sartre argues that the subject has to be aware of its impulses if one is to be able to resist the interpretations of the psychoanalyst who threatens to expose what is hidden or repressed. On this view, the unconscious censor is, in fact, conscious of what it represses, thus obviating the conscious/unconscious distinction made by Freud.

For Sartre, the fact that consciousness is reintroduced at the level of the unconscious leads to a version of the problem of reflection. Sartre argues, against Freud, that the determination of the whole subject by a part will implicitly reintroduce the whole subject as the part, thus leading either to the subversion of the initial part-whole distinction, or to a condition of infinite regress. In other words, as long as the unconscious is conceived as part of the subject that causally determines consciousness—while still being inaccessible to consciousness—a situation of infinite regress will necessarily result.

FORMULATING UNCONSCIOUS EXPERIENCE

Binswanger's criticism of the Freudian unconscious is rarely as explicit as that of Sartre. Nor is his interest in psychoanalysis limited to or determined by his philosophical predilections. Binswanger, it must be remembered, was first and foremost a clinician whose approach was indebted to Freud and psychoanalysis. He is content, in the main, to assume that his criticism of the deterministic, explanatory nature of psychoanalysis applies to more specific aspects of psychoanalytic theory such as the unconscious. For Binswanger, moreover, Daseinsanalysis is complementary to a scientific explanatory system. As such, his criticism of such concepts as the unconscious involves their claim to finality, not their practical effectiveness per se.[21]

This fact may help to explain Binswanger's puzzling response to Freud: "Needless to say, I have never managed without the unconscious." Binswanger not only acknowledges the role of unconscious processes as an explanatory hypothesis for human behavior; he also emphasizes that his criticism of the unconscious does not amount to a rejection of such key psychoanalytic concepts as wishes, fantasies, or dreams. Rather, in contrast to psychoanalysis, the emphasis of Daseinsanalysis is on understanding and treating the particular world-design of the dreamer, what Binswanger refers to as the "being-in-it," or the way in which "being-self" corresponds to this world-design.[22] As such, the importance of wishes, fantasies, and dreams are all acknowledged by the Daseinsanalytic clinician, though they are analyzed in a different manner.

For Binswanger, as we have seen, the main goal of psychopathology is to achieve knowledge and scientific description of the patient's world-designs. On this basis, Binswanger distinguishes between two "very different scientific endeavors":

One is phenomenological [Daseinsanalysis] and devotes itself to the phenomenal content of every verbal expression, every mode of action, every attitude, and attempts to understand it from basic modes of human existence prior to the separation of body, soul, and mind, and of consciousness and unconsciousness; and the other [psychoanalysis] is the objectifying natural-scientific one, which according to Freud himself subordinates phenomena to the "hypothetically postulated strivings," investigates the verbal content not with respect to the world-design which emerges in it, but with respect to those strivings or "natural" instincts, and which thus projects the being of man upon the conceptual level of the being of "nature."[23]

In other words, Binswanger does not interpret a patient's experiences in terms of intrapsychic drives or a mental apparatus. Nor does he seek simply to elaborate the physical reality of the patient's world. Rather, clinical phenomena must be understood and examined within the field of existence in which they take form.

It thus is the way in which Binswanger conceptualizes unconscious experience that separates Daseinsanalysis most sharply from psychoanalysis. For Binswanger, to begin with, the term *unconscious* is adjectival; it is merely descriptive of a facet of human experience. In contrast to Freud, who sees the unconscious as the product of repressed drives, desires, and wishes, Binswanger examines an individual's unconscious experiences within the particular world-designs in which they take place. A case example will help illustrate this approach.

Binswanger provides an example from the *Jahrbuch* of Bleuler and Freud of a young girl who at the age of five experienced a puzzling attack of anxiety and fainting when her heel got stuck in her skate and separated from her shoe.[24] Thereafter the girl experienced spells of overwhelming anxiety whenever the heel of one of her shoes appeared loose or when someone touched the heel or even spoke of heels.

Binswanger suggests that psychoanalysis has shown the way in which these fears can signify anxieties about being separated from her mother. According to Binswanger, Freud demonstrated that it was the fantasies connected with the initial incident—not just the incident itself—that caused the pathogenic effect. From Binswanger's Daseinsanalytical perspective, however, the aim is to investigate the world-design that made these fantasies and phobias possible in the first place.

Binswanger suggests that the young girl's experience of "continuity" became constricted to such a degree that all of her experiences were subjected to this single category. It was this single category, in turn, that determined her world. Consequently, any experience of disruption or separation became very anxiety producing. As Binswanger puts it:

The emergence of the phobia should not be explained by an overly strong pre-oedipal tie to the mother. Rather, we should realize that such an overly strong filial tie is only possible on the premise of a world design based exclusively on connectedness, cohesiveness, and continuity. Such a way of experiencing the world and being attuned does not have to be "conscious." Neither must we call it "unconscious" in the psychoanalytic sense, since it is outside the contrast of these opposites.[25]

For Binswanger, then, the narrowness of this girl's world-design helps to explain the fact that she is unable to integrate the meaning of her phobia of heels. It is not the memory of the original event that is repressed, but, rather, the meaning of it that remains unarticulated and outside of her awareness.

If the young girl's constricted world-design is neither conscious nor unconscious, as Binswanger suggests, then what is it? According to Binswanger, the experiential data to which the descriptive term *unconscious* refers, represents that aspect of Dasein that Heidegger calls thrownness:

> Psychoanalysis, as we know, interprets the unconscious from the perspective of consciousness. But it is clear that a doctrine that does not proceed from the intentionality of consciousness, but that, rather, shows how this intentionality is grounded in the temporality of human existence, must interpret the distinction between consciousness and unconsciousness temporally and existentially. The point of departure for this interpretation cannot be consciousness. It can, instead, only be the "unconscious," the thrownness and determinateness of Dasein.[26]

According to Heidegger, thrownness is constitutive of Dasein as being-in-the-world. As interpreted by Binswanger, thrownness refers to Dasein's facticity. In other words, Dasein continually finds itself in a particular time and space, and in some way determined and limited by them. For Binswanger, it is this sense of having been "thrown" into a situation that is the object of what psychiatry investigates: the way in which we find ourselves determined by the past and the present—the place and situation in which we currently exist.

In reference to the case of the young girl, therefore, we see that for Binswanger her experience was unconscious in that sense that she found herself in a situation (thrownness) that led her to view the world exclusively in terms of "connectedness, cohesiveness, and continuity." This constricted world-design, in turn, determined the nature of her experiences and helps to explain her phobia and anxieties. It was through the later dialogue of psychoanalysis that her unconscious experience of the world was eventually made known.

Another way of thinking about the notion of thrownness, at least as Binswanger uses it, is in terms of prereflective experience. *Experience that has not been reflected on, formulated, and articulated necessarily remains latent and pre-reflective. Such pre-reflective, unformulated experience might be descriptively termed unconscious.* And it is precisely this perspective on unconscious experience that is developed in the work of Sullivan, to which I now turn.

FROM BINSWANGER TO SULLIVAN

Like Binswanger, Sullivan concentrates on the ways in which a person structures reality, not on building structure within the personality. For Binswanger and Sullivan alike, the aim of psychoanalysis is not to make the unconscious conscious in the traditional Freudian sense, but to free patients from distorted or constricted modes of relating to others and the world around them. As such, Binswanger's view of the unconscious might be understood along the lines of Sullivan's notion of "unformulated experience."[27] The unconscious, for Sullivan, refers to private experience that has yet to be elaborated and fully understood in the context of psychoanalytic dialogue.

Like Binswanger, Sullivan's approach remains sketchy. This is not entirely surprising since Sullivan was chiefly concerned with the interpersonal, not the intrapsychic dimension of experience. According to Sullivan, the goal of psychoanalysis is to identify and elaborate the patient's "parataxic" mode of relating: the arbitrary, private, and frequently distorted mode of interpersonal experience. To achieve this goal, the psychoanalyst and patient attempt to achieve "consensual validation" of the patient's experience of relating to others and the world. Consensual validation signals the arrival of the patient at a "syntaxic," or interpersonally verifiable view of reality. This process of dialogue is crucial to the work of analysis because it can help patients to understand, integrate, and ultimately overcome their parataxic mode of relating.

According to Sullivan, the formulation of all experience is connected to the "self-system," which includes all experiences and ways of relating that are not associated with anxiety. The self-system effects the way in which the person will formulate new and potentially anxiety producing experience. Sullivan suggests that when experiences are too laden with anxiety, then they are not formulated: "One has information about one's experience only to the extent that one has tended to communicate it to another or thought about it in the manner of communicative speech. Much of what is ordinarily said to be repressed is merely unformulated."[28] Sullivan elaborates the defensive use of unformulated experience in a much clearer sense than Binswanger. Unlike repression, in which an experience is defensively pushed from awareness, Sullivan is suggesting that certain experiences are never known to begin with and thus remained unformulated.

The distinction drawn by Sullivan between the actual experience and the knowledge we have of that experience is important. It also relates to Sartre's distinction between the pre-reflective and reflective dimensions of experience. Sartre argues that consciousness is immediate and pre-reflective, whereas knowledge is essentially reflective.[29] In other words, if I experience pleasure, my consciousness of pleasure exists together with my knowledge of it. Yet my consciousness and knowledge of pleasure are not identical. Without an immediate awareness of pleasure it would not be possible to reflect on the experience, know that it is a state of pleasure, and articulate it as such.

The point is that pre-reflective experience often remains unformulated until it is articulated in the presence of another person. For Sullivan, as we have seen, this takes place at the syntaxic level. Experiences that remain unformulated, on the other hand, are parataxic, since they are arbitrary, private, and not usually communicable. According to Sullivan, avoidance of formulation is accomplished by means of "selective inattention." This refers to situations in which one's attention is either not sufficiently focused on what is noticed, or one is unable to draw implications from what is noticed. As Sullivan puts it: "When things go by rapid transit through awareness into memory without the development of implications, those undeveloped implications are not there for the purpose or recall."[30] Yet selective inattention should not be understood in Freud's terms as a form of repression. Rather, as Donnel Stern suggests, the experience is never fully known to begin with because the interpersonal imprimatur it would need to be cognized was never present. As a result, such experience is screened out prior to its articulation and remains undeveloped.[31]

THE INDIVIDUAL UNCONSCIOUS

Sullivan's conception of unformulated experience clearly belies his strong interpersonal perspective. Indeed, it would seem that, for Sullivan, experience is only truly valid once it is interpersonally communicated and maintained. This position is reminiscent of later Ludwig Wittgenstein, who states in *Philosophical Investigations* (1953) that so-called inner or mental states of human experience are significant to human life to the extent that they are external, publicly observable process of actions or events: "an 'inner process' stands in need of outward criteria."[32] It is precisely on this point, however, that Sullivan's position differs most sharply from that of Binswanger.

Whereas Binswanger is concerned with elaborating the structure of an individual's world as it appears to and is experienced by that individual, Sullivan states famously that the feeling of being a unique individual, and of having a uniquely individual self is nothing more than a narcissistically invested fiction.[33] Thus, while Binswanger and Sullivan would no doubt agree on the notion of unformulated experience and the role it can play in psychopathology, they part ways on the notion of an "individual uncon-scious"—and with good reason.

The problem with Sullivan's position on unformulated experience is that it discounts the role of the pre-reflective self, which is by its very nature individual. The simple example of looking at oneself in the mirror illustrates the epistemic basis of the pre-reflective self. In order to re-cognize myself in a mirror as both the knower and the known, I must already possess an initial familiarity with myself. Otherwise, I would not be able to identify the image in the mirror as my own.[34] It is this aspect of the self—an unformulated yet implicit self-awareness—that is fundamental to our ability to relate to others and the world around us. It is also inimitably connected to our use and understanding of language. Thus, when Sullivan suggests, following Mead, that meaning at the unformulated level can only be known if it is symbolized in a publically appreciable way, he overlooks an important fact.

If I cannot articulate a meaning to someone else in terms that the other person can understand, it suggests I am not yet able to reflect on that meaning in an interpersonally verifiable way. But this does not detract from the implicit validity of this meaning. Indeed, I would like to suggest that it is precisely this form of individual meaning—that which is not yet articu-lated and remains prereflective—that is the key to spontaneous artistic cre-ation, whether in music, painting, sculpture, or other art forms. Similarly, it is the poet who relies on evocative power of metaphor to bend and manipu-late language in ways that can communicate such unformulated meanings.

The problem with Sullivan's emphasis on an interpersonally verifiable view of reality is that it undervalues the way in which individual meaning can be private and significant at the same time. For example, I may find myself in love with another person but not know the words to correctly name and communicate this feeling. This does not imply, however, that my experience is any less valid than if I were able to articulate and name it. Indeed, in such cases I may rely on art, music, or poetry to communicate this experience. Moreover, if I am fortunate enough that the other person shares my feelings of love, he or she may be able to understand such nonverbal communications, even without the use of a formal, public language. My point is that in referring to the individual, private nature of unformulated experience as parataxic, there is a tendency to overlook its importance for the nature of self-experience and self-understanding. It is precisely the pre-reflective familiarity the self has with itself that is constitutive of the indi-vidual unconscious, and, as we have seen, forms the necessary basis for achieving conscious, self-reflective awareness. Ironically, in his attempt to overcome the intrapsychic dimension entirely, Sullivan neglected what Freud's perspective on the unconscious had to offer: namely, a uniquely individual form of self-experience. Binswanger's concern with articulating the individual world-designs of his patients allowed for the unfolding of this self-experience in a more nuanced way than was possible in Sullivan's interpersonal model.

The insights of Binswanger and Sullivan thus provide us with an alternative way of approaching, understanding, and ultimately elaborating the nature of unconscious experience. To be sure, the perspectives of both thinkers remain underdeveloped and in need of further discussion. My objective, in this chapter, has been to show ways in which such discussion might proceed. Although neither Binswanger nor Sullivan, in my view, satisfactorily come to terms with such fundamental issues as repression and dissociation, they expand on areas of individual experience that have remained outside the purview of traditional psychoanalytic theorizing. The ego psychological, structural model of the psyche, which dominated American psychoanalysis until recently, did not allow for elaboration of the level of experience examined by Binswanger and Sullivan. As Binswanger aptly states: "In every psychology that makes the human being into an object . . . we find a fracture, a rift through which it is apparent that what is being scientifically studied is not the whole person, not the human being as a whole. Everywhere we find something that overflows and bursts the parameters of such a psychology."[35] My elaboration of the perspectives of Binswanger and Sullivan should not, however, be read simply as an indictment of what Freud said about the unconscious. Indeed, just as Binswanger and Sullivan expand on Freud's initial insights through critique and revision, so too has psychoanalysis developed in new directions. An adequate understanding of the nature of unconscious experience must take all of these perspectives into account.

NOTES

1. Ludwig Binswanger, *Freud: Reminiscences of a Friendship*, Norbert Guterman, trans. (New York: Grune and Stratton, 1957), 64. A note on translation: the few existing translations of Binswanger are frequently imprecise. I have therefore changed translations where deemed necessary and usually quote the original German text.

2. Binswanger, *Freud*, 64.

3. Rollo May et al., *Existence: A New Dimension in Psychiatry and Psychology* (New York: Basic Books, 1958).

4. See Gerhard Fichtner, ed., *Sigmund Freud—Ludwig Binswanger. Briefwechsel, 1908–1938* (Frankfurt a.M.: Fischer, 1992), for a full account of the correspondence.

5. Binswanger, *Freud*, 69.

6. Binswanger, *Einführung in die problem der allgemeinen psychologie* (Berlin: Julius, 1922).

7. Martin Heidegger, *Being and Time*, John Macquarrie and Edward Robinson, trans. (Oxford: Blackwell, 1927/1962).

8. Heidegger was initially intrigued by Binswanger's work and the two men entered into a correspondence in the late 1920s, which was punctuated by personal visits over the next four decades. For a detailed discussion of the Binswanger–Heidegger relationship, see: Roger Frie, "Interpreting a Misinterpretation: Ludwig Binswanger and Martin Heidegger," *Journal of the British Society for Phenomenology* 29 (1999): 244–257. Binswanger began sending Heidegger his texts in the early 1930s, and the philosopher responded in kind. From the late 1940s onward, however, Heidegger

worked closely together with another Swiss psychiatrist, Medard Boss. Today the term *Daseinsanalysis* is commonly used to refer to the work done by the Daseinsanalytical Institute in Zurich, which was founded by Boss. In contrast to Boss, Binswanger was critical of some aspects of Heidegger's philosophy. Binswanger's interpretation of *Being and Time*, which for a time set the standard for interested psychologists and psychiatrists, did not remain loyal to the philosopher's text. In addition, Binswanger drew on other thinkers to develop a theory of human interaction that he felt was missing in Heidegger's fundamental ontology. This led to Heidegger's and Boss' later critique of Binswanger's work; see Martin Heidegger, *Zollikoner Seminare*, Medard Boss, ed. (Frankfurt a.M: Vittorio Klostermann, 1987).

9. Binswanger, "Traum und Existenz." In *Ausgewählte werke band III: Vorträge und Aufsätze*, M. Herzog, ed. (Heidelberg: Asanger, 1930/1994), 95–120.

10. Binswanger, *Über Ideenflucht*. In *Ausgewählte werke band I: Formen missglückten daseins*, M. Herzog, ed. (Heidelberg: Asanger, 1933/1992), 1–232; Binswanger, *Schizophrenie* (Pfullingen: Günter Neske, 1957).

11. R. Frie, The Existential and the Interpersonal: Ludwig Binswanger and Harry Stack Sullivan, *Journal of Humanistic Psychology* 40 (2000): 108–129.

12. Binswanger. *Ausgewählte Werke Band 2: Grundformen und Erkenntnis menschlichen Daseins*, M. Herzog and H. J. Braun, eds. (Heidelberg: Asanger, 1942/1993).

13. Binswanger, *Freud*, 96.

14. Binswanger, *Ausgewählte Vorträge und Aufsätze, bd. II* (Bern: Francke, 1955), 181.

15. Binswanger, *Ausgewählte werke band I: Formen missglückten daseins*, M. Herzog, ed. (Heidelberg: Asanger, 1992) 221.

16. This fact has not stood in the way of innovative, if ultimately unsuccessful attempts to locate the place of the unconscious in Heidegger's work. See William Richardson, "The Place of the Unconscious in Heidegger." In K. Hoeller, ed., *Heidegger and Psychology* (Seattle: Review of Existential Psychology and Psychiatry, 1988), 176–198.

17. Binswanger, "The Case of Ellen West." In R. May et al., *Existence: A New Dimension in Psychiatry and Psychology* (New York: Basic Books, 1958), 326–327.

18. Binswanger, "The Case of Ellen West," 326.

19. Binswanger, *Ausgewählte Vorträge und Aufsätze, bd. I* (Bern: Francke, 1947) 117.

20. Jean-Paul Sartre, *Being and Nothingness*, Hazel Barnes, trans. (New York: Philosophical Library, 1956), 52.

21. For a similar perspective on Binswanger's approach to Freud's unconscious, see Jacob Needleman, *Being-in-the-world* (New York: Souvenier, 1964), 88.

22. Binswanger, "The Case of Ellen West," 327.

23. Binswanger, "The Case of Ellen West," 327.

24. See Binswanger, "Über die daseinsanalytishe Forschungsrichtung in der Psychiatry." In *Ausgewählte Vorträge und Aufsätze, Vol. 1*, 190–217, for a more detailed discussion of this case.

25. Binswanger, "Über die daseinsanalytishe Forschungsrichtung in der Psychiatry." In Ausgewählte Vorträge und Aufsätze, Vol. 1, 198.

26. Binswanger, "Heidegger's Analytic of Existence and Its Meaning for Psychiatry." In Needleman, *Being-in-the-World*, 219.

27. Harry Stack Sullivan, *Conceptions of Modern Psychiatry* (New York: Norton, 1953), 185.

28. Sullivan, *Conceptions of Modern Psychiatry*, 185.

29. Sartre, *Being and Nothingness* (New York: Philosophical Library, 1956).

30. Sullivan, "Selective Inattention." In H. S. Perry et al., *Clincial Studies in Psychiatry* (New York: Norton, 1956), 58.

31. Donnel Stern, *Unformulated Experience* (Hillsdale, NJ: Analytic Press, 1997), 60.

32. Ludwig Wittgenstein, *Philosophical Investigations* (Oxford: Blackwell, 1953), sec. 580.

33. Sullivan, "The Illusion of Personal Individuality." In *The Fusion of Psychiatry and the Social Sciences* (New York, Norton, 1971) 198–226.

34. This was the so-called "original insight" expounded by the early German Romantic philosopher J. G. Fichte; a similar perspective on self experience was elaborated in the German Romantic philosophy of F. W. J. von Schelling and Friedrich von Hardenberg, also known as the poet Novalis. See Roger Frie, *Subjectivity and Intersubjectivity in Modern Philosophy and Psychoanalysis* (Lanham, MD: Rowman and Littlefield, 1997/ 2000) for a more detailed discussion of the relevance of early German Romantic philosophy to current debates on subjectivity in philosophy and psychoanalysis.

35. Binswanger, *Freuds Auffassung des Menschen im Lichte der Anthropologie*. In *Ausgewählte Vorträge und Aufsätze, Bd. I* (Bern: Francke, 1947), 179.

THREE

TRUTH, MIND, AND OBJECTIVITY

Marcia Cavell

UNTIL RECENTLY, we conceived the mind as essentially monadic, containing entirely within itself much of its content as well as the rudiments of its structure. In recent years, however, a number of psychoanalysts and philosophers have begun to view the mind as constituted by an interactive, interpersonal world. (The new discovery that connections in the infant brain are made through the infant's earliest interplay with responsive adults is a graphic neurological correlate of this thesis.) We think of the observational stance as *within* an intersubjective field (Mitchell, 1988), and hold that knowledge is achieved through a process of dialogue in which every person's contribution is necessarily partial. I will refer loosely to these and kindred beliefs as the Intersubjective view of the mind, though in both psychoanalysis and philosophy there are important differences among the view's various proponents.

It is a shift with enormous clinical implications, affecting how we think about resistance (Spezzano, 1993), the unconscious (Atwood, 1992), psychic change (Hoffman, 1983), and of course the analytic relationship. The 'neutral' analytic observer, situated somehow outside the analyst-analysand pair where he or she has privileged access to the truth, has disappeared; between analyst and patient, we recognize, interpretation goes two ways (Hoffman, 1983).

I think that in general the intersubjectivists are on the right track. All the more reason for protecting their position against some mistaken inferences they themselves occasionally draw that actually undermine it. The following passages from recent psychoanalytic writers, all of whom I am generally in sympathy with, represent the sorts of mistakes I have in mind:

(1) " 'Reality,' as we use the term, refers to something subjective, something felt or sensed, rather than to an external realm of being existing independently of the human subject" (Atwood, 1992, pp, 26, 27). (2) The idea of analytic 'objectivity,' Fogel suggests, is "an intellectual remnant of the one-person psychology paradigm." He continues: "Might reducing the object of analysis to the 'interaction' between patient and analyst not mislead us, if it predisposes us to imagine that there is an objective reality, 'out there' between analyst and patient, that one can be 'objective' about?" (Fogel, 1996, p. 885). (3) "If an observation or measurement could establish a truth, that truth could never become untrue. Yet this happens all the time in science" (Spezzano, 1993, p. 30).

Each of these passages says something important. The first and second insist that the only 'reality' we can investigate, know, deceive ourselves about, must be within the realm of someone's potential experience. So Kant said, and on this point few philosophers would disagree. But it does not follow that reality is subjective. On the contrary, in the absence of a distinction between what I 'subjectively'—or even we, putting our 'subjectivities' together—believe to be the case (a belief that itself is as much a part of reality as the chair I am sitting on), and what *is* the case, however that is ascertained, the concept of reality loses its sense. In what follows, it will emerge, I hope, that objective reality is a concept indispensable to human affairs.

The third passage warns that *what we take to be a truth* can always be called into question at another time, or under other circumstances; that our claims to truth must always be provisional; that a truth claim is always that, a claim, requiring support; that between the best evidence and *what is the case* there will always be a gap; that a justified belief and a true belief are, unfortunately, not necessarily the same; that talk about 'the truth,' especially 'sincere,' self-righteous talk, is often a way of dignifying one's own blind spots; that the conversational move that says 'You're wrong' or 'That is not true' is often a conversation-stopper (this last is more a question of tact than fact, however).

Yet it is what we hold true that changes, not truths themselves. The shift from the widely held twelfth-century idea that the earth is flat to the fifteenth-century idea that it is round is not a change in truth but in belief. We now hold that our ancestors had very good reasons for believing what they did about the shape of the earth—indeed little reason for believing anything else. Their beliefs were amply justified, yet wrong. We suspect, furthermore, that if these ancestors were here now and knew what we do, they would agree with us; that between us and them there would be room for dialogue.

So what is truth? We might think, confusedly, that answering this would deliver all the particular truths there are. But as I understand it, the question seeks a clarification of the concept of truth, and this clarification will not tell us which particular propositions are worthy of belief. In short, we cannot give a definition of truth that will allow us to pick out just those propositions that are true. That would be a bit of magic. Nevertheless, we can say clarifying things like the following: truth is a property of sentences, beliefs, propositions, such that if a person's belief that the earth is round is true, the world is round. (Philosophers put it this way: 'P' is true if and only if *p*. For example: The sentence 'Miriam is Adrian's sister' is true if and only if Miriam is Adrian's sister.) I will call this idea that truth depends on the way things are, not on how people think they are or wish they were, the homely view of truth. (It is because of this dependency that some philosophers have viewed truth as correspondence. The trouble with this view, however, is that it does not even begin to explain truth, for there is no way of carving out just that part of the world that makes a belief true. This is where coherence comes in. We cannot say that truth just is coherence either, for coherence is only one constraint on rationality. A system of beliefs might be perfectly self-consistent, yet inconsistent with another system. To this, coherentists sometimes respond that any coherent system of beliefs must be appropriately responsive to the way the world is, a response that returns us to the homely idea of truth. For a fuller discussion of truth, correspondence, and coherence, see Cavell, 1993, ch. 1.) Of course to investigate the truth of any belief or sentence we must first know its meaning, which is constructed by us. Meaning is constructed; so are theories. Furthermore, the meaning of a belief or sentence is constrained by its place in a network of other sentences in the language or beliefs in the person's mind. But truth is not constructed.

Truth is objective in the sense that the truth of a sentence or belief is independent of us; what is true about a particular matter may be different not only from anybody and everybody's opinion about its truth, but also from its utility: a belief that works for me, even for us, may turn out to be false. (When pushed on this point, pragmatists often retort that 'useful' must take in the longest possible run, and everything we will ever know about the way things are, a retort that once again collapses 'useful' back into 'true.')

Here is my claim: Subjectivity, in a certain key sense of the word to be defined later, goes hand in hand with intersubjectivity; but also, a concept of intersubjectivity that floats free from the ideas of objectivity and truth is no intersubjectivity at all. This is because of what I see as necessary conditions for the mental. Many psychoanalysts have been saying in different ways that the 'space' within which thinking can occur is triangular in character. (I return later to some of these authors.) So I say also; but the space I see is triangulated by one mind, other minds, and the objective world, discoverable by each of them, existing independent of their beliefs and will, a world they share in fact, and which they know they share. The argument I am going to work out is that two minds can know each other *as* minds only on the same condition. Take away this third point of the triangle, the objective world, and we are left with no minds at all. Give up the idea of an objective reality, 'out there' between analyst and patient that we can be more or less objective about, and what we are left with *is* "the one-person psychology paradigm." Forego the idea that analyst and patient share a common world, despite the differences in their experiences of it, and we make the idea of interpretation unintelligible; for interpretation requires that there be public things, like the words we say, the things we do, the common room that patient and analyst inhabit, to give a common reference from which interpretation can get started, a ground for either agreement or disagreement. I cannot disagree with you about the shape of the earth, for example, unless I know more or less what you mean by 'the earth,' and believe that we are talking about, more or less, the same thing. If we are not, then we are not disagreeing but talking past each other. The separateness of analyst from patient that is an essential aspect of the psychoanalytic situation is a function of the fact that there is an objective world out there, larger than the two participants, to allow them a perspective beyond their own.

In the first two sections, I elaborate a certain shift that has taken place in twentieth-century philosophy from what I will call a subjectivist view of meaning and mind to an intersubjectivist view, and I argue for the latter. We find versions of the first in philosophy from Plato, on whom I touch very briefly, through Descartes, my central focus, all the way to the contemporary philosopher, John Searle. My discussion of subjectivism attempts to make clear that it is only the Cartesian view of truth from which we need to distance ourselves.

For versions of the intersubjectivist view I single out George Herbert Mead, V.S. Vygotsky, Ludwig Wittgenstein, and Donald Davidson. Psychoanalysts familiar with other philosophers who might seem equally well to deserve consideration here, for example, Husserl, Gadamer, Habermas, or Putnam, may wonder why I omit them. I do so for the sake of brevity, and because my view of intersubjectivity is tendentious. The philosophers I discuss are en route to the following specific ideas that I think are crucial: (1) The concept of mind can be elucidated only by reference to the normative concepts of truth, objectivity, and reason. This of course does not mean that all thought even of a propositional sort is rational; much is not. It means, first, that a creature lacking these concepts altogether could not be said to have any thoughts *of a propositional sort*; it means, second, that so long as there is a mind at all, that mind must be rational to some extent, where by 'rationality' I do not mean a narrow capacity to draw logical conclusions, but to appreciate concepts like 'evidence,' 'reason for,' 'commitment.' (2) When a child can be said to have propositional thought, she has made a qualitative leap from the on-the-way-to-thought child that she was before. The leap describes her, and also our vocabulary for understanding her. (3) To make this leap the child must have been in communication with other (thinking) creatures. This is the sense in which the mind is constituted by an interactive, interpersonal world.

Considerably shorter, the third and fourth sections discuss unconscious fantasy and some problems facing psychoanalysis now. The theme of truth threads through all four sections.

I should make three things clear at the start. First, when I talk about thought, I have in mind desires and emotions as well as beliefs. Second, my concern is specifically with the capacity for thought that is symbolic and propositional in character. Of course much goes on in the infant prior to the development of this capacity that affects what sort of thinker the child will be. Third, I take for granted that many thoughts even of a propositional character are unconscious, and that we all have many thoughts that cannot be captured in words.

THE SUBJECTIVIST VIEW

Plato was struck by the fact that whenever we make a judgment about something—as we do, for example, in believing that this is a table—we use predicates that are general in character. Words and particular ideas mean what they do, Plato thought, by invoking the corresponding general Forms, which transcend material reality and antedate all human minds. Plato was struck also by the fact that a judgment says something that is in principle true or false. When we know *for certain* which it is, then apropos that judgment, and only then, Plato thought, do we have knowledge; and certainty, like meaning, points to our acquaintance with the transcendent world of Forms. Thus, Plato accounts for meaning, truth, and knowledge by appealing to a realm of being that is perfect, timeless, and from which our very corporeality distances us. One important source for the later Christian ideas of original sin, and of atonement (at-onement) as requiring an act of divine grace, is here in Plato. (Read 'the spatiotemporal body' as what deprives us of godly knowledge.) Nietzsche's famous attack on Truth was fired in part by his belief that the idea of truth is inevitably linked to subservient self-loathing and a denigration of the 'merely' human.

Some of Plato's view is discernible in Descartes: for example, the ideas that any knowledge worthy of its name must be certain, and that certainty is underwritten by a transcendent order of reality, which for Descartes was God. But whereas Plato envisaged knowledge as a relation between Mind and the Forms, Descartes substituted a relation between individual mind and its inner ideas or objects. Descartes held that typically our ideas (a term that as he uses it is ambiguous between 'idea' as mental image, as concept, as proposition) purport to be representations of things in the external world. When these ideas are accurate, so are our beliefs about the external world. But even in the absence of this correspondence, I can at least be certain of knowing what I think, that is, be certain of what my mental representations are. I may be mistaken in believing that the room is hot or that the table is red; I cannot be mistaken in thinking that I *believe* the table is red. For to know what I believe I only need turn my mental eye inwards and discern the mental objects that are there, for instance, the idea 'The table is red.' I will refer to this as the ocular model of self-knowledge.

Descartes conceives the mind on the analogy of a theater, a theater that only the person whose mind it is can enter. Therefore that person and she alone is in a position to see firsthand what is happening on the stage. But whereas my physical eye sees a table in the material world, normally the same table that you see if you are in the right position, my mental eye sees a thoroughly private, subjective object. These ideas, not the things they supposedly represent, are the only things with which the mind can be acquainted. With Descartes, subjectivity in its modern sense is born, the sense in which our knowledge of our minds is presumably not connected in any essential way with the external world, and in which knowledge of other minds is either impossible or mysterious. (It would be interesting to see how Freud's concept of 'das Ich'—'the ego'—implicitly relies on a Cartesian view of the self, even as Freud attempts to undercut it.)

Descartes's picture seems to be in accord with some important phenomena of our mental life, and, because it is, the view continues to appeal both to common sense and to some philosophers. It is true, for example, that I can often know what I am thinking about without looking outside myself. So it may seem that the content of an idea is entirely contained within it. Nevertheless, there are a number of overwhelming problems with the subjectivist paradigm. I will mention a few.

Skepticism: Since it claims that all that we are directly acquainted with is our private, internal representations, the paradigm inevitably leads to skepticism about the very existence of the external world and other minds. Descartes's escape hatch is God, who warrants our knowledge claims about the external world if we arrive at them in the right way. Thus, in His goodness, God can close the gap for us between justified belief and true belief. We should note, in passing, that the Cartesian knower resembles that 'neutral' observer of which many psychoanalysts are now rightly so skeptical, the observer who presumably sees things free of human taint, just as they are.

Meaning and mental content: By the content of a thought I mean what it concerns or is about (I believe this is what Freud meant by 'quality,' 1950 [1895]). Descartes's view of meaning is 'internalist' in the sense that he thinks there is no necessary connection, anywhere in the network of a person's thoughts, between mental content and what is outside his mind, between what one means by his words and the external world. The problem here with Descartes is this: if we have no direct acquaintance with the external world but only with our own thoughts, then what entitles us to describe them in a language of material things? What entitles us to say that a particular thought is a world-is-round-sort-of-thought? How can we even speak of our ideas as representations, since to know that one thing represents another, one must have had some experience of both? The intersubjectivists I come to in a moment are united in holding that representation cannot provide the key to a theory of meaning. Of course a belief or proposition asserts that something is the case, and in this sense represents the world as being a certain way. But a theory of meaning needs to understand how concepts have the meaning that they do, how the person herself knows what she means, how sounds acquire significance. These are questions that the concept of representation begs, by telling us, so to speak, that ideas wear their meaning on their face. We intersubjectivists hold that representation cannot play the role in a theory of mind that Descartes and later representationalists assigned to it.

Kant might seem to have gotten around Cartesian skepticism in arguing that there must be a fundamental compatability between mind and world, and that it is this compatibility that makes knowledge possible. Kant also anticipates the Wittgensteinian emphasis on the normativity of the mental, the thesis that by their nature, thoughts are constrained by norms of rationality. But the distinction Kant draws between the conceptual scheme (imposed by us) and some raw, uninterpreted Given on which this scheme is imposed, reinstates the Cartesian doctrine that the mind *represents* the external world via pictures that might have nothing to do with how things really are. (For a fuller discussion of knowledge as representation, and 'the myth of the Given,' see Rorty, 1979).

Historicity: The Cartesian view does not make room for an idea that comes to seem more and more important in the latter part of the nineteenth century—namely, that all knowing is historically situated, necessarily partial in character, the achievement of individuals who are limited by their particular places in space and time. Knowledge is never certain, we now think; and it grows not by transcending partiality altogether but through a dialogue over time.

Language: It is clearly a public phenomenon. The subjectivist begins with the private, internal, and the intrinsically subjective, and will have to account for the publicity of language by somehow matching public words to private states or objects. But since on his view these states are thoroughly internal, it is hard to see how any such matching can take place.

To be sure, there are philosophers who think these problems can be solved in ways very different from the ones I suggest. I cannot argue with them here. My aim rather is to sketch an approach to mind and meaning that to many of us looks very promising, an approach that starts with public phenomena like people doing things with each other, and works its way 'inward' to mind.

Before leaving subjectivism, I should point out that Freud unquestioningly bought into the Cartesian ocular model of self-knowledge (somewhat modified by Kant), together with its skepticism about our knowledge of the external world. Freud writes: "Consciousness makes each of us aware only of his own states of mind" (1915, p, 169). And also, "behind the attributes of the object under examination which are presented directly to perception, we have to discover something else which is more independent of the particular receptive capacity of our sense organs and which approximates more closely to what may be supposed to be the real state of affairs. We have no hope of being able to reach the latter itself" (1940 [1938], p. 196). And again: "[psychical reality] is as much unknown to us as the reality of the external world, and it is as incompletely presented by the data of consciousness as is the external world by the communication of our sense organs"(1900, p. 613).

THE INTERSUBJECTIVIST VIEW
AND THE NORMATIVITY OF THE MENTAL

One of the first thinkers to put forward an intersubjectivist position was George Herbert Mead. Influenced by Darwin, Mead attempted to give a naturalistic account of specifically human thought by tracing it to lower, simpler orders of communication (Mead, 1934). At the same time, he insisted that our symbolizing activity is categorically different from any form of communication from which it evolves. The (impossible) problem he set himself was, in effect, to reduce the irreducible (more about reducibility later).

Mead distinguishes three levels of meaning. The first he calls a conversation of gestures, seen among the higher vertebrates. The second is the signal-language level at which a single word like "Fire," for example, acts as a stimulus to behavior. The third level is fully articulated propositional thought in which symbols, which are not context-dependent, replace signals that are. In a conversation of gestures, the evolutionary starting point, two animals respond to each other reciprocally, the behavior of each acting as a stimulus to the other: In a dogfight, for example, the behavior of Fido prompts a second dog to act in a way that in turn modifies Fido's behavior; and so on. The two dogs are interacting in a way that resembles human conversation, but we don't think their 'gestures' are accompanied by ideas in their heads; it is we, the observers, who ascribe meanings to animal behavior on the basis of what function it has within a group: searching for food, defending against predators, finding a mate, and so on.

An essential difference between a mere gesture and gesture at the symbolic level, Mead holds, is that the latter is accompanied by an idea, an idea that is virtually the same for both creatures. (The patient says, "I am feeling depressed," and if the analyst catches his meaning, she thinks something like "He is feeling depressed.") To explain how symbolic communication evolves from the conversation of gestures, Mead posits an identificatory act that he calls 'taking the attitude of the other.' The basic idea is that a gesture of the first creature, A, takes on a meaning for a second creature, B, who responds to A's gesture; in so doing, B interprets A's gesture in a certain way. A did not intend his gesture to have such a meaning; he did not intend anything at all. Yet if A can now take B's attitude toward his own gesture, he becomes his own interpreter; his gesture acquires for him a meaning like that it has for B. I have cast the process Mead envisions as if it took place in the life of a single individual; but Mead thinks of it as spanning species and generations. At the end of this process, he thinks, a creature with symbolic thought has evolved.

With the ideas of 'internalizing' and 'taking the attitude of the other,' Mead hoped to have located a particular bit of behavior that would explain the rise of symbolic thought, while preserving his insight that it is irreducible to anything less complex. But it's a pseudo explanation; for either A's taking the attitude of the other just is the very thing to be explained, an act of interpretation that presumes symbolic thought, or else there is nothing yet to distinguish what A does from mimicry or imitation, and we have not left the conversation of gesture. Nevertheless, in launching an investigation of meaning from two creatures interacting in a shared world, Mead's argument moves in the right direction. By implication: Descartes's investigation was wrongheaded both because it made the solitary individual its starting point, and because it took reflection rather than purposive, worldly action as the paradigmatic expression of human thought.

During roughly the same period of time, the Russian psychologist L. S. Vygotsky was developing an idea similar to Mead's. Vygotsky also held that the individual mind emerges from a more rudimentary and collective form of life, and that the crucial turn is a kind of internalization of the other. Critical of Piaget, who held, following Freud, that first there are deeply personal, subjective, autistic mental states, which under the pressure of socialization finally yield to "social thought," Vygotsky traced a developmental scheme that proceeds from social communication, to egocentric thought, and finally to full-fledged mental states (Vygotsky, 1962). Vygotsky writes: "the process of internalization is not the *transferral* of an external activity to a preexisting internal plane of consciousness; it is the process in which this internal plane is formed" (quoted in Wertsch, 1985, p. 64). For example: the child reaches unsuccessfully for an object, and the mother comes to get the object for the child. Over time what was at first a gesture that had no significance for the child but only for the mother becomes, through that interaction, a gesture with which the child *means* to point.[1] By this route, eventually the child as well as the mother can point to the apple with the idea in mind, 'Here is an apple.' Daniel Stern's use of the idea of feedback loops in parent–infant interactions might suggest a similar process (Stern, 1995).

Like Mead and Vygotsky, the later Wittgenstein thought the traditional subjectivist picture was fundamentally wrongheaded in isolating thought from action, private thought from public speech, mind from body, and one mind from other minds. The Platonic idea that individual words or concepts have meaning all by themselves begins its investigation of meaning in the wrong place, for words come to have meaning only through the activities of actual speakers who are doing things with words in the course of carrying out communal enterprises (Wittgenstein, 1953). Attention to the ways language is actually used in daily life will free us from the temptation to hypostatize language and meanings, as Plato did in positing a heaven of Forms. There are not *meanings*, but people meaning things by what they say and do.

To see how a view of meaning might take us to the intersubjectivist claim that the mind is constituted out of its interactions with other creatures, recall Descartes's ocular view of the mind, that each of us knows what she thinks (what she means), when she does, by looking inward. The presupposition here is that the meaning of an idea is written on its face, so to speak. Ideas have the content they do through representing sonething else. But, Wittgenstein points out, the concept of representation doesn't help in explaining how words and ideas acquire meaning: for what a sign represents is not something the sign itself can tell us. Even a portrait of Marilyn Monroe that is faithful to her can be taken to be her portrait only by someone who knows something about Monroe. And of course many representations are not isomorphic with the things they represent. For a representation of an apple, say, to be a representation *of an apple*, the person for whom it represents an apple must intend for it do so, must know its meaning already. So the idea of representation leaves unexplained the very thing it was summoned for: to elucidate how signs, words, ideas, thoughts, come to have the meaning they do.

Why does Wittgenstein invest rule-following with this importance? What does he mean by following a rule? Understanding why he links mind to the having of concepts will help answer these questions, as 'following a rule' elucidates what he means by having concepts. One can define 'concept' in many ways. The sense Wittgenstein is after helps describe the concept of mind in ways that reveal both its peculiarity and its embeddedness in social practice.

By 'rule-following' Wittgenstein clearly means something other than the mere disposition to do as others do; for bees and lemmings and indeed all other creatures are so disposed, yet we can describe their behavior without ascribing to them concepts. Mere regularity of behavior, even regularity that is social in character, does not give us the rule-following Wittgenstein is trying to capture; mere regularity does not call for the concept of mind. (See Kripke, 1982, Brandom, 1994, for a discussion of Wittgenstein on rule-following.) Nor does discriminatory behavior; for sunflowers can turn toward the sun, thermostats register degrees of heat, bulls be enraged by the color red, all in the absence of mind.

The relationship between being a creature that can follow rules and being a creature whose behavior is guided by concepts is clearer if we say this: having concepts (in the sense Wittgenstein is trying to capture) presumes the creature's understanding that some things are *correctly* included under the concept and some things are not, that some applications of it are right, and some wrong. Such a creature has, in Wilfred Sellars's famous phrase, entered 'the space of reasons' (Sellars, 1956). An infant might wave its hands in a particular way only when it is handed a rattle; but many of us would not want to say that therefore the infant has the concept of a rattle. So I read Wittgenstein as suggesting that we speak of the child's having the concept of a rattle not only when it responds in a particular way to rattles, but when it can think something like 'This is a rattle' and also 'That is *not* a rattle'; that the capacity for making this distinction comes along only with the more general normative concepts of error, correct and incorrect, right and wrong, objective truth; and that these arise only through engagement in communal practices.

Descartes held that the one thing we can sometimes know for sure is our own minds, that is, what we think and feel. But one cannot think the thoughts 'I am in pain,' or 'I am feeling angry,' or 'I am afraid she has gone away for good,' without the concepts of self, pain, anger, fear, belief, and so on. So if Wittgenstein is right about what concept formation requires, one could not think these thoughts at all in the absence of contact somewhere in the course of one's life with other persons and the external world. Further- more, though I have not shown how Wittgenstein argues this, one learns to apply these mental predicates to oneself only as one learns also to apply them to others.

We use the word 'subjectivity' in many ways; in some, it is attributable to infants and creatures other than ourselves. But in the non-Cartesian sense of the word that I am singling out, subjectivity exists only where there is the having of thoughts, some of which one knows as *thoughts*, and as one's *own* thoughts. In this sense subjectivity is not a condition into which we are born but one we slowly enter through our interactions with the world and with other persons in this world. Wittgenstein is not denying that my experience of pride, or sadness, or pain, is peculiar to me, nor that we can sometimes keep our pains and thoughts to ourselves, two ideas that the concept of subjectivity captures. He is insisting that unless the child were in commun- ion with other creatures who had pains, who sometimes expressed them in their behavior, and who recognized that the child has experiences similar to the adult's, the child could not learn the concept of pain. She could not even think the thought, 'I am in pain,' or 'Mama is in pain.'

When one already has a mind of one's own, it remains the case that others can sometimes know us in a way we cannot know ourselves; this is one implication of the concept of unconscious mental processes, and one reason why other persons can play an important role in the acquisition of self-knowledge. If I am a patient in analysis, the only truths about me that will do me any good are truths I myself possess. But sometimes a first step in my knowing, for example, that I am sad, and being able to link up a feeling with the thoughts that make it comprehensible to me, may be somebody else's pointing out to me that I seem to be sad. Modell writes of the ways in which "the growing child requires the confirmation of the *other* to claim possession of her affect," and remarks that the analyst does something analo- gous for his patient (Modell, 1990, p. 72).

Wittgenstein does not investigate in detail the personal interactions leading to subjectivity; but he implies that such an investigation would include the ways in which other people's responses to the child shape his emerging sense of himself, and so the understanding that he brings to his eventual first-person thinking. These are just the sorts of interactions that, because of its essentially interpersonal character, the psychoanalytic dialogue can bring to light. For example, Winnicott tells the story of a male patient who knows himself to be male, but who talks as if what he were feeling were penis envy. Winnicott says to him: " 'I am listening to a girl. I know perfectly well that you are a man but I am listening to a girl, and talking to a girl. I am telling this girl, 'You are talking about penis envy.' " After a pause, the patient responds, 'If I were to tell someone about this girl I would be called mad.' " Winnicott claims the madness as his—that is, as that of the mother who had wanted this boy to be a girl—and goes on to say: "This madness which was mine enabled him to see himself as a girl *from my position*" (Winnicott, 1971, pp. 73, 74).

Both the claims that thinking has an essentially normative character, and that only a social situation can provide a field in which this normativity arises, are more clearly argued in Davidson. But before turning to him, we should ask: why is propositional thought so important? Because only thought of a propositional sort has implications, makes assertions, sometimes contradicts itself, commits the thinker to certain conclusions, invites challenge or trust on the part of another, makes promises and reneges on promises, is open to doubt, challenge, question, reflection. Only propositional thought makes a place for dialogue that is both interpersonal and intrapersonal: I can wonder what I mean by what I said, and I can also ask you what you mean by what you said. It is only thinking of this sort that can be rational, and also, irrational: self-deceptive, or foreclosing reflection, or repressing what one also knows, or being oblivious to the implications of one's thoughts, or dissociating certain aspects of one's experience. It is propositional thought that has departed from the realm of stimulus-response, no matter how complicated, and entered the space of reasons.

What is involved in having belief that is propositional in character, Davidson asks? His answer goes something like this: To believe that '*p*' just is to hold that '*p*' is true. Of course you can know that it might be false, can be doubtful of its truth, and so on; the point is that the concepts of belief and truth, evidence and reason, are necessarily linked. So if you have a belief of a propositional sort (the beliefs we may attribute to other animals than ourselves are presumably not propositional in character) you must have a grasp of the distinction between how you *think* things are and how they (truly) are, between right and wrong, correct and incorrect, true and false, since belief is, by definition, a state of mind *about* the world; it is the sort of thing that, by definition, can be true or false (even though one may never know in particular case which it is), and for which one adduces evidence and reasons. (Whatever conditions provide for the possibility of belief, provide also on my view for the possibility of fantasy, if by fantasy we mean a mental state ascribable only to a creature that has some beliefs.) The goal, then, is to say what we can about how a child might get hold of the distinctions between the false and the true, between how things seem and how they objectively are.

There must be a kind of triangulating process, as Davidson calls it (1989, 1992), in which child and adult communicate—at first, not in words on the child's part, of course—about an object in the physical world they share. To see how triangulation works, Davidson sketches a primitive learning situation. The mother hands the child an apple, saying 'apple' as she does. Mother and child are together interested in the apple, and interested also in each other's response to it. The child babbles, and at some point, in this or a similar transaction, the child hits on a sound close enough to 'apple' so that the mother rewards the child—with a laugh, intensified interest, more play, or any of the other kinds of responses that infant observers have described. In time we can give content to the mother's saying that the child is responding specifically to apples. The mother has in mind the apple when she says 'apple,' and apple is what she means by the word.

The question, however, was the point at which we can say that 'apple' is what the child himself means and, so far, there is nothing to distinguish the mother's response to the child from an observer's response to a trained dog. So our story about the child needs a more complex form of triangulation than the one we have yet described. What it needs is a very particular sort of interaction between child and mother, in which they can observe an object in common, and observe also each other's responses to that common object. The child must be responding to a specific object, and he must know that the mother is responding to that same object. Over time, the child can then correlate the mother's responses to the object with his own. (Winnicott's writings about the transitional object are onto a similar idea. The concept of reality is constructed for any child, Winnicott suggests, through her triangular interactions with some loved external object and a loved other person who is responding both to her and to that same object. Such an object can then become symbolic, say of the breast. Winnicott writes: "When symbolism is employed, the infant is already clearly distinguishing between fantasy and fact, between inner objects and external objects, between primary creativity and perception" [Winnicott, 1971, p. 6]. Yet while Winnicott thinks that before this time there are inner objects, I want to say that only when there are, for the child, objects that are truly public can there also be 'objects' that are truly inner in a subjective, inner world.)

So the object must be something public, discernible by both mother and child, to which, furthermore, they can give a name that will allow them both to refer to it even in its absence. They must be responding to the same object in the world; they must be responding to it in similar ways; and they must both observe that they are. In such a situation it will sometimes be the case that mother and child respond to the same thing—something they can both see to be the same thing—differently. The questions can then arise: who is right, she or I? What is the object really like? What does she see that I don't? Or, what do I see that she doesn't? It is this sort of situation that makes room for the normative concepts of error, right and wrong, true and false, 'my view of things' versus 'hers,' 'my view' versus 'the way things (objectively) are.' (It *makes room for* these concepts; it does not fully explain them, a caveat I return to in a moment. And at some point this child may learn that there is no such thing as a view of the object from *no where*). Such an interaction not only allows the mother, or any interpreter, Sarah, to say of John, 'he is seeing an *x*'; it allows John to say of himself, as it were, 'I am seeing an *x*' (or 'I want an *x*,' or 'I am thinking about an *x*.') This is the answer to a question Cartesian representationalism doesn't ask. The belief that there is an apple on the table draws a line from oneself to the world. But what fixes the terms joined by the line? If we say, 'I and the thing itself,' there is nothing to give me the idea of it as an *object* external to me which can be seen from different perspectives.

This picture of what is needed for concept formation begins with the claim, which many philosophers in this century have made, that mental content is partly constituted by the events in the world that are its cause. This is not something Descartes held. Whatever the causal relations between external and internal world, they are, on his view, not in any way intrinsic to the content of that internal world. But events in the world have causal impact on sunflowers and lemmings, without this impact taking the form of concepts. So the question is, what is needed to begin to bridge the gap between mere causal relation and an object or event in the world that the child can conceive as such? What is needed to allow the stimulus—light from an apple on the table reaching my eye—to take the form of a belief, a belief for which we can give evidence, a perception of the form 'I see *that* there is an apple on the table'? (As Robert Brandom puts it, "attitudes we adopt in response to environing stimuli count as *beliefs* just insofar as they can serve as and stand in need of reasons, and the acts we perform count as *actions* just insofar as it is proper to offer and inquire after reasons for them" [Brandon, 1994, p. 5].) What is needed to baptize this cause with a name, and a name, furthermore, that has meaning for the two players—where meaning, as we have seen, is itself a normative notion? This is the question to which the triangulation picture suggests a partial answer. As Richard Rorty wrote, "The key to understanding the relation between minds and bodies is not an understanding of the irreducibility of the intentional to the physical but the understanding of the inescapability of a normative vocabulary. For the inability by an organism to use such a vocabulary entails that that organism is not using language at all" ("Davidson Between Wittgenstein and Tarski," unpublished).

My own triangulation argument differs from Davidson's only in claiming that the child needs not just one but two other persons, one of whom,
at least in theory, might be only the child's idea of a third. To have the
distinctions between true and false, thought and world, the child must move
from interacting with his mother to grasping the idea that both his perspective on the world and hers are *perspectives*; that there is a possible third point
of view, more inclusive than theirs, from which both his mother's and his
own can be seen and from which the interaction between them can be
understood. One prerequisite for this is the experience of sometimes being
responded to in an appropriate way, as Wittgenstein also suggested. Another
prerequisite is observing disagreement between other persons.

The grasp of this third possible point of view is also part of what allows
for such perplexing adult attitudes as self-forgiveness. One can experience
forgiveness if she is forgiven by the person she feels she has wronged. But if
he does not forgive her, or if he is dead, then forgiveness can come only from
oneself, which seems to present the insurmountable problem of getting outside one's own skin. A solution is in sight when one becomes able, imagina-
tively, to occupy a position beyond herself from which her actions do not
appear as isolated 'bad' fragments, but as interactions with another person,
each with complex wishes and needs. One needs to see not only oneself as
a whole, but also the relationship between oneself and the other. In having
such a third-person perspective, the analyst can help her patient begin to
discover one like it.

Now I can say more about that sense of subjectivity which I am urging
comes only with intersubjectivity. A creature has subjectivity in this sense
when it knows some of its beliefs as *beliefs*, and as its *own* beliefs. This means,
as Wittgenstein and others have argued, that it is able to make attributions
of mental states to others (see Strawson, 1963, Part III, and Evans, 1982, ch.
6); it understands that the mental states of another are available to him in
a way they are not to one's self, as one's own thoughts are accessible to one's
self in a way they are not to others. It is not only interpretable by others but
is also an interpreter of them. Such a child, as Fonagy puts it (following
Premack and Woodruff), has 'a theory of mind' (Fonagy, 1989); and only
such a creature can distinguish, some of the time, between playing and
reality, fantasy and fact. (I would say, furthermore, that only when that
distinction is in place does the concept of fantasy have any clear meaning,
but I am not arguing that here.)

Of course these knowings that characterize the very having of a mind,
a mind that is one's own, are fragile, vulnerable, easily disturbed. We do not
always recognize a fantasy for what it is (that we do not is one of the defining
characteristics of fantasy in its specifically psychoanalytic sense); particularly
if we are children, we confusedly fantasize that our own minds are transparent to others, and we confuse wishing something were so with making it so.
But these are vicissitudes of mind, not the natural condition of a particular

sort of (disturbed) mind. As Fonagy writes: "Although borderline patients' capacity to differentiate self and other is legitimately described as impaired and 'boundaries' between the two can be said to be blurred, those descriptions do not do justice to the complexity of the mechanisms involved. Even frank psychotics know that the person they are talking to is a separate person" (1989, p. 109).

But what about—one will rightly ask—the subjectivity of children for whom all of this is not yet in place? Can we not ask what the world is like for them? And may not the answer bear on the sort of thinking, reflective, self-aware persons they will become? Of course. Fonagy, Stern, Emde, and others who have observed infants, have asked these question and begun to suggest some interesting answers. From these writers we have learned that early infant–parent exchanges have a great deal to do, for example, with whether the child begins to feel that he can, or cannot, make himself understood; that he has or does not have something valuable to say or to give (a child who is not noticed, not listened to, may come to believe, by way of defending his parent, and himself from catastrophic anger toward her, that he is not worthy of being understood); that he is more or less at home in the world, or, dangerously omnipotent, at its edge. But I would describe all this as a matter of habits of attention or avoidance, of response and the evoking of response in others, of perception and feeling, that have a lot to do both with how the child will come to sense himself and the world, and with how reflective and thoughtful a person he will become, but that are set up prior to thought per se.

There are obvious similarities between the concept of triangulation I am urging and those of a number of psychoanalytic writers. Thus, Ronald Britton (following Bion) writes that the child's acknowledgment of the parents' relationship with each other creates 'a triangular space' in which thinking can occur (Britton, 1989). Green writes that Winnicott's 'transitional object' describes not so much "an object as a space lending itself to the creation of objects" (Green, 1993, p. 285). Ogden develops a concept of 'the analytic third,' according to which the analyst gives voice to the experience of the analysand as experienced by the analyst" (Ogden, 1994, ch. 5), thus providing, as I think of it, a third perspective from which the analysand can see himself.

My picture of triangulation differs from Britton's and Green's in insisting not only on the presence of persons besides the child, but also on a real external world, common to them both. Furthermore, language has a central place in triangulation as I conceive it, for it is through language and language-learning that triangulation takes place. Child, mother, and world interact in such a way that concepts, belief, propositional thought, come into being for the first time. Some 'knowledge' of syntax may be innate, as Chomsky and others have argued. But no one has successfully shown that mental content is innate. Language is not a robe that the child casts over his thought, but the medium through which he engages with others and the world in the way that begins to constitute mental life.

It is important to point out that the triangulation argument gives only a necessary condition for thought and not its necessary and sufficient conditions, which is to say that a creature might inhabit the situation that triangulation describes and yet not develop thought. This is one of the reasons for saying that thought is irreducible to any of the prior conditions that we can specify for it, without covertly including thought itself among them. The search for something more, for necessary *and* sufficient conditions, is very tempting: since mind obviously cannot come into being unless all the physical properties and worldly conditions necessary to sustain it are present, one might hope to identify mind with these conditions or some subset of them. The present interest in consciousness seems to be motivated by such a hope: surely there must be, some philosophers, psychoanalysts, and neurologists think, some particular set of neural connections that will explain consciousness so thoroughly that we can say, this *is* consciousness. But mind, subjectivity, thought, consciousness, truth, and so on, all confront us with what Polanyi calls 'emergent properties' (Polanyi, 1958), properties that in a developmental process arise spontaneously from elements at the preceding levels and are not specifiable or predictable in terms of them.

When we can attribute propositional thoughts to a child, I have argued, we must also be attributing to it the concepts of 'the objectively real,' 'true' and 'false,' 'my perspective' and 'your perspective,' all concepts that arise only within the language of mind; and for none of these concepts can we supply necessary and sufficient conditions in some other language. In this sense, all these concepts arise together; in particular it is not the case that the child first grasps the concept of himself and then the concept of other person. (Daniel Stern's claim [1984] that there is from the beginning a sense of self is ambiguous: a 'sense' of self' is not necessarily the recognition of oneself as an 'I,' with all that is involved in knowing the use of the first-person pronoun. In any case it is a claim that Stern acknowledges he cannot substantiate.) Wittgenstein wrote (1972, §141): "When we first begin to *believe* anything, what we believe is not a single proposition, it is a whole system of propositions. (Light dawns gradually over the whole.)" By the time the *whole* over which the dawn comes is fully lit, the child has made a quantum leap.

Mead descried a categorical difference between a conversation of gestures and one that can only be adequately described in the language of mind. He hoped to bridge the gap with an act of identification or internalization. But as I pointed out earlier, he begged the question by answering it with the very thing to be explained. This must be the fate of all attempts to specify an emergent property in terms of things at a lower level. For this reason, if Bion's project (1962) is to trace a continuous line from primitive 'thoughts' to thinking, it fails: either we have abstracted these thoughts from something that is already a thinking process, or they are so distant from it that thinking itself cannot provide a bridge. It is true that all of us are unable to think about some of our thoughts; but they occur in a mental setting in which we can think about some. We cannot extrapolate backward from fantasies or thoughts, unrecognized as such, to a time of thoughts before there was any thinking.

Nevertheless, though it does not fully explain propositional thought, the triangulation argument illuminates it in the following ways: it works against the subjectivist view of the mind in telling us that the child comes to have thoughts *about* the world or to make judgments about it only as he comes to be an interpreter of others; and it indicates that such acts of interpretation require a shared world and the concept of objectivity. Mead 's deep insight was that there is an intrinsic connection between being interpreted by another and being an interpreter oneself, between interpretation and symbolic thought. Neither interpreting others nor thinking for oneself could exist in isolation. To think, to have a belief in the sense that distinguishes human responsiveness to the world from that of other creatures and inanimate objects, one must have learned the interpersonal moves that count as asking for and giving reasons. Since reason is in this way a parameter of any conversation between creatures who think, I will call it a dialogue to distinguish it from a conversation of gestures. Unlike the latter, dialogue creates and presumes a shared conceptual space in which something of common interest can be talked about together; and only a dialogue is genuinely inter-subjective in the sense that each participant knows himself as a 'I,' a subject who can think of himself as a self, and knows the other as a subject, a 'I' for himself.

Toward the beginning of this chapter I said that the concept of reality loses its sense in the absence of a distinction between how things seem to me or to us, and how things are, and I promised to say why we need such a concept for our human lives. The answer is that a creature who could not grasp this distinction, in principle (though not always in a particular case), would necessarily lack the idea that another's experience of the world is different from one's own, so lack both the idea of subjectivity and that capacity for empathy that takes for granted the uniqueness of every person's perspective. Such a creature could not recognize its beliefs as *beliefs*, rather than simply the way the world is. So it would lack also the concepts of evidence and reasons, the capacities for reflection and for dialogue.

Here is how things look on the intersubjectivist account I am presenting. The concepts of right and wrong, true and false, do not enter our minds from some Platonic or Judeo-Christian heaven, but emerge from within an interpersonal, worldly, situation.[2] This does not mean that truth is just a convention, or what the majority holds true; it is perfectly possible for the majority to be mistaken on any particular issue. On just this possibility the distinction between things as they appear to me, *or to us*, insists. A convention is a practice we can change, or can imagine changing; but there is no imaginable alternative to the concept of truth that will do the job we human creatures need to do—argue things out, assess evidence, look for reasons, disagree with each other, find a consensus, questions our own convictions, and so on. Which beliefs we hold true of course differ from person to person; so also our ways of discovering the truth, and what we count as evidence. But the concept of truth does not. Both the proverbial Trobrian Islander and the speaker of Standard American English implicitly understand that a claim about *what is*, calls for evidence and reasons (they may differ about whether a particular reason is bad or good, or whether a particular test captures evidence that is relevant to the issue at hand). In short, both believers share roughly the same methodology. Then having come into a condition of dialogue with the other, the anthropologist might even discuss with his informant whether his beliefs *are* true, just as the psychoanalyst may also with her patient. This is not necessarily a dead-end question, since an ongoing conversation in which you and I come to understand better *what* each of us believes, may in fact lead to a change of mind. It is in just this way that changes in what we *hold* to be true come about.

The seventeenth-century ideal of scientific objectivity posited an observer who does not affect or intrude on the object of his investigation. We have abandoned that ideal. But another, to which I think all analysts do hold fast, asks us to try to distinguish between fantasy and reality and to take the viewpoints of others into account. With Aron, we might now view analytic neutrality as "the analyst's openness to new perspectives, a commitment to take other perspectives seriously, and a refusal to view any interpretation as complete, or any meaning as exhaustive" (Aron, 1996, p. 28).

Our developmental picture looks something like this: From the very beginning, infants make sounds and gestures that their caretakers take as signs of the infant's wants and needs. But the infant only gradually becomes able himself to mean something by what he says and does. The implication is not that before the infant has propositional thoughts and intentional states, nothing at all is going on in its head. Infants have feelings, emotions, sensations, purposes, instincts; they communicate, perceive, and learn. Once again, infant research is useful here in showing how patterns of interaction between infant and caretaker can very early establish habits of response that later might be expressed as core beliefs such as 'I had better not let on that I know what I know,' or 'I deserve every bad thing that happens to me,' or 'I am [or am not] able to cope with new tasks,' or 'the world is a fearful [or an exciting] place.'

The practices of interpreting another, asking him and oneself for evidence and reasons, pointing out that this remark or this judgments is not consistent with others, mark the very space of reasons the child enters, and must enter, in learning how to think. Of course the interpersonal relations that initiate the child into it are not coolly rational but fraught with other lessons about loving and losing, abandoning and being lost, wanting and not having, and these lessons often fetter one's thinking ability. Psychoanalysis very well describes our initiations into thought, not by picturing a space alternative to that of reasons, but more of what the space of reasons is like.

FANTASY AND THE FORECLOSURE OF THINKING

I have said that subjectivity in a certain specific sense—my having thoughts that I sometimes know as thoughts and as mine—comes along with some understanding of the world as public and shared, which we interpret in some shared ways. I now want to distinguish this general sense of subjectivity from another. The first words the child learns are public; the language she grows up speaking is also sufficiently public for her often to make herself understood. But because no two people are alike, any concept quickly acquires resonances that are unique to the child; so at the same time as she learns to mean something by her words and communicate that meaning to others, the child is acquiring an idiolect, a way of thinking, that is hers alone. Some of this is unconscious.

The trouble with that part of the inner world that is neurotic is that dialogue, intersubjective testing, even reflection by the agent herself, are foreclosed. This is the status with neurotic fantasies: they are fixed, frozen in time; apparently (so they seem to the person herself) among the *givens* of the world, like the objects that we find there. We do not recognize them as our thoughts about the objects that we find. (Whether one accepts Melanie Klein's account of the infant's inner world, it aptly depicts the way in which unconscious fantasies can strike the person herself as things embedded in the mind, or as the lining of the mind, rather than as the mind's own thoughts.) As distinct from fantasizing, thinking allows for self-reflection and for appraising one's own thoughts as true or false, realistic or unrealistic, and so on. We think with thoughts, about things, and we cannot think about these things unless we recognize our thoughts about them as thoughts. Someone gripped by a fantasy has for the moment put aside the possibility that what he thinks might be false, or a case of wishful thinking, or just a partial view of things. He has put questions of evidence and reasons. One of the therapist's tasks is to engage him in such a way that what was a fantasy can become instead a belief, and as such, subject to reflection and doubt; to free important other persons in his world from their frozen status in fantasy so that, in Loewald's memorable image, ghosts (haunting the patient's mind) can become ancestors (in the real and public world).

The goal may be accomplished partly through the way in which, in transference, the patient attempts to plug the analyst into the world as he, the patient, has unknowingly constructed it. The analyst feels, through countertransference, something of what the patient wants from her; at the same time she is learning his idiolect through listening to his dreams, images, and associations. So the analyst both learns to speak in a way the patient can understand, and refuses to play the role that she is asked to play in his fantasy world. The analytic process is sometimes described as giving the patient more choice. Before, he did not know what he was doing; now that he does, he can for the first time choose whether to go on doing it. But as Jonathan Lear (1993) points out, this misdescribes the process: When one sees that what one had taken as just the way things are is instead one's own way of looking at the world, 'just the way things are' can no longer survive as *simply that*. This world collapses. It is replaced by a space for thinking about the way things are.

The claim that all experiences are equally subjective—though trivially true—has the effect of flattening, *for the analyst*, the distinctions she needs between the publicly available and the privately constructed. The claim can also lead to confusions about the nature of empathy, which I understand as the ability, temporarily, to experience the world more or less as another does, not by forgetting the other's particular vantage point but precisely by having a good sense of it, at the same time as one holds on to one's own perceptions and one's own methodology for testing them, *a methodology that in the broadest sense is the same as the patient's*. The patient's fantasies are *fantasies* because he does not, or refuses to, query them in the way we query, at least when the occasion arises, our fully conscious beliefs and desires. If the analyst treats all the patient's convictions as having equal validity among themselves, and with her own, she in effect colludes with him in keeping his fantasies untested (Grossman, 1996); she is in no position to point out that some of his convictions conflict with his own beliefs, and also with his own understanding of what gives a belief validity, which is not its actual truth (this is always open to question) but his having submitted it to dialogue, with another or himself. These are ways in which analyst and patient share a common methodology.

There are of course other forms of irrationality than unconscious fantasy; and all of them make sense only linked to the concepts of truth and falsity. Self-deception, for example, sometimes consists in allowing oneself to hold onto a belief in one part of one's mind, so to speak, that in another one thinks is false. Resistance sometimes consists in holding at bay a perception one fears may be true.

WHERE WE ARE NOW

Why would anybody deny the homely view of truth, as the pragmatists Pierce, James, Dewey, and recently, Rorty, have seemed to do? And why would many psychoanalysts, particularly those who count themselves as 'relationalists' or as 'intersubjectivists,' have jumped on the pragmatist bandwagon? My remarks on the history of philosophy were an attempt to answer the first question by saying that the pragmatists were reacting to a view of meaning that ignores its roots in human interests, and holds that reason, divinely guided, can find certainty. We can call this truth with a capital T. Rorty, in particular, thinks we have to turn our backs on the philosophical tradition that thought of truth as correspondence with something outside the mind, something to which we do not have direct access. So we have done.

The second question has to be set in the context of the very difficult problems now facing psychoanalysis. Viewing therapeutic change as to some extent brought about by new, collaborative constructions of the present rather than by accurate reconstructions of the past, seeing insight as a creating as much as a finding, psychoanalysts are confronted with some philosophical puzzles about what the self and self-discovery are. And in the course of questioning many of the hypotheses Freud thought definitive of his 'science'—among them, drive theory and the centrality of the Oedipal complex—psychoanalysts have generated a plurality of theories, some of which are clearly incompatible with each other. In thinking about the important question, What is it this particular patient is warding off? for example, the analyst has to make some choices, as she does also in sorting through the various competing theories, both about the mind and about how it can change through therapy.

In his discontent with the imperfections of human knowledge, Descartes turned away from the external world. He replaced external objects and real other minds with internal objects that we can know, he thought, for sure. The 'two-person' psychology of the intersubjectivists is at war with old-fashioned (Cartesian) authoritarianism. It insists that what matters to us is not some timeless other world but the human here-and-now. Yet, interestingly, to say that 'reality' refers only to something 'subjective' is just the 'about-face' that Descartes made. And it suggests, with Descartes, that if we play our cards right, we need no longer be troubled that another person, or the future, may prove us wrong.

If we cannot get rid of truth, then we cannot abandon the sorts of questions that a concern with truth asks, like: What evidence is there to think that a particular theory is true? Is it compatible with something else we hold true? And, Are you and I perhaps both deluded, or thinking wishfully? As Glen Gabbard has recently pointed out (1997), the question of analytic 'objectivity' is not without its clinical implications. My guess is that in their practice, most psychoanalysts honor the distinctions between justified belief and true belief, also between what works and what is the case. These distinctions call, however, for a different account of truth than the one some psychoanalysts have championed, often in the name of openness to other points of view. There is talk now of the way in which analyst and patient 'co-construct reality.' Each of us constructs *a picture of* reality. Reality is what keeps pulling us back to the drawing board.

NOTES

1. Ferenczi was onto a similar idea in "Three Stages in the Sense of Reality" (1956). In the third, he says, the infant learns that some of its wants will be answered if it makes the right signals. Putting Ferenczi's point in another way: what is initially

a cry without meaning to the crier becomes meaningful to him in part through the behavior it produces in another.

2. Only in the final phase of writingt this chapter did I read Robert Brandom's *Making I Explicit* (1994). It makes a number of the points I have but from a slightly different angle.

REFERENCES

Aron, L. (1996). *A Meeting of Minds, Mutuality in Psychoanalysis*. Hillsdale, NJ: The Analytic Press.

Atwood, G. S. R. (1992). *Contexts of Being*. Hillsdale, NJ: The Analytic Press.

Bion, W. R. (1962). The Psycho-Analytic Study of Thinking, *Int. J. Psycho-Anal.* 43:306–310.

Brandom, R. B. (1994). *Making It Explicit*. Cambridge: Harvard University Press.

Britton, R. (1989). The missing link: Parental sexuality in the Oedipal complex. In *The Oedipus Complex Today*, J. Steiner, ed. London: Karnac Books.

Cavell, M. (1993). *The Psychoanalytic Mind: From Freud to Philosophy*. Cambridge: Harvard University Press.

Davidson, D. (1989). The conditions of thought. In *The Mind of Donald Davidson*, J. Brandland, J. B. W. Gombocz, eds. Atlanta/Amsterdam: Rodopi.

———. (1992). The second person. *Midwest Studies in Philosophy* XVII:255–267.

Evans, G. *The Varieties of Reference*. Oxford: Oxford University Press.

Ferenczi, S. (1956). Stages in the development of the sense of Reality. In *Sex in Psychoanalysis*, C. Newton, trans. New York: Dover.

Fogel, G. I. et al. (1996). A classic revisited: Loewald on the therapeutic action of psychoanalysis. *J. Amer. Psychoan. Assn.*, 44: 863–924.

Fonagy, P. (1989). On tolerating mental states: theory of mind in borderline personality, *Bull. Anna Freud Centre* 12:91–115.

Freud, S. (1900). *The Interpretation of Dreams*. *S.E.* 5.

Freud, S. (1915). Instincts and their vicissitudes. *S.E.* 14.

Freud, S. (1925). Negation. *S.E.* 19.

Freud, S. (1940 [1938]). An Outline of Psycho-analysis. *S.E.* 23.

Gabbard, G. O. (1997). A reconsideration of objectivity in the analyst, *Int. J. Psychoanal.* 78: 15–27.

Green, A. (1993). *On Private Madness*. Madison: International Universities Press, Inc.

Grossman, L. (1996). 'Psychic reality' and psychic testing, *Int. J. Psychoanal.* 77:508–517.

Hoffman, I. Z. (1983). The Patient as Interpreter of the Analyst's Experience, *Contemp. Psychoanal.* 19:389–422.

Kripke, S. A. (1982). *Wittgenstein on Rules and Private Language*. Cambridge: Harvard University Press.

Lear, J. (1993). An interpretation of transference, *Int. J. Psychoananal.* 74:739–755.

Mead, G. H. (1934). *Mind, Self, and Society, vol. I*. Chicago: University of Chicago Press.

Mitchell, S. A. (1988). *Relational Concepts in Psychoanalysis, An Integration*. Cambridge: Harvard University Press.

Modell, A. H. (1990). *Other Times, Other Realities*. Cambridge: Harvard University Press.

Nietzsche, F. (1974). *The Gay Science*. W. Kaufmann, trans. New York: Vintage Books.

Ogden, T. H. (1994). *Subjects of Analysis*. Hillsdale, NJ: Jason Aronson, Inc.

Polanyi, M. (1958). *Personal Knowledge*. Chicago: University of Chicago Press.

Rorty, R. (1979). *Philosophy and the Mirror of Nature*. Princeton: Princeton University Press.

Sellars, W. (1956). "Empiricism and the Philosophy of Mind." *Minnesota Studies in the Philosophy of Science*, 1. H. Feigl and M. Scriven, eds. Minneapolis: University of Minnesota Press.

Spezzano, C. (1993). *Affect in Psychoanalysis, A Clinical Synthesis*. Hillsdale: NJ: Analytic Press.

Stern, D. (1984). *The Interpersonal World of the Infant: A View from Psychoanalysis and Developmental Psychology*. New York: Basic Books.

———. (1995). *The Motherhood Constellation: A Unified View of Parent-Infant Psychiatry*. New York: Basic Books.

Strawson, P. F. (1963). *Individuals, An Essay in Descriptive Metaphysics*. New York: Anchor Books.

Vygotsky, L. S. (1962). *Thought and Language*. E. Hanfmann and G. Vakar, trans. Cambridge: M.I.T. Press.

Wertsch, J. V. (1985). *Vygotsky and the Social Formation of Mind*. Cambridge, Mass.: Harvard University Press.

Winnicott, D. W. (1971). *Playing and Reality*. New York: Basic Books.

Wittgenstein, L. (1953). *Philosophical Investigations*. G. E. M. Anscombe, ed. Oxford: Blackwell.

———. (1972). *On Certainty*, G.E.M. Anscombe, trans. Oxford: Blackwell.

FOUR

FREUD AND SEARLE ON THE ONTOLOGY OF THE UNCONSCIOUS

David Livingstone Smith

> Our mind is so fortunately equipped that it brings up the most important bases for our thoughts without our having the least knowledge of this work of elaboration. Only the results become conscious. This unconscious mind is for us like an unknown being who creates and produces for us and finally throws the ripe fruits into our laps.
>
> —*Wilhelm Wundt*

FOR MANY YEARS the American philosopher John Searle has been engaged in a campaign against computationalist cognitive science that includes an attack on the notion of unconscious mental phenomena. In this chapter I will demonstrate that Searle's criticisms of the notion of the unconscious are poorly taken, and that his general approach to the unconscious is the revival of a theory that was widely embraced during the late nineteenth and early twentiety century, which was decisively refuted by Sigmund Freud early in the twentieth century.

In the first part of this project I will briefly describe Searle's theory of the unconscious and point out some philosophical problems with his arguments. In the second part, I will describe the background to Freud's thinking about the unconscious and show how he managed to refute Searle-style arguments against his theory of occurrent unconscious mental events. Finally, I will use Freud's argument against Searle and draw out some of its further implications.

SEARLE'S ONTOLOGY OF THE UNCONSCIOUS

All of us possess an intuitive grasp of what it means to experience a conscious mental state. But what about unconscious mental states? For many people, including many philosophers, mind and consciousness seem so intimately bound up with one another that the idea of an unconscious mental state sounds strange. Many feel that consciousness is actually *constitutive* of the mental, and that the idea of an unconscious mental state is blatantly incoherent. Others do not share these intuitions, and can cheerfully accept the idea that an unconscious mental state is just like a conscious mental state except that it is not conscious.

Searle is not one of the latter, and although he stops short of completely discarding the idea of the unconscious, he treats it with considerable caution.[1] For Searle, conscious mental states are always *occurrent*, whereas their unconscious counterparts are *dispositional*: they are simply configurations within the brain that, under the right circumstances, will generate real, full-blooded, truly and indubitably mental conscious states. Searle refers to this general relationship between conscious and unconscious states as the "Connection Principle." I will refer to this particular version of the Connection Principle as Searle's dispositionalist thesis. On this account, it is the causal relationship between unconscious neural states and conscious mental states that legitimates calling the former mental. However, sometimes Searle gives another version of the relationship that turns on its logical rather than its causal features. "The crucial connection between consciousness and the unconscious can be stated as follows: There is a logical connection between the notion of consciousness and the notion of the unconscious such that in order for a state to be an unconscious *mental* state it must be the sort of thing that could be conscious in principle."[2]

This logical version of the Connection Principle has very different implications than the causal version. It neither entails that unconscious states cannot be occurrent, nor does it rule out the possibility that unconscious states are intrinsically mental. Whatever its philosophical virtues, the logical variant of the Connection Principle is too weak to underwrite the dispositionalist thesis. Searle makes use of the concept of supervenience to support the causal version.

> Mental states are supervenient on neurophysiological states in the following respect: Type-identical neurophysiological causes would have type-identical mentalistic effects. Thus, to take the famous brain-in-a-vat example, if you had two brains that were type-identical down to the last molecule, then the causal basis of the mental would guarantee that they would have the same mental phenomena. On this characterization of the supervenience relation, the supervenience of the mental on the physical is marked by the fact that physical states

are causally sufficient, though not necessarily causally necessary, for the corresponding mental states. That is just another way of saying that as far as this definition of supervenience is concerned, sameness of neurophysiology guarantees sameness of mentality; but sameness of mentality does not guarantee sameness of neurophysiology.[3]

There is something strange going on here: Searle is mixing up supervenience with causation, two concepts that are normally treated as quite distinct. As we will see, this ambiguity proves to be crucial for his argument. Of course, as a philosopher Searle could not fail to address it. After mentioning Hare's theory of ethical supervenience, which is constitutive rather than causal, he goes on to remark:

> So there are at least two notions of supervenience: a constitutive notion and a causal notion. I believe that only the causal notion is important for discussions of the mind-body problem. In this respect my account differs from the usual accounts of the supervenience of the mental on the physical. Thus Kim . . . claims that we should not think of the relation of neural events to their supervening mental events as causal, and indeed he claims that supervening mental events have no causal status apart from their supervenience on neurophysiological events.[4]

Philosophers normally conceive of body-mind supervenience as an "inter-level metaphysical determination relation," claiming that the physical properties of a system *constitutively fix* (rather than cause) its mental properties.[5] Searle's causal conception of supervenience is highly idiosyncratic. On strictly conceptual grounds, it is not at all clear how 'causal supervenience' differs from plain constitutive supervenience, apart from the seemingly mysterious invocation of causality. In other words, saying that something is *causally* supervenient on something else doesn't seem to add anything to the description except ambiguity. This ambiguity becomes even more opaque as we examine Searle's wording more closely. Notice that he speaks of supervenient *events*. In standard philosophical accounts, the relation of supervenience holds between *properties* (or predicates, or descriptions depending on one's philosophical taste) rather than between events, whereas causal relationships hold between events (not between properties, description, or predicates). So, causal supervenience is beginning to sound even more like ordinary causation and less like supervenience.

What kind of causation is involved in causal supervenience?

> It seems to me obvious from everything we know about the brain that macro mental phenomena are all caused by lower-level micro phenomena. There is nothing mysterious about such bottom up

causation; it is quite common in the physical world. Furthermore, the fact that the mental features are supervenient on neuronal features in no way diminishes their causal efficacy. The solidity of the piston is causally supervenient on its molecular structure, but this does not make solidity epiphenominal.[6]

Searle refers to the supervenience of mental features on physical features, and features sound a lot more like properties than they sound like events. Does causal supervenience encompass both events and properties? It seems that Searle's bottom-up causation is, in the end, just what philosophers normally call instantiation or realization. The molecular structure of the piston does not *cause* its solidity, it *is* its solidity. It is the causal relations that hold together the molecules from which the piston is composed that constitutively fix its solidity and provide it with its specific casual powers.[7] Searle's confusion of causation with instantiation leads him to claim that causal relations hold between properties in the piston example but between events in his more theoretical account of supervenience.

Now comes the kicker: "My conclusion is that once you recognize the existence of bottom-up, micro to macro forms of causation, the notion of supervenience no longer does any work in philosophy. The formal features of the relation are already present in the causal sufficiency of the micro-macro forms of causation."[8] Supervenience has been swallowed up by causation, which has become inflated so as to include instantiation. Given that causal relations hold between events, Searle's commitment to a causal account of the dependent relation between mental and physical seems to force the event thesis. But, as Searle often really means instantiation when he uses causation, he is naturally impelled to revert to talk of properties.

Let us now momentarily leave behind the vexed issues of causation and supervenience and move on to consider Searle's views on the ontological subjectivity of mental states. Searle describes his theory as causally reductive, meaning that notwithstanding the causal bond between brain and mind, mental properties cannot be ontologically reduced to neural properties. Mental states are irreducibly subjective, and therefore resist reduction to the (objective) neural level. The intrinsic subjectivity of the mental is exemplified in what he calls the aspectual shape of mental experiences. Searle describes his theory as causally reductive, but not ontologically property reductive. By this he means that although mind is caused by brain, mental properties cannot be reduced to neural properties. The irreducibility of mental properties is said to lie in their intrinsic subjectivity. Searle claims that the 'ontological subjectivity' of mental properties is displayed in their possession of 'aspectual shape.'

Every intentional state has what I call an 'aspectual shape.' This just means that it presents its conditions of satisfaction under some aspects and not others. Thus, for example, the desire for water is a different desire from the desire for H_2O, even though water and H_2O are identical. If I represent what I desire under the aspect 'water,' that is a different aspectual shape from representing the same substance under the aspect 'H_2O.' What is true of this example is true generally. All intentional states represent their conditions of satisfaction under some aspects and not others; and this has the consequence that every intentional state, conscious or unconscious, has an aspectual shape.[9]

Aspectual shape could be described as 'As-ness.' Subrena understands H_2O as water, whereas Rob mistakenly regards it as white rum. The fact that Subrena and Rob see the very same item as two different things demonstrates their essential subjectivity, which "cannot be exhaustively or completely characterised solely in third-person, behavioural or even neurophysiological predicates."[10] Now, let us reconsider the dispositionalist story about unconscious mental states in light of the notions of subjectivity and aspectual shape. If unconscious 'mental' states are actually nothing more than neural dispositions for conscious mental states, and if neural states can be exhaustively characterized in objective, third-person terms, then it seems to follow that unconscious 'mental' states do not possess aspectual shape, are not ontologically subjective, and are not really mental at all. Unconscious states possess 'an objective neurophysiological ontology' which is somehow able to "cause conscious subjective mental phenomena."[11] As Searle sums it all up: "the ontology of the unconscious is strictly the ontology of a neurophysiology capable of generating the conscious."[12] These unconscious dispositions do not possess real intentionality, which ever since Brentano has been regarded as the distinctive stamp of the mental. At best, they possess a secondhand, derivative sort of intentionality that Searle calls 'as-if' intentionality. As-if intentionality is ascribed rather than intrinsic. It is the kind of intentionality possessed by computers or, worse, by thermostats. Asking us to consider the example of a man in a sound, dreamless sleep Searle points out that we know that this man possesses all sorts of beliefs. For instance, we can imagine a sleeping man who believes that he lives in Biddeford, Maine; that Bush is president; and that moose normally possess four legs. Now, Searle asks, "*what fact about him makes it the case that he has these unconscious beliefs?*"[13] Well, given that the man is totally unconscious—he is not even dreaming about Biddeford, Bush, or moose—we are forced to conclude that neural states and processes are solely responsible for his having these beliefs. These cannot be occurrent beliefs because neural activation vectors do not possess subjectivity and aspectual shape. It must be, then, that we are dealing with his possessing neural dispositions to have these beliefs, rather than his having these beliefs themselves.

Searle asks us to accept his intuition that neurophysiological states cannot encompass aspectual shape, but he does not provide any kind of supporting argument. Consider the example of the sleeping man. Searle simply asserts that because he is unconscious there is nothing with aspectual shape going on inside his head. But why can't neural representational systems represent objects under aspectual shapes? Why not propose that the neurophysiological processes occurring within the man instantiate supervenient mental functions? Of course, these functions cannot be exhaustively characterised using neuroscientific language, but this is equally true of *conscious* mental states. The issue of the unsuitability of neuroscientific language for fully characterizing intentional states has no bearing on the issue of the token identity of mental events, complete with aspectual shape, with neurophysiological events.

It now becomes clear how Searle's strategic ambiguity with regard to the concept of causation provided him with the conceptual slack that he needs to get to his conclusion. The claim that mental events are *caused* by neural events leads effortlessly to the conclusion that the neural states of the sleeping man are simply failing to realize their dispositional powers. However, if we bear in mind that Searlean 'causation' includes instantiation, it is obvious that the man's unconsciousness need not interfere with his brain instantiating mental functions. If by saying that mental events are 'caused' by neural events, we leave it open that this may mean that they are *instantiated* by neural events, it follows that Searle's conclusion that, while unconscious, one possesses only dispositions toward mentality is not secured by his premises.

FREUD'S ONTOLOGY OF THE UNCONSCIOUS

During the late nineteenth century, dualism was virtually the only game in town when it came to understanding the mind. Several forms of dualism were current during this period, including classical Cartesian interactionism, psychophysical parallelism, and the new doctrine of epiphenominalism introduced by Huxley in 1874.[14] The neo-Cartesian dualist package contained four basic assertions: (1) that mind and body are radically distinct; (2) that the mind is entirely conscious; (3) that the mind is directly aware of its own contents and cannot be mistaken about those contents; and (4) that introspection is therefore the most appropriate tool for psychological investigation. Although there were some dissenters, the majority of neuroscientists, philosophers, and psychologists seem to have adhered to one version or another of the neo-Cartesian package.

During the latter part of the nineteenth century Cartesianism was becoming more and more difficult for an educated, philosophically sophisticated thinker to coherently entertain. This was mainly due to major scientific advances that called some of its doctrines into question. Meyer, Helmholz, and Joule had discovered the law of the conservation of energy in 1847, and by the latter half of the century philosophically aware scientists, such as the British neurologist John Hughlings Jackson, noticed that this law effectively ruled out classical Cartesian body–mind interactionism. Darwin's *On the Origin of Species* and *Descent of Man* obliterated Descartes's sharp demarcation of animals from human beings, which was closely linked to his substance dualism, and suggested that the human mind itself was forged on the anvil of strictly physical selection pressures.[15] The new discipline of neuroscience had demonstrated that at the very least the human mind is highly dependent on the slimy grey ball of massively interconnected neurons residing between our ears, and it was becoming clear that the brain itself—like the rest of the body—was animated not by a mysterious life force, but rather by strictly material electrochemical processes. The centerpiece of nineteenth-century neuroscience, the arena where the most dramatic discoveries were being made, was the field of aphasiology. Aphasiology had immense philosophical significance because it demonstrated that the language function, which Descartes had described as a function of the immaterial mind, was localized in particular regions of the cerebral cortex. Neuroscience was also noticing that cerebral lesions resulting in those neurological disorders called the agnosias contradicted the Cartesian claim that the mind is necessarily incorrigibly aware of its own contents. The emergence of hypnotism out of the ashes of mesmerism enabled experimenters to demonstrate that an individual may harbor unconscious ideas within his or her own mind that have a decisive impact on their behavior.

Historians of psychology have rightly emphasised that the concept of the unconscious was widely discussed and widely accepted in philosophical and scientific circles during the second half of the nineteenth century, a fact often invoked as a deflationary move calling into question the originality of Freud's contributions.[16] However, these writers generally pay relatively little attention to just what nineteenth-century writers meant by the term *unconscious*. A notable exception was Roland Dalbiez, who deserves credit as perhaps the first scholar to recognize the two theoretical positions I will now delineate.[17]

Nineteenth-century thinkers who were committed to the neo-Cartesian paradigm, but who were nonetheless aware of the evidence suggesting that mental processes can occur unconsciously, were in a philosophical bind. How could the empirical evidence be squared with their metaphysics? How can something truly mental also be unconscious?

One option was to affirm that the phenomena are mental, but to deny that they are unconscious. Advocates of this view, which I call *dissociationism*, proposed that a single skull can house two or more minds, all of which are conscious. In other words, a single mind can be split or 'doubled.' Once the mind has been doubled. both portions are fully conscious, but neither has introspective access to the other's mental contents. A person's consciousness is therefore 'unconscious' of the contents of the contents of their secondary or tertiary consciousnesses in much the same way that the conscious mind of one person is 'unconscious' of the contents of the conscious mind of another person. The dissociationist theory was modeled on the clinical phenomenology of multiple personality disorder and was particularly widespread in France, where research into multiple personality was enjoying great popularity. Advocates of the dissociationist approach included Paul and Pierre Janet, Azam, Ribot, Binet, and Taine in France, and William James and Morton Prince in the United States. Donald Davidson's philosophical reconstruction of the Freudian unconscious can be viewed as a contemporary variant of the dissociationist story.[18]

Another solution to the philosophical dilemma posed by the recognition of apparently unconscious mental states was to affirm that they are genuinely unconscious but deny that they are genuinely mental. This approach, which I call *dispositionalism*, makes the claim that what seem to be unconscious mental events are actually nonmental neurophysiological dispositions which, under the right circumstances, realize their causal powers to produce conscious mental phenomena.[19] In the words of psychophysicist Gustav Fechner: "Sensations, ideas, have, of course, *ceased actually to exist* in the state of unconsciousness, insofar as we consider them apart from their substructure. Nevertheless something persists within us, i.e. the body-mind activity of which they are a function, and which makes possible the reappearance of sensation, etc."[20]

The dispositionalist approach was most popular in England, Germany, and Austria. Its advocates included the philosophers Franz Brentano and John Stewart Mill, the neuroscientists William Carpenter, John Hughlings Jackson, and Gustav Fechner, and the psychiatrist Henry Maudsley. John Searle's theory of the unconscious is a contemporary representative of this school of thought, although he does not seem to be aware of his predecessors.

Both of these approaches to the conundrum of the unconscious were able to cope with the problem of the unintrospectability of seemingly unconscious mental events. The dissociationists argued that such material is unintrospectable not because it is unconscious, but because it is housed in a mind separate from the one doing the introspecting. The dissociationists proposed that the unintrospectability of unconscious phenomena was due to their nonmental character. The two solutions had interesting disciplinary implications. For the dispositionalists, the study of unconscious phenomena typically came within the purview of neurophysiology, whereas for the dissociationists it remained within the domain of psychology.

During the earliest phase of his career, from 1886 until 1895, Sigmund Freud adhered to the neo-Cartesian paradigm just like almost all his colleagues, and made liberal use of both dissociationist and dispositionalist theories in his attempts to come to grips with unconscious mental phenomena.[21] In 1895, while writing the *Project for a Scientific Psychology*, he underwent a philosophical transformation rejecting these views in favor of a theory of radically unconscious yet occurrent mental states, and simultaneously abandoned body–mind dualism for a materialist conception of mind.[22] After this revolution in his thinking, which was intimately tied to the creation of psychoanalysis, Freud was sharply critical of both dissociationist and dispositionalist approaches. Given that the present project concentrates on a Freudian critique of Searle's theory, I will set aside his criticisms of dissociationism, which has in any case been discussed elsewhere, and will concentrate on his critique of dispositionalism.[23]

Freud used a philosophical argument against dispositionalism that I call the *Continuity Argument*.[24] The Continuity Argument appears at many points in Freud's writings. Here is how he set it out in 1915:

> The data of consciousness have a very large number of gaps in them; both in healthy and in sick people psychical acts often occur which can be explained only by presupposing other acts, of which, never-theless, consciousness affords no evidence. . . . Our most personal daily experience acquaints us with ideas that come into our head, we do not know from where, and with intellectual conclusions arrived at we do not know how.[25]

The stream of consciousness runs through tunnels and under bridges, disappearing on one side and suddenly reappearing on the other. One particularly common and dramatic example is the daily hiatus of sleep. During sleep, our normal conscious thinking is suspended, only to be miraculously restored on awakening. The Continuity Argument goes on to assert that in some cases, when conscious thinking has been either suspended or discontinuously occupied with some other matter, it is pos-sible to infer the existence of continuous *unconscious* cognition. In other words, conscious discontinuity is at least on some occasions undergirded by unconscious continuity. Freud was well aware that the dispositionalist approach would interpret these events very differently, and went on to remark that "At this very point we may be prepared to meet with the philosophical objection that the latent conception did not exist as an object of psychology, but as a physical disposition for the recurrence of the same psychic phenomenon."[26]

Consider the experience of laboring fruitlessly over an intractable in-tellectual problem, giving up all hope of solving it, and after an interval of time having the solution drop into one's mind "as is shown when someone finds, immediately after waking, that he knows the solution to a difficult mathematical problem with which he had been wrestling in vain the day before."[27] There are many examples of unconscious problem solving in the history of science. The German mathematician Gauss, for one, recorded an example which he attributed to divine intervention: "Finally, two days ago I succeeded not on account of my painful efforts, but by the grace of God. Like a sudden flash of lightning, the riddle happened to be solved. I myself cannot say what was the concluding thread which connected what I previously knew with what made my success possible."[28]

A particularly unambiguous and instructive example, which I will use as a paradigm case, was provided by the French mathematician and physicist Henri Poincaré.[29] Poincaré records how

> For fifteen days I strove to prove that there could not be any functions like those I have since called Fuchsian functions. I was then very ignorant; every day I seated myself at my work table, stayed for an hour or two, tried a great number of combinations and reached no results.
>
> One evening, contrary to my custom, I drank black coffee and could not sleep. Ideas arose in crowds. I felt them collide until pairs interlocked, so to speak, making a stable combination. By the next morning I had established the existence of a class of Fuchsian functions, those which come from the hypergeometric series; I had only to write out the results, which took but a few hours.[30]

After this, Poincaré decided to go on vacation. However,

> Having reached Coustances, we entered an omnibus to go some place or other. At the moment I put my foot on the step the idea came to me, without anything in my former thoughts seeming to have paved the way for it, that the transformations I had used to define the Fuchsian functions were identical to those of non-Euclidian geometry. I did not verify the idea; I should not have had time, as, upon taking my seat in the omnibus, I went on with a conversation already commenced, but I felt a perfect certainty. On my return to Caen, for conscience's sake I verified the result at my leisure.[31]

From a Freudian perspective the only plausible interpretation of this sequence of events is that although Poincaré stopped working on the problem consciously the cognitive effort continued unconsciously and the solution was eventually served up to consciousness. Freud argued that the philosophically motivated rejection of this interpretation turns on a semantic issue.[32]

> I am aware that anyone who is under the spell of a good academic philosophical education, or who takes his opinions long-range from some so-called system of philosophy, will be opposed to the assumption of an "unconscious psychical" . . . and will prefer to prove it's impossibility on the basis of a definition of the psychical. But definitions are a matter of convention and can be altered.[33]

The flimsiness of the semantic objection stands in almost comical contrast to the elegance of its Freudian rival. Compare this simple inference to the intellectual contortions required when the dispositionalist approach is applied to the same case, which requires us to accept the highly implausible conclusion that Poincaré's thoughts about non-Euclidian geometry were *not* caused by his prior preoccupation with the problem of Fuchsian functions because once Poincaré had stopped consciously thinking about the problem he was left with nothing more than neurophysiological dispositions to think about it. But, if no cognitive work was done on the problem during the intervening period, what caused an answer to suddenly drop into his consciousness 'out of the blue'? As Freud puts it, if we confine ourselves to the conscious dimension we find "broken sequences" that are "obviously dependent on something else."[34]

Somewhat more formally, let us use the notation T_1 to denote the time when Poincaré stopped working consciously on the problem and T_2 to refer to the moment when he suddenly realized that the transformations defining Fuschian functions are identical to those of non-Euclidean geometry. According to the dispositionalist thesis, there was no *mental* work on the problem during the period between T_1 and T_2. All that occurred during this period were nonmental neurophysiological processes. But, argues Freud, if we assert that neurophysiological processes provide continuity between the events at T_1 and T_2, we must also accept that these. same unconscious neurophysiological processes are also genuinely and occurrently mental. This conclusion is secured by means of the following argument.

1. *There are discontinuities in the flow of conscious mental events.*

This point is intuitively obvious. In the paradigmatic example given earlier, there is a gap in conscious mental continuity between Poincaré's work on the mathematical problem at T_1 and the idea that suddenly entered his mind while on vacation in Coustances at T_2.

2. *Only mental processes can provide mental continuity.*

We say that there are 'gaps' in conscious mental continuity when there are *semantic* discontinuities in the flow of conscious thought. The principle that the possession of intentionality distinguishes mental from nonmental phenomena entails that semantic continuity is supplied only by mental processes. Nonmental processes do not possess semantic content and therefore cannot provide semantic continuity.

3. *All mental events are caused.*

This expression of Freud's doctrine of psychical determinism is just a special case of the view that all nonquantum-level events are caused.

4. In cases where an attempt to consciously solve an intellectual problem at T_1 is followed by:

   a. a period of conscious mental activity semantically discontinuous with it, or a period during which conscious mental activity has ceased entirely, and

   b. which is in turn followed by the involuntary occurrence of a conscious mental event at T_2 the content of which provides a solution to the problem addressed at T_1, which

   c. cannot reasonably be attributed to any cause other than the subject's own mental activity, then:

   d. the subject's unconscious mental activity is a necessary cause for the event at T_2.

5. Therefore, unconscious mental states can be occurrent

In the Poincaré example, the thought at T_2 that the transformations he had used to define the Fuchsian functions were identical to those of non-Euclidian geometry could not, given the information at our disposal, be plausibly attributed to any cause other than his own mental activity. This justifies the particular conclusion that Poincaré unconsciously thought about the problem during the interval between T_1 and T_2, and therefore the more general conclusion that occurrent unconscious mental states exist. It should be borne in mind that this example was chosen as a paradigm for Freud's Continuity Argument because it is a particularly strong and unambiguous candidate. Although it does not follow that Freud's argument can be applied with equal force to other examples of semantic discontinuity, the Poincaré example demonstrates the superiority of Freud's conception of occurrent unconscious processes vis-à-vis its Searlian dispositionalist alternative, and therefore refutes Searle's *global* claims on its behalf.

Note the elegance with which the Continuity Argument kills two Cartesian birds with one logical stone: not only does it provide a powerful argument for the existence of unconscious mental events, but it also gives us reason to accept a materialist conception of mind,[35] Freud does not reject physicalism, and he fully accepts the claim that there is neurophysiological continuity between T_1 and T_2. He claims, however, that this neurophysiological continuity, made up of causal chains of occurrent neurophysiological events, must instantiate equally occurrent causal chains of unconscious mental events.

FREUD'S ANTI-DISPOSITIONALIST ARGUMENT
APPLIED TO SEARLE

As we have seen, the pedigree of Searle's analysis goes right back to the nineteenth-century dispositionalists. I will now bring Freud-style criticisms to bear on it and show that, like its predecessors, it is vulnerable to the impact of the Continuity Argument.

Consider the following situation. An ancient astronomer is perplexed about the relationship between two celestial bodies, the Morning Star and the Evening Star. Exactly two days later he awakens from a deep and dreamless sleep with the realization that the Morning Star is identical to the Evening Star. It is difficult to escape the conclusion that real, occurrent unconscious cognitive work occurred while the astronomer was asleep. The Searlian dispositionalist has two obvious moves at this point: one can deny that the intervening events were content-bearing or one can assert that neural dispositions somehow enter into occurrent mental processes. Let us consider how these options pan out.

Putting it baldly, the first option would amount to saying that although the astronomer's thoughts at time T_1 were about the Morning Star and the Evening Star, and his thoughts at time T_2 were about the Morning Star/ Evening Star, he did not think about these stars at all during the intervening period. The neurophysiological processes that occurred were not *about* anything at all: they were merely capable of producing thoughts about stars. In fact, this is a forced move for Searle in light of his insistence that content cannot be exhaustively characterized in third-person neuroscientific terms. However, Searle is also committed to the seemingly contradictory thesis that there must be some sense in which the aspectual shape of a mental item is latent in the neurophysiological disposition that gave rise to it. How otherwise could a neurophysiological state produce some determinate conscious state, replete with aspectual shape, without possessing features that vary systematically with the aspectual shapes of the conscious mental events that they bring about? But if this is the case, then Searle's claim that neurophysiological dispositions do not possess aspectual shape is at best true only in a trivial sense. Neural dispositions must have aspectual shape latent within them or else the resultant aspectual shape of conscious mental items remains inexplicable.

So, it is clear that Poincaré underwent some sort of mental process between T_1 and T_2. Is it possible that this involved operations on performed on neurophysiological dispositional capacities instead of occurrent mental states? Searle writes: "This sort of dispositional ascription of causal capacities is quite familiar to us from common sense. When, for example, we say of a substance that it is bleach or poison, we are ascribing to a chemical ontology a dispositional causal capacity to produce certain effects."[36]

We need to look more closely at the causal powers of dispositions. The latent dispositions of bleach and poison are realized through their objects. I have to poison something (or someone) to realize the dispositional potential of a vial of arsenic. In contrast to this, neurophysiological dispositions do not act on separate objects to produce conscious states. Wherein lies the difference? The distinction reflects the fact, noted earlier, that Searle deploys an overextended conception of causation, which encompasses both standard causation (which he calls *horizontal causation*) and instantiation (which he calls *vertical causation*). The bleach/bleached, poison/poisoned relations are examples of standard 'horizontal' causation. In contrast, by his own account, the alleged relationship between neural dispositions and occurrent mental states holds by virtue of 'vertical' causation (instantiation). Environmental factors play a crucial role in both forms of 'causation.' Substances like bleach and poison can only release their dispositional powers when embedded in the appropriate causal circumstances, and their dispositional properties are inert in the absence of such causal circumstances. A poison can only do its job if it comes into the right sort of contact with the right kind of living organism. Poison and bleach possess *relational* dispositions, that is, they are realized through 'horizontal' causation. 'Vertical' causation involves *nonrelational dispositions*. Consider the example, given by Searle, of the relationship between the molecular structure of water and its property of liquidity. The molecular structure does not act on the water like bleach acts on a T-shirt because we are dealing with the relationship between microscopic and macroscopic properties of a single substance. Furthermore, those features of an item that instantiate its nonrelational properties are never simply inert, although their effects will vary with the causal circumstances surrounding it. Furthermore, it makes no sense to say that the microscopic features by means of which a macroscopic property is instantiated provide nothing more than a mere disposition for the realization of the macroscopic feature.[37] Given the right causal circumstances, such as an appropriate temperature, there is simply no way that the microproperties of water could not be realized as the macroproperty of liquidity. Change the causal circumstances (e.g., change the temperature) and the way in which the microproperties are realized as macroproperties will vary systematically with them, but in all instances the microproperties are realized in one form or another.

AN ADDITIONAL IMPLICATION OF THE
FREUDIAN CRITIQUE OF DISPOSITIONALISM

As Searle remarks, the dispositional properties of a poison supervene on its chemical ontology. A poison remains a poison irrespective of whether or not it ever poisons anything. A chemist may transform a poison into an innocuous substance by changing its chemical structure. By the same token, a modification in the neurophysiological state disposing our imaginary astronomer to think that the Morning Star and the Evening Star are distinct celestial bodies might result in a neurophysiological state disposing him to think that the Morning Star and the Evening Star are one and the same. If this is the case, then what seems to be occurrent unconscious thought taking place between T_1 and T_2 are actually systematic transformations of nonmental neurophysiological states. What real grounds are there for justifying the assertion that the systematic transformation of neurophysiological states that at the very least correspond to logically ordered sequences of thought are themselves nonmental? Freud adhered to the broadly functionalist notion that mental operations can be realized in a variety of mediums.

> It will soon be clear what the mental apparatus is; but I must beg you not to ask what material it is constructed of. That is not a subject of psychological interest. Psychology can be as indifferent to it as, for instance, optics is to the question of whether the walls of a telescope are made of metal or cardboard. We shall leave entirely on one side the material line of approach, but not so the spatial one. For we picture the unknown apparatus which serves the activities of the mind as being really like an instrument constructed of several parts . . . each of which performs a particular function and have a fixed spatial relation to one another: it being understood that by spatial . . . we really mean in the first instance a representation of the regular succession of the functions.[38]

If one accepts the broadly functionalist notion that thinking is as thinking does, or, more technically, that cognitive operations can be realized through any suitable medium, then the transformation of the disposition to think that the Morning Star and the Evening Star are distinct into the disposition to think that the Morning Star and the Evening Star are identical seems inescapably mental. A defender of Searle's position might suggest that these operations are mental only because they involve states with dispositional powers to produce conscious mental events. However, Searle's argument about dispositional powers is based on his claim about aspectual shape: it is precisely because aspectual shape cannot be exhaustively characterized neurophysiologically that he concludes that a dispositional relationship holds between neurophysiological states and their corresponding conscious mental states. But what of the principled, logically ordered transformation of one disposition into another? Must logical algorithms also possess aspectual shape? If not, does it mean that they are not mental? Even if we conceive of it as a transformation occurring between dispositions, the process by means of which the astronomer comes to think of the Morning and Evening Stars as identical seems to be an unmistakably mental process even though in Searle's view it must be regarded as devoid of aspectual shape.

CONCLUSION

Searle's dispositionalist approach to the unconscious is the most recent expression of an older tradition in the philosophy of psychology. His contention that the unconscious 'mental' contents possesses a purely neural ontology and as such lack aspectual shape, that they are therefore dispositional rather than occurrent, and essentially non mental, is effectively refuted by Freud's Continuity Argument. Whatever the virtues of the causal version of Searle's Connection Principle, it's validity is not secured by his argument for the dispositionalist theory of unconscious mental events.

NOTES

1. J. Searle, *The Rediscovery of the Mind* (London: Bradford/MIT, 1992).
2. J. Searle, Searle. In S. Guttenplan, ed., *A Companion to the Philosophy of Mind* (Oxford: Blackwell, 1995), 548.
3. J. Searle, *The Rediscovery of the Mind* op. cit., 124–125.
4. Ibid.
5. T. Horgan, From supervenience to superdupervenience: Meeting the demands of a material world, *Mind* 102 (1993): 555–586.
6. J. Searle, *The Rediscovery of the Mind*, op. cit., 125–126.
7. J. Heil. *The Nature of True Minds* (Cambridge: Cambridge University Press, 1992).
8. J. Searle, *The Rediscovery of the Mind*, op. cit. 126.
9. J. Searle, Searle, op. cit., 548.
10. J. Searle, *The Rediscovery of the Mind*, op. cit., 157–158.
11. Ibid., 168
12. Ibid., 172.
13. Ibid., 159.
14. T. H. Huxley, On the hypothesis that animals are automata. In G. N. A. Vesey, ed., *Body and Mind* (London: George Allen and Unwin, 1874).
15. C. Darwin, *The Origin of Species* (London: Penguin, 1859, 1968); *The Descent of Man, and Selection in Relation to Sex* (London: John Murray, 1871).
16. H. Ellenberger, *The Discovery of the Unconscious: The History and Evolution of Dynamic Psychiatry* (New York: Basic Books, 1970); L. L. Whyte *The Unconscious Before Freud* (London: Julian Friedman, 1979).
17. R. Dalbiez, *Psychoanalytical Method and the Doctrine of Freud, Vol. II.* Trans. T. F. Lindsay (London: Longmans, Green and Co., 1941).
18. D. Davidson, Paradoxes of irrationality. In R. Wollheim and J. Hopkins, eds., *Philosophical Essays on Freud* (Cambridge: Cambridge University Press, 1982); D. L. Smith, *Freud's Philosophy of the Unconscious*, (Dordrecht & Boston: Kluwer Academic Publishers, 1999).
19. D. L. Smith, *Freud's Philosophy of the Unconscious*, op. cit.
20. Fechner, cited in F. Brentano. *Psychology from an Empirical Standpoint* (London: Routledge & Kegan Paul, 1973), 104.
21. D. L. Smith, *Freud's Philosophy of the Unconscious*, op. cit.; Freudian science of consciousness: then and now. *Neuropsychoanalysis* 2, no. 1 (2000): 38–45.
22. S. Freud, Project for a scientific psychology. *S.E.*, 1.
23. D. L. Smith, *Freud's Philosophy of the Unconscious*, op. cit.
24. S. Freud, The unconscious. *S. E.*, 14; (1926) The question of lay analysis. *S. E.*, 20; (1940) An outline of psychoanalysis. *S.E.*, 23.
25. S. Freud, The unconscious. *S. E.*, 14: 166–167.
26. S. Freud, The unconscious. *S. E.*, 14:167.

27. S. Freud, The ego and the id. S.E., 19:26.

28. Gauss, cited in J. Hadamard, *The Psychology of Inventing in the Mathematical Field* (Princeton: Princeton University Press, 1949), 15.

29. H. Poincaré, *Last Essays*, J. W. Bolduc, trans. (New York: Dover Publications, 1963).

30. Ibid., 383–394.

31. Ibid.

32. S. Freud, Jokes and their relation to the unconscious. S. E., 8; A note of the unconscious in psycho-analysis. S.E., 12; The claims of psycho-analysis to scientific interest. S.E., 13; Introductory lectures on psycho-analysis. S.E., 15 & 16; The ego and the id. S.E., 19:26; An autobiographical study. S. E., 20; An outline of psycho-analysis. S.E., 23.

33. S. Freud, 162.

34. S. Freud, Jokes and their relation to the unconscious. S. E., 8: 158.

35. D. L. Smith, *Freud's Philosophy of the Unconscious*, op. cit.

36. J. Searle, *The Rediscovery of the Mind*, op. cit., 161.

37. D. Papineau, *Philosophical Naturalism* (Oxford: Blackwell, 1993).

38. S. Freud, The question of lay analysis. S. E., 20: 194.

FIVE

PARANOIAC *EPISTEME*

Jon Mills

IF YOU WERE TO randomly open any text of Lacan's and begin to read, you might immediately think that the man is mad. In a word, his writing is psychotic: it is fragmentary, chaotic, and at times incoherent. First of all, his style of spoken discourse, given in lecture format before appearing in print, is infamously troublesome. Second, his fragmented texts obstinately oppose conforming to formal articulate systematization. As a result, Lacan is not very accessible, either as a stylist or a theoretician. For these reasons he invites controversy and is often misinterpreted.[1]

As a fearsome polemicist, radical eccentric, and unorthodox practitioner bordering on the scandalous, within mainstream psychoanalysis, Lacan's name has become a dirty word. While hailed as the "master" by his adherents, vociferous criticism of the "French Freud" mounted vast condemnation for his exploitation of psychoanalytic technique labeled as manipulative, abusive, unethical, and perverted. It comes as no surprise that he would be inevitably blamed for the suicide of some of his analysands, thus leading to his eventual expulsion from the psychoanalytic community (Haddad, 1981; Lacan, 1964a). Although the recognized genius that often accompanies his legend has by no means vanished from academic circles, due to the arcane and inconsistent nature of his writings, Lacan's theoretical oeuvre has been dismissed by some as a "delusion" (Roustang, 1990).

It is rather ironic that Lacan's theoretical innovations are sometimes characterized by the language of the psychoses, for his theory of knowledge is tinged with a psychotic hermeneutics. 'Paranoia' is derived from the Greek, *para*—outside of or beside—as in *'beside* oneself'—and mind (*nous*, νόος), thus beyond intelligible thought (*noēsis*), hence madness. It can also be said that Lacan's splintered, disparate, and often implicit theoretical structure personifies his very notion of desire: desire is beyond structure, beyond words—it is merely the unutterable, ineffable. That which remains nameless, indescribable—unknown—is surely what haunts us; and it is ominous precisely because it is alien.

Like Lacan's conception of the Real—which has no formal text—his comments on paranoiac knowledge are limited to only a few fragments in his *Écrits* and his *Seminars*, thus lacking clarification and systematic rigor. Because his scant remarks on the subject have genuine theoretical and clinical value, it is my intention to provide a conceptual model explicating the scope, breadth, and process of paranoiac knowledge thus showing how Lacan's insights have clinical utility. By way of illustration, I will examine a case of paranoia.

PROLEGOMENA TO LACAN'S SYSTEM: THE RELATION BETWEEN KNOWLEDGE AND PARANOIA

Lacan is very difficult to understand, which makes the interpreter's task ever so daunting. Such difficulty is in no doubt why, in part, most psychoanalytic clinicians in North America remain confused about—if not oblivious to—his theoretical visions. Even worse, there is no unified agreement among Lacanians on how we should interpret Lacan. His invented jargon is highly esoteric, drawing on and reappropriating concepts from many different fields of study including philosophy, anthropology, semiotics, and mathematics, and thus can evoke both admiration and dismissal. Here I am reminded of a decorative centerpiece: it's nice to look at, but no one dares to touch it. The confusional aspects of Lacan's discourse become particularly vexing when Lacan himself declares that he is intentionally trying to confound the very audience who seeks to understand him (Lacan, 1955–1956c, p. 164). For these reasons, Lacan's technical jargon cannot be easily converted into a user-friendly guide. Moreover, many of his concepts have multiple meanings that even oppose each other when viewed from different contexts within his system. While I will attempt to mitigate some of the confusion surrounding his discourse, it will be necessary for me throughout this project to retain much of his technical language, without which many of his theoretical distinctions would go unrecognized.

It is not necessary to adopt Lacan's entire system, which is neither essential nor desirable, to appreciate what he has to offer to our topic at hand. In fact, many of Lacan's positions—such as the decentering of subjectivity for the reification of language—radically oppose contemporary psychoanalytic thought to the degree that Lacan becomes essentially incompatible. Notwithstanding, with the ever-increasing linguistic turn in psychoanalysis, Lacan becomes an important figure to engage. Because language is a necessary condition (albeit not a sufficient one) for conceptual thought, comprehension, and meaning to manifest (see Frie, 1997; Mills, 1999), human knowledge is linguistically mediated. But the epistemological question—that is, the origin of knowledge—requires us to consider pre-linguistic development, intrapsychic and interpersonal experience, and the extra- or nonlinguistic processes that permeate psychic reality, such as the constitutional pressures of the drives (*Triebe*) and affective states (from the monstrous to the sublime) that remain linguistically foreclosed as unformulated unconscious experience. When these aspects of human life are broadly considered, it becomes easier to see how our linguistic-epistemological dependency has paranoiac a priori conditions. From Freud to Klein and Lacan, knowledge is a dialectical enterprise that stands in relation to fear—to the horror of possibility—the possibility of the *not*: negation, conflict, and suffering saturate our very beings, beings whose self-identities are linguistically constructed.

The relation between knowledge and paranoia is a fundamental one, and perhaps nowhere do we see this dynamic so poignantly realized than in childhood. From the 'psychotic-like' universe of the newborn infant (e.g., see Klein, 1946), to the relational deficiencies and self-object failures that impede the process of human attachment, to the primal scene and/or subsequent anxieties that characterize the Oedipal period, leading to the inherent rivalry, competition, and overt aggression of even our most sublimated object relations—fear, trepidation, and dread hover over the very process of knowing itself. What is paranoid is that which stands in relation to opposition, hence that which is alien to the self. Paranoia is not simply that which is beyond the rational mind, but it is a generic process of *noēsis*—'I take thought, I perceive, I intellectually grasp, I apprehend'—hence have *apprehension* for what I encounter in consciousness. With qualitative degrees of difference, we are all paranoid simply because others hurt us, a lesson we learn in early childhood. Others hurt us with their knowledge, with what they say, as do we. And we hurt knowing. 'What will the Other do next?' We are both pacified yet cower in extreme trembling over what we may and may not know—what we may and may not find out; and this is why our relation to knowledge is fundamentally paranoiac.

For Aristotle (1958), "all men by nature desire to know" (p. 108). This philosophic attitude is kindled by our educational systems, perhaps informing the popular adage, "Knowledge is power." But whose? There is no doubt that the acquisition of knowledge involves a power differential, but what if knowledge itself is seen as too powerful because it threatens our psychic integrity? In the gathering of knowledge there is simultaneously a covering over, a blinding to what one is exposed to; moreover, an erasure. I ~~know~~ (No)! Unequivocally, there are things we desire to know nothing about at all; hence the psychoanalytic attitude places unconscious defense—negation/denial and repression—in the foreground of human knowledge, the desire not to know.

When we engage epistemology—the question and meaning of knowledge—we are intimately confronted with paranoia. For example, there is nothing more disturbing when after a lifetime of successful inquiry into a particular field of study it may be entirely debunked by the simple, arrogant question: How do you know? Uncertainty, doubt, ambiguity, hesitation, insecurity—anxiety!: the process of knowing exposes us all to immense discomfort. And any epistemological claim is equally a metaphysical one. Metaphysics deals with first principles, the fundamental, ultimate questions that preoccupy our collective humanity: What is real? Why do I exist? Will I *really* die? Metaphysics is paranoia—and we are all terrified by its questions: Is there God, freedom, agency, immortality? *Is? Why? Why not? Yes but why?!* When the potential meaning and quality of one's personal existence hinge on the response to these questions, it is no wonder why most theists say only God is omniscient. And although Freud (1927) tells us that the very concept of God is an illusory derivative of the Oedipal situation—a wish to be rescued and comforted from the anxieties of childhood helplessness, He—our exalted Father in the sky—is *always* watching, judging. Knowing this, the true believer has every reason to be petrified. For those in prayer or in the madhouse, I can think of no greater paranoia.

THREE REALMS OF BEING

Human knowledge is paranoiac—it torments, persecutes, *cuts.* This is essentially what Lacan (1953–1954) means when he says "my knowledge started off from paranoiac knowledge" (p. 163), because there are "paranoid affinities between all knowledge of objects as such" (1955–1956b, p. 39). To understand what Lacan means, it is necessary to provide a preliminary overview of his ontological treatment of the human condition that he situates in three realms or contexts of being, namely, the Imaginary, Symbolic, and Real. By closely examining a few of Lacan's key works, it will become increasingly clear that aggressivity suffuses the very fabric of human knowledge, a paranoiac residue of the dialectic of desire.

It may be useful to think of three main periods that characterize Lacan's work. While his early period (1932–1948) focused on the role of the imago, his middle period (1948–1960) concentrated on the nature of language that subordinated the world of images to linguistic structures and practices. During his late period (1960–1980), Lacan was preoccupied with a formal systematization of psychoanalysis via logic and mathematics that sought to provide a coherent explanatory framework involving the three realms or registers of mental life. As a cursory definition, we might say that the Imaginary (*imaginaire*) is the realm of illusion, of fantasy, belonging to the sensuous world of perception. In contrast, the Symbolic (*symbolique*) is the formal organization of psychic life that is structured through language and linguistic internalizations, thus becoming the ground of the subject; while the Real (*réel*) remains foreclosed from epistemic awareness within the abyss of unconscious desire. The Real is delimited—the *Ding-an-sich*: it remains the mysterious beyond, the heart of desire.[2] For Lacan, desire is persecutory by virtue of belonging to the Other, first originating in a specular imago, then constituted through the domain of language and speech.

According to Malcolm Bowie (1991), the imaginary, symbolic, and the real are not mental entities, rather they are *orders* that serve to position the individual within a field that traverses and intersects him or her. The word *order* suggests a number of important connotations for Lacan. Analogous to botanical or zoological taxonomy, (1) there is a hierarchical arrangement of classes whereby (2) internal principles of similarity and congruence govern membership in each class. Furthermore, (3) higher levels of classification have superior cognitive status, suggesting that (4) a series of commands or orders are being issued from some undetected source—presumably the real—the night of the mind. No limitations are placed on the Lacanian orders; they may be used to explain any form of human condition from the most banal mental mechanism to the most severe forms of psychopathology. Within the three Lacanian orders, each perspective is realized from its own unique vantage point, revealing an insight into psychic organization that forecloses the others, yet envelopes them. However, by themselves, each fail to fully represent and articulate the greater dynamic complexity that characterizes the parallel processes and temporal unification of the three orders.

As multiple processes, the Lacanian three orders are not stable, fixed entities—rather they are under the constant pressure of evolution, vacillating between antithetical movements of progression and regression, construction and decay. The three orders pressurize each other constantly, having short-term moratoriums. In other words, the three orders are in conflict with each other and, when operative, attempt to exert their own unique influence over the other orders. This in turn creates overdetermined and multiple, dynamic levels of psychic reality. In their dialectical transitions, each order encroaches on the other—the symbolic defining and organizing the imaginary, the imaginary hallucinating the real. Furthermore, the real always wedges its way through the gaps of conscious intentionality, giving desire a voice through the medium of perception and speech. At any given moment we live in all three realms of being, each operative and dynamic within their own orders parallel to each other, yet they are integrative, structured, and complex. While the real is the most obscure concept for Lacan, it reintroduces a vibrant theoretical life to psychoanalytic inquiry that underscores the primacy of an unconscious ontology that Freud was so instrumental to advance. Despite its mysterious appeal shrouded in inconceivability, the real is the reverberation of its own truth disclosed on its own terms and understood through its own language, the idiom of desire.

THROUGH THE LOOKING GLASS

Lacan's inaugural theory of the self was formally introduced in 1936 to the fourteenth International Psychoanalytic Congress and published the following year under the title "The Looking-Glass Phase." This single contribution launched a radical new portrait of ego formation in psychoanalytic thought. One reason why his theory is so radical and controversial is that, for Lacan, the ego, with qualifications, does not exist—at least not in the ordinary sense psychoanalysis has come to view the notion. The ego is a mistake (*méconnaissance*); thus, it is merely an illusory projection of autonomy and control. In other words, the ego (*moi, Ich*) or 'I' is merely a *wish*—itself the product of social construction.

At this point, it may be useful to distinguish between what Lacan means by the self, the ego, the and subject. The 'self,' 'ego,' or 'I,' which is used synonymously throughout much of Lacan's writings, is typically equated with our conscious perceptions and definitions of ourselves. Therefore, when Lacan (1955–1956b) says that "meaning is imaginary" (p. 65), he is saying that our ego is conceptually bound to our conscious self-*image* or self-representations. The term 'subject,' on the other hand, always refers to the unconscious—that which is alien and lies outside of conscious self-awareness. Lacan, as does Freud, privileges the unconscious over the conscious ego, and hence emphasizes that all foreign desires, thoughts, parapraxes, and so on that slip out during acts of speech are tantamount to revealed id (*Es*) processes (Fink, 1997). However, Lacan does not make the distinction between the conscious and unconscious portions of the ego as Freud (1923) does, nor is he inclined to attribute 'agency' to the unconscious, even though he concedes we have a tendency to attribute subjectivity to it. While Freud (1933, p. 6) spoke of the trichotomy of the psyche or "Soul" (*Seele*)—not the 'mental apparatus,' which is a mistranslation—as the temporal unification of the dynamic processes that constitute psychic life, Lacan makes the unconscious subject completely nonpersonal. For our purposes here, however, it may be less confusing if we think of the subject as the whole human being composed of both conscious and unconscious organizations.

The mirror stage is the initial point of self-discovery, hence the dawn of the nascent ego insofar as the 'I' is discovered in the eyes of the other. From the recognition of the self through the looking glass, or through another as its metaphorical representation, the emergence of self-consciousness is constituted in and through alienation. Taken over from Hegel's (1807) theory of desire and recognition, Lacan (1953–1954) states that "the original, specular foundation of the relation to the other, in so far as it is rooted in the imaginary, [is] the first alienation of desire" (p. 176). In the realm of the imaginary, the budding ego first recognizes itself in an object outside of itself, in the mirror image of the other. This illusory order is the initial constitution of the self, as the first matrix of the ego, which is the psychically formative period that occurs between the ages of six to eighteen months of infancy.

Through Kojève, Lacan was deeply influenced by Hegel, especially by his lordship and bondage chapter outlined in the *Phenomenology of Spirit*. For Hegel, one's sense of self is contingent on the recognition of the other, and this contingency itself fosters a paranoid dynamic. We all seek recognition— this is a basic human need. The ego is affirmed by the other, but not at first. There is originally the experience of inequality, whether this be the child's relation to the parent or the servant's relation to the master. Ultimately the desire for recognition becomes a fundamental battle for dominance and validation in which each subject struggles to overcome the objectification of the other. From this standpoint, the sense of one's fundamental contingency on recognition is basically paranoiac and may regress to that paranoid state whenever one becomes acutely aware of that contingency.

Drawing on the ethological research of Tinbergen and Lorenz regarding the perceptual functions of animal behavior, and on Freud's thesis of identification, Lacan emphasizes the organizing function of the imago as the perceptual *Gestalten* that forms the most elemental contours of psychical structure. For Lacan, as for Hegel, the initial recognition of the 'I' does not entail the subject's self-awareness of itself as a fully self-conscious agent. This is a developmental achievement mediated by its burgeoning modes of identification. For Lacan, however, this primordial form of identification "situates the agency of the ego . . . in a fictional direction" (1936, p. 2), namely, in the gaze of the other which gives the illusory semblance of self. In other words, images symbolize, reflect the 'I,' and thus resemble a constituted self that are the initial stimuli for ego boundaries and body differentiation to be forged. The mirror phase is therefore the world of perception, forever cast under the penumbra of the imaginary.

As early as his essay on "The Mirror Stage," Lacan's mature theory of desire is already implicit, it is already prepared. The mirror experience functions as the coming into being of identity, the initial formation of the self—a self that is dialectically and intersubjectively constructed through desire, as the relation of being to *lack* (*manque*). Lacan emphasizes the "internal thrust" of desire within the presupposed subject, yet desire is always *caused* or given over, through internalization, by the Other. As a result, desire is always characterized by absence and incompleteness. Such void, such hole in being clamors in "anticipation" for presence, for fulfillment of its lack, facilitated by the parental imagos that the premature ego identifies with, thus giving an illusory sense of totality and completeness. We may say that such illusory completeness is fantasized, hallucinated *as* reality, thus the fulfillment of a wish. However, the dislocated images mirrored in the other subjected to the illusion of cohesiveness of identity are in fact *defensive* processes enacted to ward off fragmentation anxiety: the genesis of ego development is the life of desire.

THE OTHER AS PERSECUTORY

Lost in its alienation, the Lacanian subject discovers itself in the imaginary, recovered through the mediation of the other, giving itself meaning through the symbolic, struggling on the threshold of the real. But for Lacan (1936), there can never be an absolute self, no autonomous 'I' or transcendental ego that exists apart from the Other; the 'I' is always linked "to socially elaborated situations" (p. 5) mediated by linguistic structures ontologically constituted a priori within its social facticity. Thus the *I* is the *Other*.

It is through the image of the other that the infant comes to grasp awareness of its own corporeal integrity and seize the first measure of control over its body movements. The imago serves as an "alter-ego," an organizing, stabilizing function that coordinates cohesiveness out of internal chaos and provides homogeneity out of primal discord. Through the imaginary, the ego is no more than a return of an image to itself. The paradoxical structure of the imaginary is therefore the polarity between alienation and recognition. Lacan sees recognition as the recovery of the alienated image facilitated through the mirroring of the other. As the subject finds or recognizes itself through an image (insofar as recognition is the misrecognition of its autonomous ego as an illusory mastery), it is concurrently confronted with its own alienated and alienating image; hence this process becomes an aggressive relation.

Lacan describes the degree of "aggressive disintegration" that torments the inchoate ego in "the form of disjointed limbs, or of those organs represented in exoscopy, growing wings and taking up arms for intestinal persecutions" (1936, p. 4). The persecutory fantasies that accompany early ego development may indeed take the form of "images of castration, mutilation, dismemberment, dislocation, evisceration, devouring, bursting open of the body, in short, the . . . *imagos of the fragmented body*" (1948, p. 11). Feldstein (1996) notes that the imago allows the infant to elide a fundamental rupture in which "anxiety-producing images of the fragmented body are disavowed because such untotalizable self-differences could give rise to paranoid perceptions . . . [thus] paranoia is related to the mirror-stage attempt to manufacture a future-perfect mastery" (p. 135). It becomes essential for the ego to split, compartmentalize, and/or project its negative introjects from its internal experiences and internalize soothing ministrations to defend against such hostile intrusions. Thus, the stabilizing and "fixating" quality of the positive imago serves a cohesive function. As the imago (accompanied by maternal ministrations and validating presentations) helps constitute the burgeoning 'I,' the salutary power of the specular image becomes a unifying and integrating activity.

The organizing and synthesizing functions internalized over maturation become unifying yet mobile fixtures of the child's inner representational world. Such internalizations are fortified through ongoing identifications that provide the illusion of self-cohesion that further serve to ward off primordial anxiety associated with fragmentation, decomposition, and loss of undifferentiated bliss with the imago. This is also a prevalent theme for Klein (1946) and post- Kleinians (Bion, 1959; Segal, 1957): ego organization is besieged by the horrors of persecutory-annihilation anxiety. Unlike Klein, however, the self is the introjection of the other, not the projection of the self discovered in the other. For Lacan, the self is causally given over by the other; thus the self is the other internalized in all its variegated forms.

Given the plethora of images and fantasies that populate the early stages of the imaginary, it becomes increasingly clearer to see how the other becomes a persecutory object. The other, and particularly the other's desire, is always a potential threat to the subject because it is an alien force that stands in firm opposition to the subject, an antithesis that evokes rivalry and competition. This is why Lacan (1955–1956b) says that "all human knowledge stems from the dialectic of jealousy, which is a primordial manifestation of communication" (p. 39). The subject first encounters the other as *opposition*—an opposition that *desires*. As such, the other is in possession of something the subject lacks. We are jealous of what the other has that naturally evokes feelings of rivalry, competition, and envy. This naturally leads Lacan to conclude that "the object of human interest is the object of the other's desire" (p. 39). What the subject desires in otherness is the other's desire, thus bringing about a primordial confrontation with death: in opposition there is always the possibility of being annulled. "The dialectic of the unconscious always implies struggle, the impossibility of coexistence with the other [is] one of its possibilities" (p. 40). Whether the other is the object of desire that enjoys a degree of liberty that the subject lacks, or whether the Other is the symbolic order imposing an austere reality on the subject's inner world through the violation and demands of speech, the acquisition of knowledge becomes a paranoiac enterprise.

AGGRESSIVITY AND IDENTIFICATION

Within the initial phases of the imaginary, aggressivity becomes paramount for Lacan. The image as an alienating presence may be an ominous, rivalrous threat that the subject fears as dangerous. While the imago may be a validating-soothing-sustaining introject that provides the self with illusory stability, it may also become colored by the projection of the one's own innate destructive impulses organized in one's paranoiac relation to the imago. The doubling function of the imaginary, as the medium for both self-recognition and self-alienation, serves as the initial developmental impetus behind the dialectical unfolding of desire.

The interface between identification, aggression, and the captivation of the specular imago in the imaginary register serves paradoxical functions. For Lacan, the "captation" of the mirror image is both entrancing and intrusive; it fascinates yet it captures. As the image of oneself is given over by the other, there is a new psychical action, that of identification, which for Lacan is the moment of the inception of the ego. While Freud (1921, 1933) envisions identification as the development of an emotional bond with a significant figure, Lacan focuses on the dialectical capacity to form judgments of identity and difference. Through identification, the baby finds the image a captivating albeit imprisoning force chained to the pull of the imaginary. For Lacan, this incarcerating point of attraction implies that the ego momentarily becomes fixed and static. Unconscious fantasy systems largely serve a defensive function in the pre-Oedipal child, fueling illusory misrecognitions as a way of fending off the aggressive violation of the imago's encroachment.[3]

There is an a priori manifestation of destruction within the imaginary order: aggressivity is ontologically constituted within any dyadic relation. The imaginary capture of the mirror is mired in destruction, for as Lacan emphasizes, any imaginary relation generates rivalry and conflict. Recall that what we identify in opposition is the other's desire that we long to possess. Identification therefore generates an ambivalent tension between possession and lack. Identification with a rival evokes the dialectic of presence and absence, mastery and servitude; thus the initial point of confrontation entails the recognition of what one has not yet procured or mastered. For example, we may say that the mother's image is castrating because it is more powerful. Fear, dread, or shame may be evoked by a simple look: the other's desire is exposed through a gaze. Thus, the boundary of the imaginary becomes difference. For Lacan, this dual relation between the infant–mother dyad encases desire within an interminable narcissistic battlefield.

It is important to note that aggressivity and aggression are not the same. For Lacan, aggression is a derivative of the death drive (*Todestrieb*) while aggressivity is the acting out of aggression through the symbolic and imaginary orders. Following Freud (1920), aggressivity is both the deflection of self-destruction and a defensive, protective reaction to an external threat. Lacan (1948) shows that aggressivity is immured within the structures of subjectivity "by its very constitution" (p. 9), and avouches that "aggressivity in experience is given to us as intended aggression and as an image of corporeal dislocation" (p. 10). As we have said, imagos can be noxious and disfiguring, thus leading to fragmentation and a fracturing of the body. The ego attempts to fantasize the illusion of mastery and unity in the face of these dislocated and contrary experiences characteristic of the child's fragmented bodily states that are displaced as aggressivity directed toward others. Richard Boothby (1991) argues that "aggressivity is a drive toward violation of the imaginary form of the body that models the ego. It is because aggressivity represents a will to rebellion against the imago that aggressivity is specifically linked in fantasy to violations of the bodily integrity" (p. 39). Thus, for Lacan (1966), "the notion of aggressivity corresponds . . . to the splitting of the subject against himself" (p. 344). Such "dehiscence" in the nascent ego gives rise to persecutory anxiety, hence the origins of knowledge are paranoiac in their "most general structure." "What I have called paranoic knowledge is shown, therefore, to correspond in its more or less archaic forms to certain critical moments that mark the history of man's mental genesis, each representing a stage in objectifying identification" (1948, p. 17).

Knowledge—the other's knowledge—is always lurking with pernicious intent to get in and *kill* the ego. The objects of identification are inherently baneful: they eviscerate desire simply because they are the other's desire. As the child's identificatory powers increase, so does the capacity for aggressivity. When the burgeoning ego identifies with the other's desire, it models the other and hence enters into an aggressive rivalry over the object of the other's desire. Following Hegel (1807), Lacan (1953–1954) sees this process as a competition for recognition: "The subject's desire can only be confirmed in this relation through a competition, through an absolute rivalry with the other, in view of the object towards which it is directed. And each time we get close, in a given subject, to this primitive alienation, the most radical aggression arises—the desire for the disappearance of the other" (p. 170). Lee (1990) aptly tells us that "aggression directed toward others is found at the very center of the *moi's* structure, as it comes into being through the dialectic of the child's narcissistic identifications with various visual images" (p. 27). Such identification, says Lacan (1948), is also an "erotic relation, in which the human individual fixes upon himself an image that alienates him from himself, that are to be found the energy and the form on which this organization of the passions that he will call his ego is based" (p. 19).

For Lacan, the aggressivity injected into the very process of ego identification itself "determines the awakening of his desire for the object of the other's desire" (1948, p. 19). Lacan essentializes aggression as an ontologically indispensable psychic process that infuses narcissistic ego development. Aggressivity breaches the margin of libidinal self-investment as it falls on the fringe of self-destruction. Such "narcissistic suicidal aggression" operative with the formation of the ego is due to the alienated and lethal assault of the imago that unleashes a violence on the subject to the point of self-extinction. As the other, *objet a* (sometimes referred to as *objet-petit-a*) is the signifier of desire; thus the subject is an-*other* plundered by the object's desire. Bowie (1991) explains that "the original act of identification is the original narcissistic declaration too; into the very constitution of the ego its destruction is already woven; the only escape from alienation is an aggravation of the alienated state" (p. 34).

For Freud, narcissistic object-choice is the process of conversion (*Umwandlung*) of aggressivity into love, a process that hinges on the repression of the drive toward aggression in the face of socialization and object attachment. For Lacan, this two-phase process is compressed into one: narcissism and aggressivity are correlatives. Julien (1994) expatiates on this claim: "Narcissism, in which the image of one's own body is sustained by the image of the other, in fact introduces a *tension*: the other in his image both attracts and rejects me. I am indeed nothing but the other, yet at the same time, he remains *alienus*, a stranger. This other who is myself is other than myself" (p. 34).

As the ego is formally laid down in the imaginary relations of the mirror stage, aggressivity is embedded in love by virtue of this dual relationship. Duality implies difference, exclusion, antithesis. My desire is *their* desire!—it is already tainted with ugliness. A fundamental dichotomy is already constituted by this a priori relation, a rigid *either/or* leading to what Lacan calls the "fraternal complex": *either* I kill the other *or* the other will kill me. As the immature ego is imperiled by perceived hostile and persecutory advances by the other's desire, the child is immersed in a destructive reality that it must endeavor to deflect, project, and keep at bay. At the same time aggressivity contaminates the inner I; the ego is subjected to its own libidinal and relational strivings to attach to an ideal love object. From a Kleinian perspective, the oscillation between ideal and persecutory object relations is further enhanced during the depressive position. As paranoid anxiety gradually devolves into (yet remains subsumed within) depressive anxiety, the ego is besmirched by fears of destruction and loss of love. This is very much in keeping with Lacan's position: the ego's ambitendent, aggressive-erotic structure is the narcissistic foundation for *jouissance*—the realm of excess—desire's pleasures in death.[4]

For Lacan, death plays a pivotal role in the organization of the psyche: "aggressivity gnaws away, undermines, disintegrates; it castrates; it leads to death" (1948, p. 10). Schneiderman (1983) suggests that desire itself is the desire for death, one that is "cultivated to the extend that death is kept at a distance" (p. 74). The pleasure of death is not to be experienced as a real death, rather as the euphoria of *jouissance*, the pleasure of its sublimation. This sublimation, however, is not bound to the homeostatic laws that govern the pleasure-principle, rather it exceeds it. We might say that death satisfies desire, but only if it is sustained, prolonged. Death is only satisfying if it is protracted. The pleasure of death, hence the process of death, makes the experience of satisfaction satisfying.

Boothby (1991) cogently shows that Lacan's treatment of the death drive is pivotal in his theoretical innovations that intimately link death with the functions of speech, language, and desire. As Lacan (1954–1955b) states, "the death instinct is only the mask of the symbolic order" (p. 326). Thus, the death drive hides behind the veil of speech. Language castrates *jouissance*, it alienates desire from satisfaction and thus introduces a division within the subject leaving a palpable void (Ragland, 1995). Lacan's repositioning of death provides us with a hermeneutics of unconscious desire. With reference to Freud, Lacan (1958) suggests that "life . . . has only one meaning, that in which desire is borne by death" (p. 277). Desire is the spawn of intrusion, violation, and laceration from the Other—speech and language are by nature aggressive, they *cut*.

THE *DE*-STRUCTURE OF LANGUAGE

As we have seen, Lacan's developmental picture of the ego is clearly imbued with a negative dialectic: imagoes are alien and threatening, identification is formed in relation to lack, object relations are primarily aggressive and rival-rous, and desire is always imposed. From this account, the ego is vigilant and suspicious; hence it takes a paranoid relation toward the world at large that becomes unconsciously fortified. But when the ego acquires language, para-noia takes a symbolic turn signified through the demands of speech. The notion of the symbolic order of mental functioning came to the fore during the Rome Report.[5] Developed by Saussure and Jakobson, and taken over by Lévi-Strauss' formalization of the elementary structure of kinship with its reliance on Jakobson's binarism, Lacan's (1977) emphasis on symbols refers not to icons or stylized figurations, but rather to signifiers that he extends into a general definition with differential elements; in-themselves without meaning, signifiers acquire value only in their mutual relations that form a closed order (p. ix). Language lends structure to the psyche, thus, it is the symbolic that gives order to the subject. In fact, for Lacan, the subject is ultimately *determined* by the symbolic function of signifiers, speech, and lan-guage. The relationship between the imaginary and the symbolic is con-trasted by the experiences of the ego and its images on the one hand, and the fortification of linguistic attributions on the other. We are thrown into the realm of the symbolic: language is already constituted a priori within a preexisting social ontology, predefined, predetermined. Lacan (1957) tells us: "language and its structure exist prior to the moment at which each subject at a certain point in his mental development makes his entry into it" (p. 148). Symbolization attempts to give desire structure and order. Submitted to its systemic facticity, desire is molded by linguistic ontological pressures.

The introduction of the symbolic category marks a radical departure from Freud's metapsychology, indeed a rewriting of the structure of the psyche. Bore out in "The Agency of the Letter in the Unconscious or Reason since Freud," Lacan (1957) deliberately refigures Saussurian linguistics, insinuating the radical claim that not only is the unconscious structured like a language, but the unconscious *is* language (also see 1955–1956, pp. 11, 119, 166). For Lacan, the unconscious is not just conceived metaphorically as language, it is literally the Letter, thus the signifier. He states: "But how are we to take this 'letter' here? Quite simply, literally ... the unconscious is the whole structure of language" (1957, p. 147). More specifically, letters (words) func-tion as an infinite deferral within the signifying chain. This infinity in the link of signifiers shares affinities with Freud's concept of primary process thinking: signifiers break through obstacles, they know no limits, there is merely a constant flow. The agency (*instance, Instanz*) of the letter suggests that there is an authority to language, indeed an 'insistence.' Furthermore, Lacan's reference to 'reason since Freud' refers to what reason has become since Freud due to his insistence on the agency of the unconscious; hence the unconscious is our reason why the illusory is our consciousness.

The symbolic order was important to Lacan precisely because it was inclusive and versatile, capable of referring to an entire range of signifying practices (Bowie, 1991; Fink, 1995; Marcelle, 1992). Due to its coherence and malleability, the symbolic category links the world of the unconscious to the structures of speech, and thus even more broadly to a social linguistic ontology. While repression is the prototype of the unconscious for Freud (1923, p. 15), language is the sine qua non of Lacan's new symbolic science.

Lacan's admiration of the symbolic is clearly contrasted to his derisive view of the Imaginary.[6] The symbolic is the seat of motion and heterogeneity, thus transcending the field of illusory similarity: opposition and difference are firmly retained. The symbolic gives rise to the subject distinct from the imaginary ego, as an order of being that is always intermittent and disjoined (Bowie, 1991). Thus, the symbolic is characterized by the ontology of absence, negativity, and nothingness. The relation between absence and presence, vacuity and abundance accents the power of signification. Lack has as much signifying potency as excess and none may operate alone without evoking antithesis. For Lacan (1953, 1957, 1960), the signification of lack parallels castration, as the "Name-of-the-Father" is the symbol for an authority that is both punitive and legislative. As the "paternal metaphor" that inheres in symbolization, lack is given significance in relation to otherness structured in symbolic opposition to the subject. Without such dialectical positionality, desire would succumb to a psychotic universe imprisoned within an absence of signification.

The imaginary is determined by signifiers, thus language is crucial in the construction of identity (Sarup, 1992). For Lacan, words are interpreted and given meaning retroactively; the behavior and verbal communication of another is always in need of interpretation, refracted through language. Lacan (1960) emphasizes the interpersonal demand for recognition that operates within the dialectic of desire. Within contemporary psychoanalysis, Kohut (1971, 1977, 1984) has made the need for validation and recognition the pinnacle motive force of desire: the subject craves attunement and mirroring from its selfobject milieu. While Lacan's (1953, 1958) mature period deifies the symbolic at the expense of decentering the subject, his approach nevertheless underscores the "lack of being" that characterizes desire, the "want-to-be" (manque-à-être) that characterizes the dialectic of recognition (pp. 259, 274).

While Lacan (1964c,d) says that "the unconscious is structured like a language" (pp.149, 203), language itself can be dialectically destructive: the symbolic has the capacity to de-structure as it imposes order and meaning. The symbolic is an imposition, it places a demand on the subject. Language by its very nature is assaultive: through distinctions, disjunctives, and classifications it makes exclusions and omissions, thus dividing particulars from universals as it discriminates, separates, and categorizes. The order and structure of the letter as an insistence are only possible in the wake of disorder and destruction that are determined by its dialectical relation. The metonymy of what *is*, is defined by what it is *not*. Language breaks up meaning and fractures it through negation, an act of de-structuring based on engagement with opposition. While the symbolic order frames, composes, and constructs, it can conversely displace one meaning for another.

The very structure and imposition of the symbolic can geld and dismember. Words take on signifying functions that activate cognitive, affective, and fantasy systems that rip through the very core of our being. Speech—the spoken word—is the medium of caustic oral aggression that can be so acerbic and devaluing that it may scar one's self-concept and inner representational world. Negation—"No!"—by its very definition and execution introduces lack, absence, and deprivation. This is why so often we see conflicted individuals fixate on what was said or unsaid by others, thus assuming obsessional forms and repetitions. The perseveration of thought affixed to lack can be a living hell. Speech creates psychic pain through the affliction of desire and lack, as does silence—a poignant withholding. This may be why we all have "paranoid affinities" in relation to how the other uses language and speech: we fear evaluation and judgment—the other's desire, hence the unknown.

THE DESIRE NOT TO KNOW

We have shown that the paranoiac process of acquiring knowledge has its genesis in the imaginary, first as the subject's misidentification with its alienated image in the reflection of the other, and second as the fundamental distortion and miscognition of external objects (also see Muller & Richardson, 1982). Human knowledge is paranoiac because the subject projects its imaginary ego properties into objects that become distorted and perceived as fixed entities that terrorize the subject with persecutory anxiety in the form of the other's desire. While the terrifying part-object experiences of the dislocated body arise in the imaginary, the symbolic register introduces another form of fragmentation. Desire and speech by their very nature impose a command. Knowledge is saturated with paranoia because it threatens to invade the subject, and it is precisely this knowledge that must be defended against as the desire not to know.

Interpreting Lacan, Bruce Fink (1997) tells us that just as patients do not possess a genuine desire for change, they further lack a genuine desire for self-knowledge. While people may show interest in knowing why their lives and interpersonal relationships are unsatisfactory, and specifically what keeps interfering with their adjustment and happiness, Lacan (1955–1956a) suggests that there is a more fundamental unconscious wish not to know any of those things. "The subject's entire subsequent development shows that he wants to know nothing about it" (p. 12). In *Encore*, Lacan (1972–1973) further adds that "the unconscious is the fact that being, by speaking, enjoys, and . . . wants to know nothing more about it"—that is, "know nothing about it at all" (pp. 104-105). This is why patients often resist therapy and avoid the process of self-examination and change. They have no desire to know the root of their symptoms or neurotic mechanisms, what functions their defenses serve, and why they are instituted in the first place. This is why Lacan says that patients do not want to give up their symptoms because they provide familiarity and meaning: we enjoy our symptoms too much! (Žižek, 1992). This is the insidious structure of *jouissance*, namely, pleasure in pain, or the satisfaction individuals find in dissatisfaction to the point that they wish not to give it up. As Ragland (1995) asserts, "the inertia of *jouissance* . . . makes a person's love of his or her symptoms greater than any desire to change them" (p. 85). From this standpoint, the unconscious is first and foremost sadomasochistic: it inflicts a perverse pleasure through suffering at its own hands.

There is a self-destructive element to the enjoyment of symptoms, a revelry in the realm of excess to the point that truth or knowledge must be suspended, disavowed, or denied. This is why Lacan thinks that all knowledge of objects as such become tainted with paranoia: they threaten the subject's *jouissance*, and thus must be defended against as the desire not to know. So we may see how Lacan's theoretical insights have clinical applicability, let us now turn our attention to a case of paranoia.

THE CASE OF MRS. Z

The patient is a forty-eight-year-old white female with a presenting clinical picture of paranoid agitation, domestic violence, and suicidal gestures in response to her suspicion that her husband was having an extramarital affair. She was voluntarily admitted to an inpatient psychiatry unit of a general hospital after she was found intoxicated standing in the rain nude for approximately two hours. Upon confronting her husband about the alleged affair, Mrs. Z had reportedly slapped and hit him and then set a blanket on fire in the upstairs bedroom of their house before running outside in the cold with no clothes on, refusing to come back inside, saying she would rather die. She deliberately tried to hide from a small neighborhood search party but was eventually located and brought to Emergency by the police. This was the patient's first hospitalization and she had no previous psychiatric history.

Mrs. Z has been married to her husband for twenty-three years and has a twenty-year-old daughter who recently got married and moved out of the home. Following her daughter's marriage, the patient was removing something from her husband's car when she noticed that there was a crack in the upholstery of the driver's seat. Apparently the seat was splitting at the seam in the upper right-hand corner, yet she paid it little attention. A week had passed when she noticed that the rip in the seam had widened and with panic she immediately fantasized that her husband was having vigorous sexual relations with another woman in the car, thus causing damage to the seat. Upon having this fantasy, Mrs. Z reported that she recalled an event that took place approximately four months prior to her daughter's wedding when she thought she smelled perfume on her husband's shirt while doing the laundry, something she dismissed at the time. This recollection further revived a painful twenty-year-old memory of when her husband blurted out another woman's name during intercourse, leaving an unabated narcissistic injury; yet he assured her at the time his slip was only a fantasy and that he had never been unfaithful, an explanation that she believed.

After discovering the torn seat for the second time, Mrs. Z's suspicions started to assume more paranoid qualities, thus producing obsessional preoccupations that her husband was cheating on her each day as he went to work. She started checking and cleaning the car every night as he returned home hoping *not* to find evidence to corroborate her intuitions. One evening, however, she found a small piece of wire fencing underneath the passenger's front seat and concluded that someone had been in the car. When she asked her husband to explain how it got there, he could not, only suggesting that she must have overlooked the object when she previously vacuumed the car.

The patient now started to record the gas mileage each day as her husband drove to and from work. She had already driven the same route he normally took and recorded the mileage so she could have a baseline for comparison. When the milage on the odometer proved to be significantly higher than expected on his next return from work, she confronted her husband on the discrepancy and accused him of having an affair. He vociferously denied any such thing and told the patient that she was paranoid. Mrs. Z admitted that while she had little proof at the time, she thought her husband was lying because he could not look her directly in the eye.

Convinced of her husband's infidelity, Mrs. Z purchased a voice-activated tape recorder and secretly concealed it in her husband's car. Upon returning from work that evening, the patient retrieved the tape recorder from the car and listened to the tape in its entirety. Initially the tape played back familiar sounds of a moving car on the road, conveying common traffic noises and music from the radio. After approximately 20 minutes of listening to the tape, Mrs. Z reported that she began to feel foolish that she had mistrusted her husband. But just as she was ready to turn off the tape, she reportedly began to hear her husband converse with another woman. The conversation soon led to passion as she heard the couple engage in the act of sexual relations.

Mrs. Z immediately confronted her husband about the affair, which he point-blankly denied. When she then produced the tape recorder and explained how she had hidden it in the car recording his entire drive to work, he supposedly became frantic and disoriented. But when she played the section of the tape of the man conversing with the woman, he emphatically stated, "That's not my voice!" Steadfastly denying that he was the one on the tape, the husband conjectured that someone from work must be stealing his car during the day, driving to some undisclosed location to have sex with some woman, and then returning the car before he gets off from work. At first Mrs. Z could not believe his story, but he assured her that he was not the man on the tape. Because the sound of the recording was crude, she had reason to doubt her previous assessment. Furthermore, he informed the patient that someone could have had access to his car unbeknownst to him because he routinely leaves his keys on a hook at the office so not to lose them before he takes the company truck to the construction site each morning. However, he could not explain why two strangers would do such a thing or what possible motives they could have. He could think of no one at work with whom he had a conflict or who would be inclined to take his car.

Wanting to believe her husband, Mrs. Z accepted his story and tried to convince herself that someone was playing a prank on them. It is during this time that she began abusing alcohol on a daily basis in order to cope. A few days had passed before she secretly resumed planting the tape recorder in the car. When she listened to the tape the second time, however, she suspected that the tape had been tampered with or changed. Over the days that followed, the patient was convinced that someone was removing the tape recorder, changing the tape from side A to side B, and replacing it in its original position with an altered recording. In desperation, she confided in her daughter and other family members that her husband was having an affair, but he had convinced them that she was mistaken. Mrs. Z had continued to hide the tape recorder in the car for some time and reportedly recorded another discussion between a man and a woman. Maintaining his innocence, the husband speculated that the strangers must have made a duplicate set of keys to the car since he no longer left his keys hanging publicly on a hook in the office for people to take at their leisure.

The couple maintained this charade for a few more weeks, first getting an anti-theft device—"The Club"—and securing it to the wheel when away from his car at work, and then installing an elaborate car-alarm system. These protective devices were of no help because the alleged 'strangers' were still apparently taking the car. When Mrs. Z heard once more what she perceived to be her husband's voice on the tape conversing with another woman, she became increasing more accusatory, volatile, and inebriated on a regular basis. The patient began to secretly follow her husband to work to spy, watching to see if he would deviate from his route or if she could catch the culprits. After a few days of observing nothing unusual, she began to suspect that her husband knew that he was being followed and the car observed. Around this time, the patient reported that she started noticing objects in the house missing, and that dish towels were being removed from the kitchen drawer but returned days later folded incorrectly. Her family was convinced that she was "crazy": her paranoia was either due to an overly active imagination or alcohol, and her drunkenness was simply a means of "getting attention."

While the complexities of this case are by no means exhausted in this short description, we may nevertheless see how the patient's discovery of her husband's transgressions was tinged with paranoia. Even during her hospitalization, the patient was struggling with accepting the realization of his infidelity that persecuted her as paranoiac knowledge. She did not wish to know, and the desire not to know marked by a disavowal of the evidence at hand was experienced as a persecutory assault on her psychic integrity. Lurking in the shadows, this knowledge stalked her, prowling in the recesses of her mind in the form of fixed repetitions and fantasies thus leading to obsessional cycles of fear, dread, anxiety, and rage—violating her self-cohesion.

In discussing a case of hysteria, Freud (1893–1895) referred to the "blindness of the seeing eye" as not wanting to know (p. 117, fn. 1). But Mrs. Z's desire not to know was not merely a desire to remain ignorant of her husband's deeds, it was a desire not to know *his* desire. As Lacan (1959–1960a) puts it, "the moving force of paranoia is essentially the rejection of a certain support in the symbolic order" (p. 54)—she could not accept his desire, hence his demand. The need to mobilize specific defensive maneuvers designed to deny the possibility of the truth in the service of self-deception was exacerbated by the acute nature of her paranoiac intrusions: she was painfully exposed to the other's desire. In his lecture, "The See-Saw of Desire," Lacan (1953–1954) writes: "What is ignorance? Certainly it is a dialectical notion, since it is within the perspective of truth that it is constituted as such. If the subject does not refer himself to the truth, there is no ignorance. If the subject doesn't begin to ask himself the question what is and what is not, there is no reason for there to be a true and a false, nor even, beyond that, reality and appearance" (p. 167). The structure of human knowledge is paranoid for the simple reason that it is constituted in dialectical relation to truth: to know or not to know?—that is the question. In either instance, there is an apprehension to knowing because of the possibility of being subjected to a painful realization: in this case, the other's desire. She *sees*, she *saw*—hence 'See-Saw,' and this must be negated. Having knowledge or not is in relation to presence and lack. Paranoia is a reaction to anxiety generated in response to desire as demand and/or in relation to absence.

Mrs. Z knew the truth, but it had to be disavowed; she so desperately wanted to remain ignorant of the affair that she inverted and displaced the truth through the mechanism of misrecognition. In the most general sense, she became lost in the imaginary and could not see the real for what it was. Lacan (1953–1954) asserts: "Misrecognition represents a certain organization of affirmations and negations, to which the subject is attached. Hence it cannot not be conceived without correlative knowledge. If the subject is capable of misrecognizing something, he surely must know what this function has operated upon. There must be, behind his misrecognition, a kind of knowledge of what there is to misrecognize" (p.167). The patient's misrecognition is a function of her desire not to know what she knows. She is "attached" to her own wish. What she wishes to know is a symptom of her misrecognition, namely that her husband could not be guilty of desiring another woman. In fact, her self-deception was so entrenched that she had reportedly taken the tapes to a private investigator for a voice analysis, the results of which were still pending during her hospitalization. Because her husband denied that the voice on the tape was his, yet had no explanation to account for the alleged incidents, the patient felt this was the only way to reconcile the situation. Lacan (1953–1954) adds, "[s]he misrecognizes, or refuses to recognize . . . but everything in the way [s]he behaves indicates that [s]he knows that there is something that [s]he doesn't want to recognize" (p. 167). What Mrs. Z refused to recognize was her husband's desire. "The delusional intuition is a full phenomenon that has an overflowing, inundating character for the subject" (1955–1956b, p. 33). She so badly wanted to believe the untruth that she set out to prove him innocent: "The voice analysis will exonerate him!" she exclaimed. During her hospitalization she had still hoped that the voice match would come back negative, which would prove in her mind that unidentified strangers were the offenders, yet as Lacan informs us, deep down she had already recognized the truth that she so despairingly wanted not to believe. But as Lacan (1959–1960b) says elsewhere: "nothing is more ambiguous than belief" (p. 171). He further states: "At the basis of paranoia itself, which nevertheless seems to be animated by belief, there reigns the phenomenon of the *Unglauben* (disbelief)" (1964e, p. 238). If the voice analysis exonerated her husband, her paranoia would be confirmed only on the condition that it was not him, a wishful expression of her desire not to know. But if the results were inconclusive, she would continue to be plagued by suspicion, mistrust, and doubt.

Mrs. Z's misrecognition was maintained through periods of "transitivism," what Lacan refers to as moments of "see-sawing" in which the subject takes the other's actions (or thoughts) to be equivalent with her own. The patient's husband did not want her to know and he deliberately and calculatingly lied to cover up his deed and desire. Through projective identification, she identified with his desire, which she introjected and made her own. "He would not do such a thing because he loves only me. He would not hurt me!" Wanting to accept his story—his lie—she misrecognized his original desire for his counterintention, namely his reparatory, secondary wish for her not to know the truth. But all his reassurances and pleading could not stave off what she had already affirmed yet negated. She recognized his desire for what it was—"this other negates [me], literally kills [me]" (1955–1956c, p. 209): it gnawed on her as a slow emotional torture. Forced on her as a savage assault, violence and self-abuse was her only recourse—the destructive affliction of the other's desire.

CONCLUDING REFLECTIONS

Whether paranoiac acquisitions arise in the fragmented images and dissociated impulses that characterize the experience of the incipient ego, in the imaginary relations governing fantasy, wish, conflict, and defense, or in our confrontation with the Other, the epistemic-phenomenological process of 'knowing' is dynamically informed by unconscious paranoiac pressures. This is most evident when we confront the other's desire. As Hegel articulated nearly two hundred years ago, the desire for recognition produces a primordial confrontation leading to "the desire for the disappearance of the other" (Lacan, 1953–1954, p. 170). When we encounter impasse from the affliction of others, we simply wish for them to vanish. Desire is a demand to which we yield or oppose. Language imposes itself on us as demand to which we are enslaved, thus explaining in part why we fear knowing anything beyond our immediate control. Whether constructed or discovered, the process of examining what *is* and what is *not*—being and nothingness—is driven by paranoia—itself the dialectic of being in relation to lack.

But paranoiac knowledge is not merely a fear of the unknown, it is a trepidation of knowing a particular truth that the subject may find horrific. Whether knowing elicits revulsion, shame, envy, or hate, it is the other's desire that is revealed in relation to our own. The juxtaposition of what is known to what is concealed always evokes the affirmation-negation contrast. As Lacan (1955–1956b) says, "paranoid knowledge is knowledge founded on the rivalry of jealousy" (p. 39) due to the subject's realization of lack in relation to the object of the other's desire. "This defines, within the speech relationship, something that originates somewhere else—this is exactly the distinction between the imaginary and the real" (p. 39). The object of otherness is a primitive alienation that we wish to possess and is thus the object of a primary identification. For Lacan, desire originates from the outside—*it* speaks. This is why he says that when the other talks about himself, he speaks to us about something that has spoken to him.

But we may ask: What part of the subject speaks from within? Analysis tells us the unconscious—the realm beyond conceptualization, namely, the real. In the imaginary and symbolic domains, we are bombarded by alienation, opposition, and demand, but *the unconscious is the house of being*, and our relation to the real is a self-relation we know very little about. "The unconscious is something that speaks within the subject, beyond the subject, and even when the subject doesn't know it, and that says more about him than he believes" (1955–1956b, p. 41). Here we may say that the unconscious is even more alienating than the imaginary, because we are ultimately estranged from ourselves—from our own inner world. Elsewhere Lacan (1964b) says: "In the unconscious there is a corpus of knowledge (*un savoir*), which must in no way be conceived as knowledge to be completed, to be closed" (p. 134). Therefore, the goal of psychoanalysis may be said to be the creative discovery of ἀλήθεια. Truth is a process of disclosedness or unconcealment, a process that may never be completely actualized.

We have an ambivalent relation to the unconscious—the desire to know is opposed by the desire to remain oblivious. For Lacan, the real is that place of limit—that which is lacking in the symbolic order: it is truly most horrific by the mere fact that it can never be known in itself. There is ultimately no safety in the unknown, and that is why the phenomenology of the lived experience carries with it the paranoiac residue of the uncertainty of the life within. The imaginary and symbolic orders interpenetrate the real, which in turn inform how the unconscious interpenetrates consciousness. Consciousness becomes an appearance, an illusory articulation of what cannot be rightfully articulated. This is why consciousness can only reveal through images and symbolization the differentiated and modified forms of unconscious reality. For Lacan (1954–1955a), objects that terrify us, such as "the anxiety-provoking apparition of an image . . . summarize what we can call the revelation of that which is least penetrable in the real, of the real lacking any possible mediation, of the ultimate real, of the essential object which isn't an object any longer, but this something faced with which all words cease and all categories fail, the object of anxiety *par excellence*" (p. 164).

The real resists articulation because it is simply 'the impossible,' thus subjecting consciousness to the paranoid abyss of the ineffable. Freud (1900) was the first to insist on the primacy of the underworld: "The unconscious is the true psychical reality; *in its innermost nature it is as much unknown to us as the reality of the external world*" (p. 613). And just as the nature of symptoms have a sense (Freud, 1916–1917), Lacan emphasizes the primal communication of the real as that indescribable language, that which is *paranoos*, thus beyond mind (νόος). It is not 'I' who speaks, rather 'it' speaks in me.

NOTES

1. From his *Seminar* on the psychoses, Lacan (1955–1956c) says, "I'm not surprised that my discourse may have created a certain margin of misunderstanding. . . . I would say that it is with a deliberate, if not entirely deliberated, intention that I pursue this discourse in such a way as to offer you the opportunity to not quite understand" (p. 164).

2. The real surfaces as the third order, standing in juxtaposition to the imaginary and the symbolic, intimately intertwined yet beyond the previous domains. The real has no formal text, it is deliberately undecided. It is neither symbolic nor imaginary, rather it remains foreclosed from the analytic experience which relies on speech. The real is the domain of the unconscious, that realm of psychic territory we can never know as such in-itself; it remains beyond the epistemic limitations of the symbolic, yet is disclosed in every utterance. We may say that the real is the seat of desire whereas the imaginary and symbolic orders devolve into it. The real is the presupposed psychical reality, the raw substrate of the subject awaiting structure through

linguistic acquisitions. Lacan's notion of the real should not be confused with 'reality,' which is in some ways knowable (at least theoretically), yet the subject of desire may only suppose the real—the *Ding-an-sich*—since reality for the subject is merely phantasmatic. For Lacan, 'the real is the impossible,' it is the realm of the unthinkable, the unimaginable; and this is precisely why the real cannot be penetrated by imagination or the senses. The real is that which is missing in the symbolic order, that which is untouchable, indescribable by language, yet "the ineliminable residue of all articulation." (Lacan, 1977, p. x).

　　3. This view must be contrasted to the pleasant, soothing presence of the imago, and particularly the maternal imago, that is gradually internalized by the child, thus becoming a stabilizing and cohesive function informing psychic structure (e.g., see the various development models of Bowlby, 1980; Klein, 1946, 1957; Kohut, 1978; Mahler, Pine, & Bergman, 1975; Mitchell, 1988; Stern, 1985).

　　4. Eros has many faces, even in death. There is a perverse pleasure in death; for Freud, the fusion of libido within self-destruction, for Lacan, the experience of *jouissance*. Unfortunately there is no adequate translation of this word in English. 'Enjoyment' is suffused in its meaning but does not convey the sexual connotations retained in French. In one sense, *jouissance* denotes the intense pleasure of orgasm; *jouir* is slang for 'to come.' However, pleasure does not quite capture its precise meaning for the residues of death are encrusted in its essence. Therefore, we may say that *jouissance* is pleasure in the realm of excess: "[it] is the essence or quality that gives one's life its value" (Ragland, 1995, p. 87).

　　5. "The Function and Field of Speech and Language in Psychoanalysis" was delivered to the Rome Congress held at the Istituto di Psicologia della Università di Roma, 1953.

　　6. For Lacan, the implications of the imaginary are often pejorative, suggesting that the subject seeks to remove itself from the flux of becoming by reducing itself to the stagnant aura of illusion. While Lacan introduced some positive valence to the imaginary in later theoretical postulations, it largely remains a negative construct. It may be argued, however, that we can never escape the captivating presence of the imaginary. After all, it is the world of perception and fantasy, of wish and defense. We can never transcend the illusory.

REFERENCES

Aristotle. (1958). *Metaphysics*, Book 1, in *The Pocket Aristotle*, trans. W. D. Ross. New York: Washington Square Books.

Bion, W. R. (1959). Attacks on Linking. In E. B. Spillius, ed., *Melanie Klein Today: Developments in Theory and Practice. Volume 1: Mainly Theory*. London: Routledge, 1988: 87–101.

Boothby, Richard. (1991). *Death and Desire: Psychoanalytic Theory in Lacan's Return to Freud*. New York: Routledge.

Bowie, Malcolm. (1991). *Lacan*. Cambridge: Harvard University Press.

Bowlby, J. (1980). *Attachment and Loss*. London: Hogarth Press.

Feldstein, Richard. (1996). "The Mirror of Manufactured Cultural Relations." In *Reading Seminars I and II: Lacan's Return to Freud*, eds. R. Feldstein, B. Fink, & M. Jaanus. Albany: State University of New York Press.

Fink, Bruce. (1995). *The Lacanian Subject: Bewtween Language and Jouissance*. Princeton, NJ: Princeton University Press.

———. (1997). *A Clinical Introduction to Lacanian Psychoanalysis*. Cambridge: Harvard University Press.

Freud, S., & Breuer, J. (1893–1895). *Studies on Hysteria*. Standard Edition: Vol. 2. London: Hogarth Press.

Freud, S. (1900). *The Interpretation of Dreams*. Standard Edition: Vols. 4–5. London: Hogarth Press.

———. (1916–1917). *Introductory Lectures on Psycho-Analysis*. Standard Edition: Vols. 15–16. London: Hogarth Press.

———. (1920). *Beyond the Pleasure Principle*. Standard Edition: Vol.18. London: Hogarth Press.

———. (1921). *Group Psychology and the Analysis of the Ego*. Standard Edition: Vol.18. London: Hogarth Press.

———. (1923). *The Ego and the Id*. Standard Edition: Vol.19. London: Hogarth Press.

———. (1927). *The Future of an Illusion*. Standard Edition: Vol. 21. London: Hogarth Press.

———. (1933). *New Introductory Lectures on Psycho-Analysis*. Standard Edition: Vol. 22. London: Hogarth Press.

Frie, Roger. (1997). *Subjectivity and Intersubjectivity in Modern Philosophy and Psychoanalysis: A Study of Sartre, Binswanger, Lacan, and Habermas*. Lanham: Rowman & Littlefield Publishers.

Haddad, Gérard. (1981). "Une pratique" (A Practice). *L'Ane*, 3; September 20.

Hegel, G. W. F. (1807). *Phenomenology of Spirit*, trans. A.V. Miller. Oxford: Oxford University Press, 1977.

Julien, P. (1994). *Jacque Lacan's Return to Freud: The Real, the Symbolic, and the Imaginary*. New York: New York University Press.

Klein, Melanie. (1946). "Notes on some schizoid mechanisms." In *Developments in Psycho-Analysis*. London: Hogarth Press.

———. (1957). *Envy and Gratitude*. In *Envy and Gratitude and other Works, 1946–1963*. London: Hogarth Press, 1975.

Kohut, Heinz. (1971). *The Analysis of the Self*. New York: International Universities Press.

———. (1977). *The Restoration of the Self*. New York: International Universities Press.

———. (1978). *The search for the self: Selected writings of Heinz Kohut: 1950–1978*. 2 Vols., ed. P. Ornstein. New York: International Universities Press.

———. (1984). *How Does Analysis Cure?*, eds. A. Goldberg and P. Stepansky. Chicago: University of Chicago Press.

Lacan, Jacques. (1936). "The Mirror Stage as Formative of the Function of the I." In *Écrits: A Selection*, trans. Alan Sheridan. New York: Norton, 1977.

———. (1948). "Aggressivity in Psychoanalysis." In *Écrits: A Selection*, trans. Alan Sheridan. New York: Norton, 1977.

———. (1953). "The Function and Field of Speech and Language in Psychoanalysis." In *Écrits: A Selection*, trans. Alan Sheridan. New York: Norton, 1977.

———. (1953–1954). "The See-Saw of Desire." In *The Seminar of Jacques Lacan, Book I: Freud's Papers on Technique, 1953–1954*, trans. John Forrester, ed. Jacques-Alain Miller. Cambridge: Cambridge University Press, 1988.

———. (1954–1955a). "The Dream of Irma's Injection (Conclusion)." In *The Seminar of Jacques Lacan, Book II: The Ego in Freud's Theory and the Technique of Psychoanalysis, 1954–1955*, trans. Sylvana Tomaselli, ed. Jacques-Alain Miller. Cambridge: Cambridge University Press, 1988.

———. (1954–1955b). "A, m, a, S." In *The Seminar of Jacques Lacan, Book II: The Ego in Freud's Theory and the Technique of Psychoanalysis, 1954–1955*, trans. Sylvana Tomaselli, ed. Jacques-Alain Miller. Cambridge: Cambridge University Press, 1988.

———. (1955–1956a). "Introduction to the Question of Psychoses." In *The Seminar of Jacques Lacan, Book III: The Psychoses, 1955–1956*, trans. Russell Grigg, ed. Jacques-Alain Miller. New York: Norton, 1993.

———. (1955–1956b). "The Other and Psychoses." In *The Seminar of Jacques Lacan, Book III: The Psychoses, 1955–1956*, trans. Russell Grigg, ed. Jacques-Alain Miller. New York: Norton, 1993.

———. (1955–1956c). "The Hysteric's Question." In *The Seminar of Jacques Lacan, Book III: The Psychoses, 1955–1956*, trans. Russell Grigg, ed. Jacques-Alain Miller. New York: Norton, 1993.

———. (1957). "The Agency of the Letter in the Unconscious or Reason Since Freud." In *Écrits: A Selection*, trans. Alan Sheridan. New York: Norton, 1977.

———. (1957–1958). "On a Question Preliminary to Any Possible Treatment of Psychosis." In *Écrits: A Selection*, trans. Alan Sheridan. New York: Norton, 1977.

———. (1958). "The Direction of the Treatment and the Principles of its Power." In *Écrits: A Selection*, trans. Alan Sheridan. New York: Norton, 1977.

———. (1959–1960a). "*Das Ding.*" In *The Seminar of Jacques Lacan, Book VII: The Ethics of Psychoanalysis, 1959–1960*, trans. Dennis Porter, ed. Jacques-Alain Miller. New York: Norton, 1992.

———. (1959–1960b). "The Death of God." In *The Seminar of Jacques Lacan, Book VII: The Ethics of Psychoanalysis, 1959–1960*, trans. Dennis Porter, ed. Jacques-Alain Miller. New York: Norton, 1992.

———. (1960). "The Subversion of the Subject and the Dialectic of Desire in the Freudian Unconscious." In *Écrits: A Selection*, trans. Alan Sheridan. New York: Norton, 1977.

———. (1964a). "Excommunication." In *The Four Fundamental Concepts of Psycho-Analysis*, trans. Alan Sheridan, ed. Jacques-Alain Miller. New York: Norton, 1981.

———. (1964b). "Presence of the Analyst." In *The Four Fundamental Concepts of Psycho-Analysis*, trans. Alan Sheridan, ed. Jacques-Alain Miller. New York: Norton, 1981.

———. (1964c). "Sexuality in the Defiles of the Signifier." In *The Four Fundamental Concepts of Psycho-Analysis*, trans. Alan Sheridan, ed. Jacques-Alain Miller. New York: Norton, 1981.

———. (1964d). "The Subject and the Other: Alienation." In *The Four Fundamental Concepts of Psycho-Analysis*, trans. Alan Sheridan, ed. Jacques-Alain Miller. New York: Norton, 1981.

———. (1964e). "Of the Subject Who is Supposed to Know, Of the First Dyad, and Of the Good." In *The Four Fundamental Concepts of Psycho-Analysis*, trans. Alan Sheridan, ed. Jacques-Alain Miller. New York: Norton, 1981.

———. (1966). *Écrits*. Paris: Éditions du Seuil.

————. (1972–1973). "On the Baroque." In *The Seminar of Jacques Lacan, Book XX: Encore, 1972–1973*, trans. Bruce Fink, ed. Jacques-Alain Miller. New York: Norton, 1998.

————. (1977). *Écrits: A Selection*, trans. Alan Sheridan. New York: Norton.

Lee, J. S. (1990). *Jacques Lacan*. Boston: Twayne Publishers.

Mahler, M. S., Pine, F., & Bergman, A. (1975). *The Psychological Birth of the Human Infant*. New York: Basic Books.

Marcelle, M. (1992). *Jacques Lacan: The French Context*, trans. Anne Tomiche. New Brunswick, NJ: Rutgers University Press.

Mills, Jon. (1999). Unconscious Subjectivity. *Contemporary Psychoanalysis*, 35 (2), 342–347.

Mitchell, S. A. (1988). *Relational Concepts in Psychoanalysis: An Integration*. Cambridge, MA: Harvard University Press.

Muller, John P., & Richardson, William J. (1982). *Lacan and Language*. New York: International Universities Press.

Ragland, Ellie. (1995). *Essays on the Pleasures of Death: From Freud to Lacan*. New York: Routledge.

Roustang, F. (1990). *The Lacanian Delusion*. New York: Oxford University Press.

Sarup, Madan. (1992). *Jacques Lacan*. Toronto: University of Toronto Press.

Schneiderman, Stuart. (1983). *Jacques Lacan: The Death of an Intellectual Hero*. Cambridge: Harvard University Press.

Segal, Hanna. (1957). Notes on Symbol Formation. *International Journal of Psycho-Analysis*, 38: 391–397.

Stern, Daniel. (1985). *The Interpersonal World of the Infant*. New York: Basic Books.

Žižek, Slavoj. (1992). *Enjoy Your Symptoms! Jacques Lacan in Hollywood and Out*. New York: Routledge.

SIX

FROM MYTH TO METAPHYSICS: FREUD AND WITTGENSTEIN AS PHILOSOPHICAL THINKERS

JAMES C. EDWARDS

THERE ARE SOME CRITICS—Samuel Johnson on Shakespeare comes immediately to mind—whose judgment has the transparency of spring water. In their remarks the work of another is made to float before the reader as brightly lit, becalmed, and as perfectly suspended as the submerged basketball in *Equilibrium*: the work under examination displaces no more liquid than its volume strictly demands; its worth is weighed precisely by its buoyancy in the critical medium.[1] Such criticism seems to vanish in our use of it; all that remains is the original work itself, cleansed and gleaming in what now seems our own perfect vision. But there are other critics, equally brilliant and frequently equally useful, whose own thoughts can never disappear from view, whose judgment of another always drags into sight some portion of the critic's own projects and obsessions. Rather than transparency and exactly calibrated value, their criticism furnishes the excitement of partiality and polemic; it seems less an appraisal than an appropriation, perhaps even an assault. Speaking about Freud, Wittgenstein is the latter sort of critic.

Wittgenstein was ambivalent about Freud's achievement. In the late 1930s he would unabashedly speak of himself as a "disciple" or as a "follower" of Freud; according to his friend Rush Rhees he counted Freud as one of the few authors consistently worth reading, as a writer who always had "something to say."[2] But at the same time he considered the influence of psychoanalysis to be harmful: "[I]t will take a long time before we lose our subservience to it." Freud's work, he said, combines "great imagination and colossal prejudice."[3] What is valuable in it must be painstakingly separated from those elements that conduce to domination and befuddlement. Those latter elements form a "way of thinking" that, in Wittgenstein's view, needs combating.[4]

Ambivalence in a thinker usually so incisive should not be taken lightly; perhaps the conflict runs to matters that are, for both subject and object, profound indeed. Despite their provenance in scattered occasions, Wittgenstein's criticisms of Freud are not just the table-talk of genius, interesting to intellectual historians only because Wittgenstein is Wittgenstein and Freud is Freud. Rather, they reach all the way down to some of the foundational, and least understood, features of Wittgenstein's defining philosophical project. For him, Freud represents not just an important advance in European psychology and morals; he is also an important figure within the history of Western metaphysics, a history Wittgenstein is committed to bring to a particular sort of end. Tracing and weighing Wittgenstein's animadversions will help us to appreciate the achievements—and, perhaps, to mark the limitations—of both thinkers: that, at any rate, is the conviction of this chapter.

Wittgenstein's remarks about Freud are of two sorts. First—and most common in the two published conversations from 1943—there are criticisms of particular Freudian doctrines and techniques: for example, criticism of Freud's claim that a repressed wish of the dreamer is the latent content of a dream; or criticism of his claim that in a dream a determinate language of symbols is employed to represent that content.[5] In these passages Wittgenstein is careful and thorough, turning the Freudian thesis this way and that, looking at it from several (and sometimes quite unexpected) angles; even the convinced Freudian is likely to concede that these critical darts sometimes hit the mark. At the same time one is also likely to think that these criticisms (however successful in particular instances) fail to get over the bar he famously sets for himself in the preface to the *Philosophical Investigations*, namely, that his remarks should be instantly recognizable as his own and no one else's.[6] Here is an example: "But this procedure of free association and so on is queer, because Freud never shows how we know where to stop—where is the right solution." Here is another: "Take Freud's view that anxiety is always a repetition in some way of the anxiety we felt at birth. He does not establish this by reference to evidence—for he could not do so." And here is a third example: "Freud mentions various symbols: top hats are regularly phallic symbols, wooden things like tables are women, etc. His historical explanation of these symbols is absurd."[7] Whatever one might say about the justice of these complaints, there is nothing here that belongs exclusively to Wittgenstein. Any intelligent reader of Freud might have said as much, or as little.

There is, however, another sort of criticism found in Wittgenstein's remarks, most notably, perhaps, in the conversation with Rhees in 1946.

Here he scants particular Freudian claims in favor of an attempt to judge the character of the project as a whole. In these remarks one sees Wittgenstein judging Freud not merely as a compelling cultural figure whose work needs to be engaged by any alert reader but also—one might say—as a competitor; as one who shares the same philosophical space as the critic, has some of the same ambitions, and whose work is an impediment, or a danger, to the critic's own. Here criticism shades swiftly into polemic, and these polemical remarks about Freud will claim most of my attention. Because they are global rather than local in their focus, and because they are suggestive rather than explicit, to unlock their true force requires that they be linked to other passages in the philosopher's texts. Wittgenstein's own mark is on these sentences, and that mark is appreciable only as part of a life's work, one that is both obscure and hugely ambitious. Surely the same must be said of Freud's best sentences as well.

MYTH AS A STYLE OF THINKING

"I have been going through Freud's 'Interpretation of Dreams' with H. And it has made me feel how much this whole way of thinking wants combating."[8] "This whole way of thinking": at bottom that is the significance of Freud the psychologist for Wittgenstein the philosopher. Psychoanalysis is most remarkable not for its specific psychological and metapsychological theses, not for its cures (and botches of cures), not for its techniques of therapy and for its grand architecture of the soul; what makes it remarkable, according to Wittgenstein, is the *style of thought* that it appropriates and extends, a style of thought that traps psychoanalysis in the philosophical thickets Wittgenstein devoted his life to clearing. But what is that "whole way of thinking" Freud trades on? Where does it come from, and what makes it so seductive? And what is supposed to be wrong with it?

It is clear from the 1946 conversation that Wittgenstein's distaste for Freud's "way of thinking" is directly linked to his claim that Freud is a kind of mythmaker.

> Freud refers to ancient myths in these connections [i.e., in his therapeutic and theoretical work], and claims that his researches have now explained how anybody should think or propound a myth of that sort.
>
> Whereas in fact Freud has done something different. He has not given a scientific explanation of the ancient myth. What he has done is to propound a new myth. The attractiveness of the suggestion that all anxiety is a repetition of the anxiety of the birth trauma, is just the attractiveness of a mythology. "It is all the outcome of something that happened long ago." Almost like referring to a totem.[9]

Freud claims to explain myth psychologically; in reality, says Wittgenstein, he is portraying psychology mythically. Why, Freud asks, should the Oedipus myth have gripped human attention for so long and with such intensity? And he answers: because the myth reveals something essential and unchanging about the dynamics of the human psyche. The myth presents those psychological dynamics dramatically and in narrative; it condenses psychic processes into compelling characters and plot. But doesn't Freud in his explanations do exactly the same? Why does he characterize the psyche as a hidden realm—the kingdom of the unconscious—populated by agencies and forces in constant struggle?[10] Why does Freudian metapsychology postulate and personify an agency like the id or the superego in order to account both for normal human development and for its neurotic breakdown? Because, according to Wittgenstein, such characterization holds the same charm for us as the ancient myths it is supposed to explain and replace. Freud's representation of himself as a courageous and hard-nosed scientist, as a supplanter of wooly narrative by adamant fact, is misleading. In reality—says Wittgenstein—he is retelling the old tales in a materialist and empirical idiom; he is a mythmaker working in a vocabulary more suited to the idols of the moment.

In Wittgenstein's remarks the word *myth* is charged with quite specific force. A myth is not just a naively false account of some puzzling phenomenon, nor even a naively false account expressed in highly pictorial and personified language. When a child blames the broken cup on the clumsiness of her invisible friend, that is not mythmaking, although it may be a carefully narrated fantasy. Likewise, the adult's conviction that a certain kind of spider web will stop bleeding when applied directly to a wound is not a myth, and it would not be even if it were attached to some elaborate story about the supernatural origins and exploits of that particular sort of spider. So what, for Wittgenstein, makes a myth a myth?

Note first his claim that Freud's psychological explanations and theoretical constructions don't acquire their power for us in the same way as explanations and theoretical constructions in the established natural sciences do. In physics, for example, the power of an explanation or a theory lies first of all in its predictive power: "Physics is connected with Engineering. The bridge must not fall down."[11] The test of the adequacy of a theory or an explanation in physics is how well, when applied to some actual situation, it allows us to do what we want to do. Moreover, the theories and explanations of physics are put forth on the basis of a great deal of evidence, including experimental evidence. Before a given theory is accepted, a detailed examination of all the relevant data is patiently undertaken and a careful verdict is entered. Notice how different Freud's explanations are. They derive their force not from their powers of empirical prediction and control, and not from the careful collection of evidence that led to their adoption, but from what Wittgenstein calls their *charm*. "Many of these explanations are adopted because they have a particular charm. The picture of people having subconscious thoughts has a charm."[12] The charm is typically so strong as to sweep aside the traditional questions of evidence and prediction pressed in the natural sciences. The mark of a "charming" account is that hesitation evaporates; instead one says, "Yes, that *must* be how it is. *Of course*; it's obvious."[13]

Why should certain explanations have such immediate and forceful appeal ("charm") for us? Wittgenstein's answer begins by calling attention to the kinds of phenomena for which the mythical explanation is offered; these phenomena impress themselves on us in a quite particular and even peculiar fashion. They demand of us a certain sort of hermeneutical response; they must be shown to *mean* something. Here is an example from Wittgensteins: "There is a cathedral in Moscow with five spires. On each of these there is a different sort of curving configuration. One gets the strong impression that these different shapes and arrangements must mean something."[14] Wittgenstein compares this case directly to our common impression that our nighttime dreams must mean something, that there is an arcane language in which they speak to us, saying something we very much need (and also perhaps fear) to hear. We don't react in this way to our daydreams, he points out; in them we don't find the impressiveness—the *pathos*—that demands that we make sense of them as obscure but important communications, as omens, that must be carefully read and heeded. We dismiss our daydreams as trivial, as pure psychic excess and coincidence, the froth on the waves of self-conscious mental life.

The word he uses to characterize the *pathos* that demands this sort of interpretation is *uncanny*. (In German presumably he would have said *unheimlich*, which is of course an important word for Freud as well.[15]) A nightmare is uncanny; a daydream is not.[16] A nightmare is, to read the German literally, "unhomely." It seems to come, simultaneously, both from inside and from outside one's life; and it upsets the expectations and routines on which the sense of that life ordinarily depends. In the night-dream one's dead father is alive and one's lover has a butterfly's body, not a human one. Moreover, one is powerless to change these disturbing appearances; the dream is just as adamant and as ruthless as one's everyday experience: it will not yield to one's fear or one's horror. But not everything, not even everything puzzling and disturbing, has the particular *pathos* of the uncanny. If this afternoon I hear a knock at the front door and no one is there, I may be baffled and even a bit distressed, but the experience is not genuinely uncanny. I don't feel compelled to attribute to it some important message or meaning; it was just a strange thing to have happened: usually I am not subject to such illusions. Such a happening calls, one might say, only for *explanation*, not for *interpretation*.[17] But if, on the other hand, I come upon two children solemnly putting a live fly in the hollow head of a doll and then burying it, I know I'm in the presence of something that demands a certain sort of interpretation.[18] In that case there is the *pathos* of the uncanny. Only a certain sort of response, intellectual or otherwise, will do justice to that *pathos*.

So what gives Freudian explanations of, say, dreams or neuroses their particular charm? The general answer is that they match the uncanniness of the explanandum with uncanniness in the explanans. Wittgenstein: "A lot of things one is ready to believe because they are uncanny."[19] Of these sorts of explanations he also says, "The *attitude* they express is important. They give us a picture which has a peculiar attraction for us."[20] Thus, Wittgenstein's claim that Freud's "way of thinking" is the creation of a new myth: a myth is the kind of explanation that conserves the uncanniness of what is to be explained by reinscribing that uncanniness in the explanation itself. The point of mythical explanation is not, as might be true of an explanation in physics, to make one's puzzlement disappear and give one power over something one had been unable to predict or control. Rather, a mythical explanation is the *sublimation* of one's puzzlement: it is a conservation of the uncanniness one has experienced; a conservation that shifts that uncanniness to a higher level.

A clear illustration of this point is found in Wittgenstein's discussion of Freud's notion of the "primal scene" (*Urszene*).

> Much the same could be said of the notion of an 'Urszene.' This often has the attractiveness of giving a sort of tragic pattern to one's life. It is all the repetition of the same pattern that was settled long ago. Like a tragic figure carrying out the decrees under which fate placed him at birth. Many people have, at some period, serious trouble in their lives—so serious as to lead to thoughts of suicide. This is likely to appear to one as something nasty, as a situation which is too foul to be the subject of a tragedy. And it may then be an immense relief if it can be shown that one's life has the pattern of a tragedy—the tragic working out and repetition of a pattern which was determined by the primal scene.[21]

Notice what's happening in the case Wittgenstein sketches. Something deeply troubling to a person—perhaps his powerful desires for sex with men rather than with women—presses against him with such force that he is pushed to the brink of suicide.[22] And yet this person cannot see his situation as anything but "nasty." He is ashamed not only of the "foul" desires that so torment him; he is also ashamed of their *banality*. He is ashamed that his life is being destroyed by something so common as a particular sort of sexual desire. Other people are challenged, perhaps even brought low, by conflicts that the whole world can recognize as worthy: for example, religion and family loyalty versus the state (Antigone); friendship versus moral and political ideals (Brutus). In such struggles, even if the outcome is death, there is for the protagonist at least the consolation of nobility. These conflicts put into play all that is best about human beings; through their reach and significance they elevate all who are caught up in them. But in the case of this unhappy homosexual there is, from his point of view, only baseness. He is about to kill himself, but not because of religious duty or civil demand; he is being maddened and destroyed merely by the form and intensity of his sexual longings. His *body*, whether conceived as material substance or as historical construct, has betrayed him. What could be more demeaning?

Here there is a certain uncanniness that needs to be explained: it is the uncanniness of the power of the banal itself. What is uncanny for this man is not (just) that he is being destroyed, not (just) that he is being tormented without respite and driven to the edge of committing "the elementary sin";[23] what is most uncanny is the site and agent of this devastation: an unconventional and (let us presume) despised ("nasty") sort of sexual desire. Here is one way this person might see his situation: I am the victim of my physiology. Something is wrong with the way my brain is wired; if only it were wired differently, then my sexual desires would be just like everyone else's. Or he might see it this way: I am the victim of my family history. Something went wrong with the way I was reared; if only I had been reared differently ("normally"), then my sexual desires would be just like everyone else's.

Either of these responses might give the man a certain amount of peace; either of them might also suggest an effective therapeutic regimen. Physiology and family history, while surely very powerful, are not (we assure ourselves) beyond the reach of some technology. The brain can be rewired through drugs; family history can be recovered and reconstructed through psychotherapy. But what neither drugs nor therapy can do is to give nobility to nastiness. Neither can take the banality of family muddle or physiological design-flaw and sublimate it into tragedy. Both therapeutic regimens, the chemical and the historical, insist that the man see his unwanted desires as just so much static in the signal. Both represent him to himself as a sort of machine that needs to be fixed; as the product of essentially mechanical processes that, in his case, somehow went awry. There is optimism in that view, perhaps even a certain sort of comfort; what there is not is *dignifying drama*.

According to Wittgenstein, Freud offers an account that restores a measure of dignity to the man by representing his situation as uncanny from beginning to end. There is nothing uncanny about faulty wiring or bruising family history; there is, on the other hand, something uncanny about seeing one's present impasse as the repetition of a situation that has recurred from time immemorial. "It is all the outcome of something that happened long ago."[24] Mere mechanical breakdown is trivial and demeaning; the workings of fate, however, are uncanny and ennobling. "And it may then be an immense relief if it can be shown that one's life has the pattern rather of a tragedy— the tragic working out and repetition of a pattern which was determined by the primal scene."[25] Yes, an "immense relief": and because of that relief, which is the relief of *significance* and not (merely) the relief of potential repair, the

Freudian explanation has a "charm," a "peculiar attraction," that makes it seem obvious. "Yes, of course, it must be like that."[26]

MYTH AND THE IDOLATRY OF SCIENCE

Wittgenstein's objection to Freud's "way of thinking" is that it preserves in the explanans the uncanniness of the explanandum. In that way it is distinctively mythical, and it thereby presents itself to us with a peculiar sort of charm. An important part of that charm is the consolation, one might even say the flattery, offered by this sort of account; we are attracted to the way it sublimates the banal and the nasty into the noble and the "interesting." To be a broken machine—broken either by faulty design or rough handling—is flatly dull; no one could find it fascinating or elevating. How much more exciting it is to be the victim of fate, the pawn of ancient and obscure powers. And it is that sense of significance, of *pathos*, that the Freudian account fosters, with its appeal to the hidden, to the arcane, to the numinous unconscious forces of which we are the victims and accomplices. For all his mask of post-Enlightenment secularism, there is still in Freud the portrayal of human beings as the scene of cosmic drama, the place where the gods appear—even if now the contesting powers are taken inside both individual history and general psychic structure rather than placed in the heavens. Zeus and Leda get renamed id and ego, but the numinous character—the "charm"—of their harsh encounter does not thereby disappear.

Writing in a genre where explicit theological references are taboo, Freud is thus able to reinscribe the gods and their whims as psychic powers and their historical vicissitudes. The "laws" of the psyche become doubles for the commandments of the Divine Ones; dreams, symptoms, and parapraxes take the place of omen, scripture, and revelatory event. In this way we remain interesting to ourselves. Our sense of our own *pathos*, threatened by the steady advance of systems of mechanical (chemical, physical) explanation, is restored: not so much by a disavowal of mechanism (Freud is constantly insisting on his own scientific ambition and achievement) as by the distinctively literary presentation of it. Freud cannot have done with drama—with principalities and powers, with reversal and counterreversal—in his writing. His case histories are, first and last, compelling and uncanny stories; and the metapsychology he brings to bear in them is equally personified and narrative. All these features of Freud's thinking Wittgenstein condenses into a single description: *mythmaker*.

But why think of this—as Wittgenstein clearly does—as an *objection* to Freud? What's wrong with offering a "mythology" that gives dignity to human suffering, especially if that "mythology" offers the promise of a therapy that mitigates such pain, transforming (as Freud famously said) neurotic misery into ordinary human unhappiness? There is not a single or a simple answer to this question, but in this section and the next I want to explore two ways in which Freud's mythical "way of thinking" runs afoul of Wittgenstein's peculiar sensibility, both philosophical and ethical.

First, notice the way Freud presents his metapsychological ideas (the ego, the id, dream-language, and so forth) as candidates for our reasonable *belief*. He thinks that what he is saying is not just truthful—in the way that the *Iliad* or *Crows in a Cornfield* can be truthful—but *factually* true; our proper response to his claims is to accept them as accurate representations, to take them as pictures of the way things "really are," past the level of appearance. But "belief is a weak misreading of literature," as Harold Bloom is fond of pointing out.[27] One has a tin ear for poetry if all one can think to ask Yeats is, "Were there exactly fifty-nine swans at Coole that October? Are you sure there weren't fifty-eight?" And one sadly misunderstands still life if one looks over Cézanne's shoulder and complains, "The apples aren't really as yellow as you make them." Accurate representation is not the point. Poetry and painting do not, in the first instance, solicit our *belief*. But in just this way Freud weakly misreads himself, and he demands of us the same weak misreading. He is the inventor of a new mythology, the fashioner of a new vocabulary (and technique) of dramatic, uncanny self-understanding; but he cannot help seeing his achievement, and insist that we see it as well, as a contribution to natural science. He is a poet who wants to deny his powers of imagination, preferring instead to claim the authority of the empirical.

Freud's well-known idolatry of natural science makes this weak misreading inevitable. Listen to him in full cry: "Our best hope for the future is that intellect—the scientific spirit, reason—may in process of time establish a dictatorship in the mental life of man."[28] That remarkable, unguarded Freudian pronouncement, especially its endorsement of reason's absolute hegemony, reminds one of Nietzsche's famous remark in "The Problem of Socrates": "When one finds it necessary to turn *reason* into a tyrant, as Socrates did, the danger cannot be slight that something else will play the tyrant. Rationality was then hit upon as the savior."[29] Socrates' commitment to being "absurdly rational" bespoke his covert recognition that he himself was already the slave to another master, already subject to the tyranny of the descending instincts. His ambition to make himself the slave of reason is thus deeply fearful, and deeply self-deceptive. Likewise, Freud's paean to reason reveals his covert awareness of how far from "the scientific spirit, reason" his own original work is actually situated. He is a heretic insisting that his work represents the *true* faith, despite its apparent deviance from the traditional canons. Freud is profoundly *anxious* here: anxious to claim the patent of reason as a defense against having to ally himself with the poets to whose company he really belongs; anxious that his claim to that patent is stillborn. "We are unknown to ourselves, we knowers."[30] Yes, and we are primarily unknown to ourselves *as* knowers. Anyone (whether Socrates or Freud) so deeply committed to self-knowledge through reason is, in the character of his work, unknown to himself. One loses oneself just at the place one expects to find oneself most truly; the site of self-knowledge turns out to be the place farthest from home, the place most uncanny. Freud seeks self-knowledge through the representations of "the scientific spirit, reason," flattering himself that he has left the imagination with its anarchy safely behind, while in reality he is imposing—surreptitiously—just another of imagination's tyrannies.

This anxious and self-deceiving worship of science constitutes a large part of the "colossal prejudice" that Wittgenstein abhors in Freud. Early and late he rejected the idea that natural science could and would provide the answer to our ethical and spiritual ills. Here is the first paragraph of the preface to the *Philosophical Remarks*, written in 1930:

> This book is written for such men as are in sympathy with its spirit. This spirit is different from the one which informs the vast stream of European and American civilization in which all of us stand. *That* spirit expresses itself in an onwards movement, in building ever larger and more complicated structures; the other in striving after clarity and perspicuity in no matter what structure. The first tries to grasp the world by way of its periphery—in its variety; the second at the center—at its essence. And so the first adds one construction to another, moving on and up, as it were, from one stage to the next, while the other remains where it is and what it tries to grasp is always the same.[31]

Clearly Wittgenstein has no truck with Freud's hope that "the scientific spirit, reason" will establish itself as the absolute ruler (the "dictator") of human endeavor. Such hope, however familiar to those of us inhabiting "the vast stream of European and American civilization," is both naïve and idolatrous. From Fraser's patronizing accounts of the rituals of traditional societies to the breathless case histories in *Listening to Prozac*, there runs a common thread: it is the conviction, or at least the dream, that natural science can give us a view of ourselves that is final, complete, and morally empowering.[32] The pieces, we think, are falling into place; we are just about to enter the Promised Land of established fact and clear direction. The spirit of natural science "expresses itself in an onwards movement, in building ever larger and more complicated structures" that will enable us to grasp the world fully and finally, in all its variety.

Freud certainly sees himself as part of that "onwards movement." He is, he believes, essentially a physician and a scientist, a man defined by his commitment to *Naturwissenschaft*; and not only that: he believes *Naturwissenschaft* to be the key to a proper view of the world, both actually and practically. Freud's anticipation of the hegemony of reason is, at bottom, an ethical yearning. He belongs wholly to the Enlightenment cohort that construes the triumph of science over superstition, the displacement of dogma and fantasy by carefully substantiated fact, as the last and best chance for human virtue, and perhaps even for human survival. Only the dictatorship of intellect can provide sufficient strength to save human beings from their individual and social vices; civilization requires that we drain the fetid marshes and build our imperial cities on the dry ground. Like Nietzsche's Socrates, who famously taught that knowledge and virtue are the same, Freud fears the anarchy of the ignorant instincts. But Wittgenstein is a different kind of thinker, and a different kind of person. While he admires Freud for his "great imagination," for his power to create a new way of characterizing what it means to be a human being, he rejects both Freud's own misunderstanding of that characterization and the naïve trust in natural science that motivates it.

MYTH AND METAPHYSICS

There is a further, and I believe deeper, criticism of Freud to be found in Wittgenstein's remarks. Freud's "way of thinking" is objectionable because the structure of his metapsychological "mythology" recapitulates the deep structure of Western metaphysics; in this way, Freud belongs to the history of Western philosophy, a history Wittgenstein sees as a death trap, a "fly-bottle" from which his work is supposed to extricate us.[33]

To appreciate this criticism, one must understand the origin of Western philosophy in a single Platonic question. Here in my study right now are various kinds of things. There are chairs, books, a sleeping cat, a videotape of an Errol Morris film. That's what those things truly are, or indeed Truly Are: books; a cat; a videotape. They aren't just indeterminate, "meaningless," nonspecific blobs of being-stuff; they are determinate (kinds of) things, things self-identical over (some determinate period of) time as the (kinds of) things they are: books; a cat; a videotape. Each of these things has an "identity" as itself, defined by relations of Sameness and Difference to other things equally "identified." But—and here is the Platonic question—where do those "identities" come from? What "makes" a cat a cat? What "gives" the video its specific reality as a video? What makes them just those particular, determinate, and relatively continuous (kinds of) things; things with just those particular and determinate and relatively continuous "identities," identities recognizable as such in our sight, speech, and practice?

It's not just that I call the cat a cat and thus "make" it one.[34] No, it is, Really Is, a cat before I speak to call it so: not a dog; not a pillow; not a piece of pie. It's a *cat*, that and nothing else, and that's why I call it what I do. Again, the philosophical question is: What "makes it possible" for this (kind of) thing *to be* just the determinate and self-identical (kind of) thing it so definitely is, and that I can therefore recognize it as being? And then of course there is the even more fundamental question behind that one: the question of how *anything* is the determinate (kind of) thing it is. How (why) is What-There-Is always already *articulated* by relations of Sameness and

Difference? How (why) do things—entities, beings—originally and inevitably get their "Being" as the (kinds of) things they always already are? Why (how) is there Something—some stable structure of temporally enduring (kinds of) things—at all, rather than the Nothing of constant Heraclitean flux?

That Platonic question is, one might say, the founding question of Western philosophy; and the paradigmatic answer is of course Plato's own: what "makes" a cat a cat, or a book a book, is its relationship to some preexistent Form of the Cat or Form of the Book. The eternal and perfect existence of the Forms originally and inevitably articulates sublunar reality into its structure as determinate (kinds of) things. Plato's answer is paradigmatic because it accounts for the Being—the "identity," the significance—of a particular (sort of) being (e.g., a cat) by asserting the prior and necessary existence of another sort of being—a "perfect," "fully present" being; a being the Being of which is immediately self-given—the Form. The Being of the ordinary entity is accounted for in terms of its relation to the extraordinary entity. The extraordinary being "grants" Being—a particular identity, a particular significance, a particular "sense," one might say—to the ordinary one. One can, as Heidegger so brilliantly does, tell the story of Western philosophy after Plato as putting forth, one after another, a line of candidates for the "perfect" entities that grant determinate identity and sense ("Being") to the ordinary and imperfect ones. From the Christian God who through his creation of everything ex nihilo writes the book of Nature, to the Cartesian ego-subject meditating in its solitary splendor, and then finally to the centerless and constantly proliferating Nietzschean Will to Power, the sense of things is always and only explicable in terms of what lies "beyond" or "before" or "above" or "beneath" them. The source of Being is always *hidden*, always mysterious, always operating behind the scenes to give meaning and structure to the world we ordinarily confront and seek to manage. Western philosophy, then, is at bottom always *metaphysics*; it always is searching for something "beyond" (Greek: *meta*) the "physical," something that articulates the physical into its determinate entities and that gives cosmic and enduring pattern to what would otherwise be senseless flux. Philosophy is metaphysics, and metaphysics is Platonism.[35]

Notice the way the metaphysical question ("Why is there Something rather than Nothing?") is answered by postulating the existence of a "true world"—Nietzsche's phrase, of course—to account for the enduring, articulate structure of the one we ordinarily inhabit. What is crucial here is the basic pattern Plato fixes for our thinking: what explains what is, is something hidden behind (or above, or beneath) what is; something that "stands under and supports;" something Really Real that explains, stabilizes, and gives identity to the confusing vicissitudes of our experience.[36] Most of us, unacquainted with the details of the Western philosophical tradition, encounter metaphysical thinking primarily in our understanding of natural science. Isn't that what science does, after all: to discover the hidden realities that give substance and enduring structure to the passing world we experience? Quarks and bosons, or "strong" and "weak" forces, are not exactly Platonic Forms, of course; but don't they play essentially the same role? Aren't they invoked to account for the particular articulation of the universe, the precise way it comes apart and goes together? Aren't they the frame, or—better—the framing that makes reality a cosmos rather than a chaos? In the deepest of ways, modern natural science, with its "true world" of theoretical entities and its explanations in terms of hidden objects and powers, is a form of Platonism; *Naturwissenschaft* belongs, conceptually as well as genealogically, to metaphysics.

Metaphysical explanation has what one might call a "vertical" structure: to understand some phenomenon one must find something that stands "above" (or "below," or "behind": the particular spatial metaphor doesn't matter) that phenomenon and gives it its reality. For the metaphysical mind, to understand what is apparent requires finding something *not* apparent; something that (quoting Heidegger again) "stands under and supports" what one sees. You want to know what makes a cat a cat and not a dog or an otter? The (Platonic) answer is the Form of a cat, in which your particular Tabby "participates." You want to know why there are beautiful sunsets that lift the heart and nasty viruses that destroy the immune system? The (Christian) answer is God, who made them both for his greater glory. You want to know why rubber balls fall and why electrons attract? The (natural–scientific) answers are gravity and the "strong" force. When looking at the world, what you see may be what you get, but it's not what *gives* you what you get. What "gives" is something "behind," something hidden, something "metaphysical," something Really Real.

The "vertical" structure of Western metaphysical explanation has, therefore, three salient features. First, what "gives" determinate structure (enduring identity; particular sense; causal regularity; "True Being") to the world of our experience is itself not a part of that world; it must be looked for "behind" or "below" or "above" it. Second, this "true world" that grants Being to beings is *hidden*; it is not apparent to the (theoretically or mechanically) unaided senses; it must be searched for with diligence and ascetic self-denial. Third, the Hidden Reality that gives order ("Being") to the world is itself a kind of being: a "super-being" like a God or a Form or an ego-subject or a Higgs boson. The hidden world of the Really Real is thus in crucial ways structured like this one: the metaphysical, like the physical, is a realm of discrete beings, just very special ones.

Freud thinks in precisely these terms. He is, in this defining sense, a metaphysician. His metapsychology invokes a Hidden Reality in order to account for quotidian experience. Both normal human development and its neurotic or psychotic deviations are accounted for by appeal to a world of mysterious entities and forces beyond the one we ordinarily see, a "true world" that orders (and thus explains) the one we inhabit day to day. Freud's "mythology" of Egos and Ids, of infantile traumas that endlessly resurface and of dreams that tell us what we need to know but can't quite bear to acknowledge, of symptoms that are signs and of pasts that are not passed: all this belongs to metaphysics as surely as Aristotle's Unmoved Mover and Hegel's *Geist*. Freud is a philosopher, in the way in which a fin-de-siecle Viennese Jewish physician was taught to be a philosopher, that is, as a natural scientist and cultural theoretician, one who "adds one construction to another, moving on and up, as it were, from one stage to the next," trying to explain his own odd world—neuroses, hysterical paralyses, stories of child abuse and obsessive artistic production—by means of discovering the "true" one that lies behind it.[37]

Wittgenstein's fundamental objection to Freud's "way of thinking" instances his rejection of the basic structure of metaphysical—that is, Western philosophical and scientific—thinking. Wittgenstein was an antiphilosopher; the ambition of his philosophical work is to bring philosophy—metaphysical thinking—to an end. One way to begin to understand how that ambition is to be accomplished is to contrast the "vertical" explanations of metaphysics and science with the "horizontal" descriptions Wittgenstein himself favors. The true significance of Wittgenstein—the distance measured between him and the philosophical tradition he wants to conclude—is this other pattern of response to puzzlement, one that replaces theory/construction/"progress" with what he calls "perspicuous presentation."

Consider Wittgenstein's reflections on language, especially in the *Philosophical Investigations*. What is the meaning of a word? Is it a kind of object, hidden within the minds of speakers and hearers? How do noises or ink-marks become questions and propositions? Does their life as functioning linguistic entities derive from something above or behind or below them, something that grants them significance? A Western metaphysician would certainly say so: hidden behind the world we inhabit is always a "true" one that gives it substance and makes it work. Wittgenstein rejects this pattern. For him, meaning is granted to a bit of language not by some hidden entity or event—some inner and private act of definition, say, going on in the mind of a speaker or a hearer—but by *other bits of language*.[38] "[O]nly in the nexus of a proposition does a name have a meaning."[39] And a proposition has *its* meaning only in the context of other propositions. And so on: there is no end to such meaning-by-contextualization. Language (or Mind) is not a hidden Master Entity—a latter-day double for God—that ultimately grants sense to otherwise dead signs; language is only, as Wittgenstein saw even in the *Tractatus*, the limitless totality of propositions.[40] There is no hidden and animating "true world"; there is only more and more of this one. Moreover, the context-setting that lets us see the meaning of a word or a sentence will eventually spread to include elements that are nonlinguistic: understanding what "pain" means requires that we see the word (in its uses) in relation to groans, winces, wounds, screams, and the like. It must, that is, be seen as part of the "natural history of human beings."[41]

Wittgenstein calls such contextualization a "perspicuous presentation" (*übersichtliche Darstellung*) of a phenomenon:

> A main source of our failure to understand is that we do not *command a clear view* of the use of our words.—Our grammar is lacking in this sort of perspicuity. A perspicuous presentation produces just that understanding which consists in 'seeing connections.' Hence the importance of finding and inventing *intermediate cases*.
>
> The concept of a perspicuous presentation is of fundamental significance for us. It earmarks the form of account we give, the way we look at things. (Is this a 'Weltanschauung'?)[42]

Suppose I am puzzled by how the word *pain* gets its meaning. I seem to learn what pain is only from my own case, from my own immediate experience of the sensation, as when I smash my thumb with a hammer; yet the word is surely a common one, used in ordinary intercourse as if its meaning is public and objective. How can other people know what I mean by pain? After all, they don't have *my* painful experiences; they don't know what those experiences feel like *to me*. So it seems that a word like pain can have no public meaning; only a "private" one, or, rather, lots of "private" ones, one for each speaker. But how could such a "private" meaning be a meaning at all? How can language work if there is no common understanding of what a word like pain means? And so on: the more I think about the matter, the more lost in philosophical thickets I become. I no longer know my way about.[43]

I need to "command a clear view" (*übersehen*) of this confusing philosophical landscape and so find again my proper path. I might try to get such a view by going, so to speak, *deeper* into the landscape, by "penetrating the phenomena" (1953, *PI*, sec. 90) of language and meaning; by searching for something hidden—a peculiar sort of private mental act, for example—that philosophical examination must bring into sight. "*The essence is hidden from us*: this is the form our [philosophical] problem now assumes."[44] But if I were to take that path, I would be assuming the structure of understanding definitive for Western metaphysics and science; I would be seeking a "vertical" explanation that discovers a "true world" behind the phenomena that puzzle me. Wittgenstein provides a different "form of account" (1953, *PI*, sec. 122): "We must do away with all *explanation*, and description alone must take its place. And this description gets its light, that is to say its purpose—from the philosophical problems. . . . The problems are solved, not by giving new information, but by arranging what we have always known."[45] This "arrangement," this "perspicuous presentation" of what we have always known, generates understanding "horizontally," not "vertically." It *describes*; it does not "explain." It does not "penetrate phenomena" into a hidden realm of True Being; it presents those phenomena in a perspicuous arrangement in relation to one another, an arrangement that allows one's understanding to move easily from one phenomenon to the others easily and without cramping. In this way one "commands a clear view," one "sees comprehensively and holistically" (*übersieht*) what had—looked at in isolation—given one such fits of philosophical perplexity.

For Wittgenstein, *nothing is hidden*. "*Es ist ja nichts verborgen.*"[46] The task of philosophy is not to reveal something heretofore invisible and unknown; it is to assemble reminders for a particular purpose: and ultimately the purpose of such a "perspicuous presentation" is to bring peace to a mind obsessed by questions that bring its own defining powers into question.[47] The peace of philosophy's end means that such questions should completely disappear. For Wittgenstein as for Socrates, the questions that torment the philosopher begin with "What is . . .?" What is a proposition? What is logic? What is the meaning of a word? What is it to follow a rule? What is an intentional action? What is a game? What is language? What is X? But to understand what X is—what the meaning of 'X' is, what the significance of X is—comes to one only by seeing X in relation to Y, and to Z, and to R, and to S, and to T, and. . . .

There is logically no end to that series. Identity—sense, significance, "Being"—is granted only by context, and contextualization has no *inherent* limits. No Master Entity hidden behind the scenes gives to X its X-ness. One understands what X *is* only when one can place X in the stream of life, only when one can perspicuously locate it within that set of back-and-forth references that constitute its reality.[48] The world for Wittgenstein has no hidden logic, no secret meaning; sense is made on the surfaces of things, in what is apparent (if sometimes in philosophy forgotten) about their relations to one another.

That nothing is hidden is not, for Wittgenstein, merely a philosophical heuristic. It is an ethical insight: it marks an *ethos*; it determines a particular *character*, one might even say a particular way of life. It marks, that is, his commitment to what in the preface to the *Philosophical Remarks* he calls "clarity and perspicuity" rather than to "explanation" by way of "penetrating" the phenomena in hope of truth. *Clarity* rather than *Truth*: the opposition could of course be misleading; but—delicately considered—it does register a difference that is both fundamental and easy to overlook. For a life committed to clarity "what it tries to grasp is always the same."[49] There is no attempt to break through in thought into a new world, a "true world" that gives substance and form to this one; a life of clarity has done with any "onwards movement, in building ever larger and more complicated structures." It seeks the *essence* of things, as Wittgenstein puts it; but "*Essence* is expressed by grammar."[50] That is, essence comes to one in a perspicuous presentation of a thing in holistic relation to what lies both near and distant to it (linguistically and otherwise). Understanding—the clear view, the plain sense of things—dawns over the whole; but only when it can be seen *as a* whole. It dawns in the *übersichtliche Darstellung* of a great many things, art-fully arranged, things that cannot, so to speak, be specified in advance. And these things are not arranged around a hidden center. In the grammar of things that shows their essence, nothing is more fundamental than anything else. There are no different levels of presence. Each phenomenon is, so to speak, on the same plane; a perspicuous presentation provides an under-standing that is horizontal, not vertical.

Clarity, then, is contextual, and it constitutes its own end. When one has gained it, the problems that obsessed one have gone: "For the clarity we are seeking is indeed *complete* clarity. But this simply means that the philo-sophical problems should *completely* disappear."[51] And this clarity is paradig-matic both for the sound human understanding and for the healthy human life. It does not issue in truth, or, better, in new truths; it does not present us with answers to our questions, answers that heretofore had been hidden behind the veil of appearance. This clarity issues in nothing, one might say; it builds no "complicated structures" of the intellect. It disappears in the moment of its shining, along with our perplexities.

> The solution of the problem of life is seen in the vanishing of the problem.
>
> (Is not this the reason why those who have found after a long period of doubt that the sense of life became clear to them have been unable to say what constituted that sense?)[52]

Not forever does it vanish, of course, despite what Wittgenstein says here: if clarity is contextual, it is also all too frequently solicited. The problems of life, like the problems of philosophy, endlessly recur. Wittgensteinian analy-sis is interminable.

"NOTHING IS HIDDEN"

As a thinker Freud desires truth above all. Such truth is possible, he believes, only when "the scientific spirit, reason" will have achieved hegemony in human life. Commitment to that "scientific spirit" marks Freud as a meta-physician, the final sort of Western metaphysician, one who seeks the "true world" through careful reasoning, empirically validated hypotheses, and col-legial cooperation. What There Is will show itself to us neither in religious ecstasy nor in philosophical dialectic; it will come slowly and piecemeal, in reports scribbled at lab-benches and in case histories of folks like poor Dora or the Wolf Man. Freud is a thinker who wants to "penetrate phenomena" in hope of Truth, and in him that hope is firmly tethered to another, equally a part of the Western metaphysical tradition as far back as Socrates: the hope that through a True Account of things will come an access of freedom.

Through the lengthy and patient efforts of courageous thinkers the rock will break, water will flow, and healing will begin.

Such a vision—this goes without saying—is inspiring and rare; most of us care little enough about either truth or health. Small wonder then that Wittgenstein, who also wanted in his work to combine intellectual comprehension and therapeutic release, should consider himself a disciple of Freud. Both were concerned to free dying flies from fly-bottles; both aimed to be physicians of the soul, working to return us to the sound human understanding and life. But Wittgenstein's vision of such soundness is very different from Freud's. Clarity, not Truth, is his ambition; not to "penetrate phenomena" through sharpened theoretical vision but to change our way of looking at things by means of a "perspicuous presentation" of what we already know. "Philosophy simply puts everything before us, and neither explains nor deduces anything.—Since everything lies open to view there is nothing to explain. For what is hidden, for example, is of no interest to us."[53]

How remarkable those words are, and how hard to take seriously. How could what is hidden from us not matter? Doesn't it matter most of all? What would a therapy, or a way of thinking, or a way of life, be like that "simply puts everything before us, and neither explains nor deduces anything?" What might it mean to understand one's situation—in philosophy and in life— "horizontally" rather than "vertically"; to understand a thing not in terms of what is behind (or below or above) it but only in terms of what lies alongside it, at whatever particular distance? What would it be like to desire clarity rather than truth? Until we can answer these questions we cannot understand Wittgenstein—and neither, I think, do we fully understand a thinker like Freud, who represents a quite different intellectual and ethical point of view. One can take the measure of a metaphysician like Freud only when an alternative to metaphysical thinking is available.

We now can see the source of Wittgenstein's ambivalence about Freud. It is, in the first instance, his ambivalence about Western metaphysics; one might even say his ambivalence about Western civilization itself: metaphysics and our civilization remain unconsciously mythological. For Wittgenstein, Freud's scientism is just the metaphysician's latest attempt to break beyond the veil and reveal the original workings of our experience. Moreover, in Freud's sensibility, scientism is still in thrall to an attempt to salvage human dignity by attaching us to something both hidden and uncanny. For all his (sincere) protestations of secularism, Freud is still a religious thinker. He is still in love with the mystery of the world; he still believes in a hidden core of meaning that shows itself in dreams and slips and poems and marriages. For Freud something is always going on behind, or beneath, the world of ordinary things and their—frequently overlooked—connections. He remains a riddler; he sees the world as containing a dark and empowering riddle only he can solve.

But for Wittgenstein, early and late, the riddle does not exist.[54] The world is not a mystery; it is not to be understood by penetrating to some hidden heart, to some obscure entity or process from which significance flows, whether that Concealed One is called 'God,' 'the self,' 'will to power,' or 'libido.' *"Es ist ja nichts verborgen."* To be sure, but that does not mean that everything is always already clear. Despite its disavowal of metaphysics, Wittgenstein's work shines with a particular sensibility, one that encourages the reader in the thought that human life both deserves and supports the kind of intense, respectful, and patient attention one once might have called philosophical. *Pathos* does not disappear along with the uncanny gods that seemed to give us dignity and heft. Although the world does not contain a hidden core, theological or otherwise, it does offer the patient seeker a view of its essence, an essence presented by *grammar*: presented by, that is, the sort of connections among things one sees best in the grammar of a natural language.[55] Those connections are horizontal rather than vertical, holistic rather than individual, contingent rather than necessary, and just as capable of producing jokes and dire misunderstandings as they are capable of letting sense happen. Nevertheless, tracing those connections, whether in language or in life, can be an exercise that produces instances of clarity sufficient to the day's inevitable muddle and shadow. Clarity, not Truth: our life's *pathos* is not to be found in Freudian penetration but in Wittgensteinian perspicuity; the miracle of things is not in what they allow us to discover but in what they help us to see. Nothing is hidden; everything lies open to view.[56]

NOTES

1. To see an image of Jeff Koons's *Equilibrium*, go to www.artopos.org/ main-en.html?collections/ioannou/equilibrium-en.html&3.

2. The conversations with Rhees are published in Ludwig Wittgenstein, *Lectures and Conversations on Aesthetics, Psychology, and Religious Belief*, Cyril Barrett, ed. (Berkeley and Los Angeles: University of California Press, 1967). Page references will be to this volume, cited as 'Barrett'; the phrases cited in this paragraph are from Rhees's notes published on page 41 of the Barrett volume.

3. Barrett, 26. The reference is to the third of the "Lectures on Aesthetics."

4. Barrett, 50.

5. See Barrett, 45–50.

6. Ludwig Wittgenstein, *Philosophical Investigations*, G. E. M. Anscombe, trans. (Oxford: Basil Blackwell, 1953), x. Here is the relevant sentence: "—If my remarks do not bear a stamp which marks them as mine,—I do not wish to lay any further claim to them as my property."

7. The first of these sentences is from Barrett, p. 42; the second and the third are from Barrett, 43f.

8. Barrett, 50.

9. Barrett, 51.

10. For an essay that takes seriously Freud's reliance on what it calls "homunclular explanation," see Clark Glymour, "Freud's Androids," in Jerome Neu, ed., *The Cambridge Companion to Freud* (Cambridge: Cambridge University Press, 1991), 44–85.

11. Barrett, 25.

12. Barrett, 25.

13. On the other hand, one may also say, "Of course not. It couldn't be so." Theories that appeal to us by way of the charm of myth may provoke either of these reactions; what they will not provoke is careful, cautious weighing of strengths and weaknesses: "Well, maybe. Let's see what the evidence says." See Barrett, 26f.

14. Barrett, 45. One may connect this Wittgensteinian example to the young Marcel's experience, recounted in *Swann's Way*, of the three steeples at Martinville and his sense that they have a hidden message for him. (See Marcel Proust, *Remembrance of Things Past*, vol. 1, C. K. Scott Moncrieff and Terence Kilmartin, trans. [New York: Vintage Books, 1982], p. 196f.) Marcel's example shows, I believe, that not every phenomenon is impressive for everyone. (Such contingency is one of the great themes of the novel.) But maybe some are, for almost anyone.

15. See his essay, "The 'Uncanny,'" in Sigmund Freud, *Collected Papers*, vol. IV, Joan Riviere, trans. (London: The Hogarth Press, 1948), 368–407.

16. This is a generalization, of course, and may be false in particular instances. See note 12.

17. Though of course in some circumstances a similar event might push past the borders of the ordinary: I remember my grandmother telling me that on the first anniversary of my grandfather's death she heard his characteristic knock on the front door at suppertime, only to find—of course—no one there when she opened it. She took it as an omen of her own death, then soon to come.

18. The example is Wittgenstein's own, from a story by Gottfried Keller. See Barrett, 25.

19. Barrett, 25.

20. Barrett, 25f.

21. Barrett, 51.

22. Without claiming that here Wittgenstein is speaking autobiographically, I note that there are interesting parallels to his own life. For a good account of that life, see Ray Monk, *Ludwig Wittgenstein: The Duty of Genius* (New York: The Free Press, 1990). Of course I do not assert here that feeling same-sex desires is (or ought to be) *inherently* shameful, only that a given person might feel it to be so.

23. Suicide is called "the elementary sin" in Ludwig Wittgenstein, *Notebooks 1914–1916*, G. E. M. Anscombe, trans. (Oxford: Basil Blackwell, 1961), 91.

24. Barrett, 51. The quotation marks are in the original.

25. Barrett, 51.

26. Barrett, 52.

27. Harold Bloom, *Ruin the Sacred Truths: Poetry and Belief from the Bible to the Present* (Cambridge: Harvard University Press), 54.

28. Sigmund Freud, *New Introductory Lectures on Psycho-Analysis*, James Strachey, trans. (New York: W.W. Norton, n.d.), 212.

29. Friedrich Nietzsche, "The Problem of Socrates," in his *Twilight of the Idols*, W. Kaufmann, trans. reprinted in W. Kaufmann, *The Portable Nietzsche* (New York: Viking, 1982), 474.

30. Friedrich Nietzsche, *On the Genealogy of Morality*, M. Clark and A. J. Swensen, trans. (Indianapolis and Cambridge: Hackett Publishing Company, 1998), 1.

31. Ludwig Wittgenstein, *Philosophical Remarks*, Rush Rhees, ed., Raymond Hargreaves and Roger White, trans. (Oxford: Basil Blackwell, 1975), 7.

32. For Wittgenstein's animadversions on Frazer, see his "Remarks on Frazer's *Golden Bough*," reprinted in Ludwig Wittgenstein, *Philosophical Occasions 1912–1951*, James Klagge and Alfred Nordmann, eds. (Indianapolis and Cambridge: Hackett Publishing Company, 1993), 115–155. See also Peter Kramer, *Listening to Prozac* (New York: Penguin Books, 1994), passim. To his credit, Kramer is ambivalent about the "biological materialism" his book makes so credible.

33. See Wittgenstein, *Philosophical Investigations*, sec. 309.

34. In these paragraphs I am using material discussed at greater length in James C. Edwards, *The Plain Sense of Things: The Fate of Religion in an Age of Normal Nihilism* (University Park: Penn State Press, 1997), 115ff.

35. Martin Heidegger, "The End of Philosophy and the Task of Thinking," Joan Stambaugh, trans., in Martin Heidegger, *Basic Writings*, D. F. Krell, ed. (New York: Harper and Row, 1977), 375.

36. For details, see Martin Heidegger, "The Age of the World Picture," in Heidegger, *The Question Concerning Technology and Other Essays*, W. Lovitt, trans. (New York: Harper and Row, 1977), 139–153.

37. The quotation is from Wittgenstein, of course. See the preface to *Philosophical Remarks*.

38. The *locus classicus* of this Wittgensteinian claim is the famous (in some quarters notorious) "private language argument" of the *Philosophical Investigations*, starting at about sec. 243.

39. Ludwig Wittgenstein, *Tractatus Logico-Philosophicus*, D. F. Pears and B. F. McGuinness, trans. (London: Routledge and Kegan Paul, 1961), 3.3.

40. Wittgenstein, *Tractatus Logico-Philosophicus*, 4.001.

41. Wittgenstein, *Philosophical Investigations*, sec. 415.

42. Ibid., sec. 122. I have slightly changed the translation.

43. Ibid., sec. 123: "A philosophical problem has the form: 'I don't know my way about.'"

44. Ibid., sec. 92.

45. Ibid., sec. 109.

46. Ibid., sec. 435.

47. Ibid., secs. 127 and 133.

48. Norman Malcolm reports Wittgenstein as saying that an expression has meaning only in "the stream of life." See Malcolm, *Ludwig Wittgenstein: A Memoir* (London: Oxford University Press, 1962), 93. A very similar sort of holism can be found in Martin Heidegger, *Being and Time*, John Macquarrie and Edward Robinson, trans. (New York: Harper and Row, 1962).

49. Wittgenstein, *Philosophical Remarks*, 7.

50. Wittgenstein, *Philosophical Investigations*, sec. 371.

51. Ibid., sec. 133.

52. Wittgenstein, *Tractatus Logico-Philosophicus*, 6.521.

53. Wittgenstein, *Philosophical Investigations*, sec. 126.

54. Wittgenstein, *Tractatus Logico-Philosophicus*, 6.5.

55. Wittgenstein, *Philosophical Investigations*, sec. 371.

56. I am grateful to Jon Mills for his careful and helpful reading of this chapter.

SEVEN

THE HERMENEUTIC VERSUS THE
SCIENTIFIC CONCEPTION
OF PSYCHOANALYSIS

Adolf Grünbaum

THE CONSTRUCTION OF BRIDGES between the natural and social sciences is a laudable aim. But bridges that do not hold up should not be built. This chapter argues that the so-called hermeneutic reconstruction of psychoanalytic theory and therapy proposed by Karl Jaspers, Paul Ricoeur, and Jürgen Habermas fails multiply as a viaduct and alleged prototype for the study of human nature. One key to that failure is the misconstrual of so-called meaning connections between mental states in their bearing on *causal* connections between such states.

INTRODUCTION

According to the so-called hermeneutic reconstruction of classical psychoanalytic theory, the received scientific conception of the Freudian enterprise gave much too little explanatory weight to "meaning" connections between unconscious motives, on the one hand, and overt symptoms on the other. Thus, in a paper on schizophrenia, the German philosopher and professional psychiatrist Karl Jaspers wrote: "In Freud's work we are dealing in fact with [a] *psychology of meaning*, not *causal explanation* as Freud himself thinks."[1] The father of psychoanalysis, we are told, fell into a "confusion of meaning connections with causal connections."

139

The noun *hermeneutics*, which derives etymologically from Hermes the messenger, was *usefully* introduced in the seventeenth century as a name for *biblical exegesis*, and was then broadened to refer to *textual* interpretation generally. Alas, at the hands of those continental European philosophers who wanted to rehabilitate the nineteenth-century *dichotomy* between the natural and the human sciences, the term was *extended* to label the interpretation of *psychological* phenomena or *mentation as such*, to the exclusion of *non*mental ones. And, in that vein, the French philosopher Paul Ricoeur told us the following: "Psychology is an *observational* science dealing with the facts of behavior; psychoanalysis is an exegetical [interpretive] science dealing with the relationships of meaning between substitute objects [i.e., symptoms] and the primordial (and lost) instinctual objects [i.e., repressed instinctual wishes]."[2]

Yet obviously we interpret overt human behavior, no less than thoughts and feelings, but also such *physical* phenomena as X-ray films, clicks on Geiger counters, tracks in Wilson cloud chambers, and geological strata. In daily life, it is an *interpretation* or hypothesis to say that the table salt I taste at lunch is sodium chloride, just as it is an interpretive hypothesis to infer *psychologically* that a certain eye movement is a flirtatious, sexual gesture. Furthermore, insofar as merely *some kind or other* of interpretation is involved, it is trivial and unenlightening to note that there is that kind of *similarity* between the *semantic* interpretation of a written text, on the one hand, and the psychoanalyst's *motivational* interpretation of the patient's speech and gestures in the doctor's office as having so-called *unconscious* "*meaning*," on the other. In short, *etymologically*, the term *hermeneutic* is just a *synonym* for the word *interpretative*. But it is also used *ideologically* and indeed ambiguously so.

Further serious confusion is introduced by the different *philosophical* uses of the term hermeneutics as follows: Whereas some philosophers apply it, as we have seen, to render *opposition* to the unity of the natural and human sciences, others use it to *endorse* such *unity* as follows:[3] *All* these sciences are *alike* hermeneutic, we learn, in the sense of employing Kuhnian paradigms of *understanding* across-the-board to provide *explanations*. Thus, Paul Feyerabend, Mary Hesse, and Richard Rorty, for instance, welcomed Kuhn's delivery of a so-called *hermeneutic* unity of science. Yet others, like Karl Popper, saw this hermeneutic sort of unity of science as a descent into irrationalism and intellectual barbarism.[4] The deplorable use of the term hermeneutics to render *incompatible* philosophical positions just compounds the liabilities of the ambiguous and obfuscatory employment of the term *meaning*.

After Jaspers, Paul Ricoeur, and Jürgen Habermas have elaborated the patronizing claim that Freud basically misunderstood his own theory and therapy. As these European philosophers would have it, psychoanalysis can snatch victory from the jaws of the scientific failings of Freud's theory by abjuring his scientific aspirations as basically misguided. Claiming that Freud himself had "scientistically" misunderstood his own theoretical achievement, they misconstrue it as a *semantic* accomplishment by trading on the weasel word *meaning*.

I can give immediately just one of the reasons for rejecting the use of the multiply ambiguous term *meaning* to characterize the psychoanalytic enterprise. In a 1991 article entitled "Hermeneutics in Psychoanalysis," James Phillips told us à la Jaspers that Freud made a great "hermeneutic" discovery, which was to uncover hidden "meaning" where no "meaning" was thought to exist before.[5] But clearly what Freud claimed to have discovered is that behavior, such as those slips (or *Fehlleistungen*) that were previously *not* thought to be *psychologically motivated*, were *caused* by specific sorts of *unconscious motives* after all. In Freud's view, motives were clearly a *species of causes*.

In his account, an overt symptom manifests one or more underlying unconscious causes and gives evidence for its cause(s), so that the "sense" or "meaning" of the symptom is constituted by its latent motivational cause(s). But this notion of "meaning" is different from the one appropriate to the context of *communication*, in which *linguistic* symbols acquire *semantic* meaning by being used intentionally to designate their referents. Clearly, the relation of being a manifestation, which the symptom bears to its hypothesized cause, differs from the semantic relation of designation, which a linguistic symbol bears to its object. This fact is blatantly overlooked in much recent psychoanalytic literature. Thus, in a 1994 letter to the editor of the *Journal of the American Psychoanalytic Association* Philip Rubovitz-Seitz complained that "Freud portrayed his interpretations as the necessary causal inferences of a natural science, rather than as the construal of meanings employed in the human sciences."[6]

The "hermeneutic" reconstruction of psychoanalysis slides illicitly from one of two familiar senses of "meaning" encountered in ordinary discourse to another. When a parent is told by a pediatrician that a child's spots on the skin *"mean* measles," the "meaning" of the symptom is constituted by one of its *causes*, much as in the Freudian case. But when a bus driver tells us that three rings of his bell "mean" that the bus is full, these rings—unlike the symptoms of measles or neurotic symptoms—are *intended to communicate* a certain state of affairs.

Thus, the British psychoanalyst Anthony Storr conflates the fathoming of the *etiologic* "sense" or "meaning" of a symptom with the activity of making *semantic* sense of a text, declaring absurdly: "Freud was a man of genius whose expertise lay in semantics." And Ricoeur erroneously credits Freud's theory of repression with having provided, *malgré lui*, a veritable "semantics of desire."

Yet the proposed hermeneutic reconstruction of the psychoanalytic enterprise has been embraced with alacrity by a considerable number of psychoanalysts no less than by a fair number of professors in humanities departments at universities. Its psychoanalytic adherents see it as buying absolution for their theory and therapy from the criteria of validation mandatory for causal hypotheses in the empirical sciences, although psychoanalysis is replete with just such hypotheses. This form of escape from accountability also augurs ill for the future of psychoanalysis, because the methods of the hermeneuts have not spawned a single new important hypothesis! Instead, their reconstruction is a negativistic ideological battle cry whose disavowal of Freud's scientific aspirations presages the death of his legacy from sheer sterility, at least among those who demand the validation of theories by cogent evidence.

My indictment is shared by the well-known academic psychoanalyst Marshall Edelson[7] who writes lucidly:

> For psychoanalysis, the *meaning* of a mental phenomenon is a set of unconscious psychological or intentional states (specific wishes or impulses, specific fears aroused by these wishes, and thoughts or images which might remind the subject of these wishes and fears). The mental phenomenon substitutes for this set of states. That is, these states would have been present in consciousness, instead of the mental phenomenon requiring interpretation, had they not encountered, at the time of origin of the mental phenomenon or repeatedly since then, obstacles to their access to consciousness. If the mental phenomenon has been a relatively enduring structure, and these obstacles to consciousness are removed, the mental phenomenon disappears as these previously unconscious states achieve access to consciousness.
>
> That the mental phenomenon substitutes for these states is a manifestation of a causal sequence.[8]

Yet Ricoeur relies on the double-talk as to "meaning" to *misdepict* Freud's theory of repression as furnishing a so-called *semantics* of desire. Then he compounded that misrepresentation by introducing a *pseudo-contrast* when claiming that the natural scientist and the academic psychologist *observe* phenomena, whereas the psychoanalyst *interprets* the productions of patients. Thus, in his book *Freud and Philosophy*, Ricoeur tells us that, contrary to Freud, psychoanalytic theory—which he *reduces wantonly* to the interpretations given to patients undergoing analysis—is a so-called hermeneutic endeavor *as opposed* to a natural science.[9] By reducing psychoanalytic *theory*, which is far-flung and composite, to Freudian *therapy*, Ricoeur puts aside most of what Freud himself deemed to be his major and lasting contributions. As Freud put it: "The future will probably attribute far greater importance to psychoanalysis as the science of the unconscious than as a therapeutic procedure."[10]

It is true, but philosophically unavailing to the hermeneutic reconstruction of psychoanalysis, that the challenge of *puzzle solving* is presented alike by *each* of the following three different kinds of interpretive activities:

1. Fathoming the psychoanalytically hypothesized unconscious causal factors behind a symptom, dream, or slip by means of psychoanalytic interpretation.

2. Elucidating the *semantic* meaning of a *text*.

3. Doing detective work to solve a murder.

After all, the *common* challenge of problem solving in each of these *cognitive* activities hardly licenses the assimilation of the quest for so-called *psychoanalytic* meaning to the search for the *semantic* meaning of a text. Yet some hermeneuts latched on to a statement of Freud's (S.E., 1913, 13, pp. 176–178)[11] in which he avowedly "overstepped" common usage, when he generalized the term "language" to designate not only the verbal expression of thought but also gestures "and every other method . . . by which mental activity can be expressed" (S.E., 1913, 13, p. 176). There Freud declared that "the interpretation of dreams [as a cognitive activity] is completely analogous to the decipherment of an ancient pictographic script such as Egyptian hieroglyphs" (S.E., 1913, 13, p. 177). But surely this common challenge of *problem solving* does not license the assimilation of the *psychoanalytic* meaning of manifest dream-content to the *semantic* meaning of spoken or written language.[12]

Hermeneuts (or hermeneuticians) have tried to invoke the fact that the title of Freud's *magnum opus* is "The *Interpretation* of Dreams," or—in German—"Die Traumdeutung." The German word for meaning is *Bedeutung*. But even in German commonsense discourse, that term, as well as its verb *bedeuten*, are each used in *both* the Freudian *motivational* sense *and* in the *semantic* sense, as shown by the following illustrations: (1) There is a German song whose opening words are: "Ich weiss nicht was soll es *bedeuten*, dass ich so traurig bin"—translated: "I don't know what it *means* that I am so sad." (And it continues: "Ein Märchen aus alten Zeiten, das kommt mir nicht aus dem Sinn"—translated: "I am obsessed by an ancient fairy tale.") Clearly, the song does *not* express puzzlement as to the *semantic* meaning of the term *so sad*, which is known all too well. Instead, the song expresses curiosity as to the *motivating psychological cause* of the sadness. (2) The *semantic* sense occurs when someone asks: "What does the word *automobile* mean?" An etymological answer might be: "It actually means 'self-mover.' " No wonder that C. K. Ogden and I. A. Richards wrote a whole book entitled "The Meaning of 'Meaning.' "

But unfortunately "hermeneutic" philosophers such as Ricoeur and Habermas have fallaciously *misused* the following two sets of facts: (1) The interpretation of a text is, at least in the first instance, the construction of a *semantic hypothesis* as to what it asserts. (2) By contrast, a very different sort of "interpretation" occurs when the psychoanalyst bases imputations of unconscious motives on the patient's conscious *speech*, rather than, say, on behavioral indicators like weeping or gestures. In that *psychoanalytically interpretive* situation, the *semantic content* of that speech is *only* an *avenue* to the analyst's *etiologic* inferences of *causally explanatory* motives; for example, the patient's speech may be a deceptive cover for resistance to the disclosure of hidden motives.

Thus, Ricoeur misleadingly and fallaciously misdepicted Freud's theory of repression as a *semantic* achievement by misassimulating the following two sets of different relations to one another: (1) the way in which the effect of an unconscious cause can *manifest* it and provide *evidence* for it, and (2) the way in which a *linguistic symbol* represents its referent semantically or *designates* the attributes of the referent. It is precisely this misassimulation, together with abundant misunderstandings of the natural sciences, that have served Ricoeur and Habermas to manufacture a methodological *pseudo-contrast*. That pseudo-contrast is between the epistemology of causal hypotheses in the natural sciences, on the one hand, and the psychoanalyst's search for the so-called unconscious *meaning* of the patient's symptoms and conduct, on the other. In this way, they gave psychoanalytic trappings to the old nineteenth century false dichotomy between the natural and human sciences.

Similarly, in a criticism of my views, the American psychologist and hermeneutic Freudian Matthew Erdelyi fatuously offered the following platitudinous *irrelevancy* to discredit the *causal* content of psychoanalytic interpretations: "When one establishes the meaning of an unknown word from its context, one does not establish that the context has caused the unknown word." However, this truism enables Erdelyi to overlook that the psychoanalyst generally knows the contextual *dictionary* meanings of the patient's words very well; instead, the analyst has the difficult task of using the patient's words as merely *one avenue* to hypothesizing the *unconscious causes* of the patient's personality dispositions and life history! And it is bathetic to use the term *meaning* to convey the banality that psychoanalysis is concerned with *mentation* and its behavioral *manifestations*.

Similar mischief is wrought by trading on the ambiguity of the term *to signify*, as in the following example. Suppose that the sight of a small cat evokes associatively an unconscious thought of a huge, menacing tiger. Clearly, in Freud's account, this evocation is a *causal* process whose relata are mental, whatever the underlying brain process. This process of causal evocation has been misassimulated to *linguistic* reference by using the semantic term "signification" as follows: It is said that the sight of the little cat unconsciously *signifies* the tiger, as if that sight functions like a *word* or English noise, which refers semantically to the tiger. But clearly, even if the person who sees the small cat links that sight to the word *cat*, such a linkage is hardly tantamount to the unconscious *semantic* reference of the sight to the ominous tiger. Yet Lacanians tell us that the unconscious is structured like a language. In this way, they may well facilitate a misleading semantic account of an infelicitous statement such as: "To the person who saw the small cat, it unconsciously *meant* a menacing big tiger." For Freud, the sight of the small cat actuated a *causal* process of evoking the unconscious thought of a huge tiger. And the explanatory question is *why* it did so in the given case.

In a book that appeared before,[13,14] Achim Stephan[15] takes issue with some of my views.[16] He does not endorse Ricoeur's "semantics of desire."[17] But he objects[18] to my claim that "In Freud's theory, an overt symptom manifests one or more underlying unconscious causes and gives evidence for its cause(s), so that the 'sense' or 'meaning' of the symptom is constituted by its latent motivational cause(s)."

Stephan does countenance my emphasis on the distinction between the relation of manifestation, which the symptom bears to its cause, and the semantic relation of designation, which a linguistic symbol bears to its object.[19] Yet his principal objection to my view of the psychoanalytic "sense" of symptoms as being causal manifestations of unconscious ideation is that I assign "exclusively non-semantic significance" to them by *denying* that they also have "semiotic" significance like linguistic symbols.[20] He grants that Freud did not construe the sense or meaning of symptoms as one of semantic reference to their causes. Yet according to Stephan's own reconstruction of Freud's conception, "he did assume that the manifest phenomena [symptoms] semantically stand for the same thing as the (repressed) ideas for which they substitute," that is, "they stand semantically for what the repressed (verbal) ideas stand (or rather would stand, if they were expressed verbally)."[21]

According to Franz Brentano, the essential characteristic of the mental is to be *about* something, to be representational, to be directed toward something else, to be referential.[22] Brentano used the adjective "intentional" to render what he thus took to be common and peculiar to all instances of the mental, although that term also has the different meaning of "deliberate." In Brentano's view, the phenomenon of intentionality, thus construed, constitutes the criterion of demarcation between the mental and physical worlds.

Husserl objected that states of pain, and sensory qualities like red, though mental, are not "intentional" or directed toward something in Brentano's sense. Yet, Carrier and Mittelstrass[23] point out that Brentano[24] anticipated Husserl's objection by noting that "After all, *something* hurts, and *something* is perceived as red."

But as Searle has rightly argued, "undirected" (i.e., diffuse) anxiety is not representational and yet mental.[25] As he put it: "there are forms of elation, depression, and anxiety where one is simply elated, depressed or anxious without being elated, depressed, or anxious about anything."[26] Thus, intentionality à la Brentano is not a necessary condition for the mental. In any case, Aviva Cohen has noted (private communication) that the later Brentano gave up his "intentionality" as the essence of the mental.

Searle[27] has noted illuminatingly[28] that, unlike many mental states, language is *not intrinsically* "intentional" in Brentano's directed sense; instead, the intentionality (aboutness) of language is *extrinsically imposed* on it by deliberately "decreeing" it to function referentially. Searle points out that the mental states of some animals and of "pre-linguistic" very young children do have intrinsic intentionality but *no* linguistic referentiality.[29]

I maintain that Stephan's fundamental hermeneuticist error was to slide illicitly from the *intrinsic, nonsemantic* intentionality of (many, but *not* all) mental states to the *imposed*, semantic sort possessed by language. Moreover, *some* of the neurotic symptoms of concern to psychoanalysts, such as diffuse depression and manic, undirected elation even *lack* Brentano-intentionality.

Finally, the aboutness (contents) of Freud's repressed conative states is avowedly different from the intentionality (contents) of their psychic manifestations in symptoms. But Stephan erroneously insists that they are the same.

As I have earlier indicated, the common aim of the hermeneuts is to make philosophic capital out of their semantic misemphasis by buying *absolution* for psychoanalytic motivational hypotheses from the criteria of validation that are applied to *causal hypotheses* in the empirical sciences. In short, they want to escape *critical* accountability. Ironically, they cheerfully describe their philosophy as "*critical theory*" in self-congratulatory fashion. Yet since Freud's interpretations of the so-called unconscious meanings of symptoms, dreams, and slips are obviously offered as *explanatory causal hypotheses*, they call for scrutiny as such. Hence we must address the following *pivotal issue*: just what kind of *validation* do causal hypotheses require? And what sorts of causal hypotheses are at issue?

It is of major importance to realize that the very content of *causal* hypotheses prescribes what kind of evidence is required to validate them as such. And it is easy to show that the required mode of validation must be the same in the human sciences as in the physical sciences, despite the clear difference in their subject matter.

A causal hypothesis of the sort encountered in psychoanalysis asserts that some factor X is *causally relevant* to some occurrence Y. This means that X *makes a certain kind of difference* to the occurrence of Y in some reference class C. But let me emphasize that claims of mere causal relevance do not necessarily presuppose causal *laws*.

To validate a claim of causal relevance, we must first divide the reference class C into two subclasses, the X's and the non-X's. And then we must show that the incidence of Y's among the X's is *different* from what it is among the non-X's. But it is of cardinal importance to appreciate that *this requirement is entirely neutral as to the field of knowledge or subject matter. It applies alike in medicine, psychology, physics, sociology,* and elsewhere. The belief of the hermeneuts that causality as such is "owned" by the physicists, as it were, is born of ideological special pleading.

Alas, just that error was abetted by the pernicious ordinary language philosophy that faded away in the 1960s. It is illustrated by Stephen Toulmin's writings on psychoanalysis in the 1950s. But once we appreciate, as Freud did (S.E., 1895, 3, pp. 135–139), the stated *ontological neutrality* of the relation of causal relevance as between the mental and the physical, it is plain that a person's conscious or unconscious motives are no less causally relevant to her or his action or behavior than a drug overdose is to a person's death or than the blow of a hammer is to the shattering of a windowpane. As we recall, in Freud's view, motives are clearly a species of the genus cause (S.E., 1909, 10, p. 199; 1900, 5, pp. 541–542, 560–561, and 4, pp. 81–82). Thus, to speak of our motives as "reasons" does not invalidate their status as a *species* of cause.

But Stephen Toulmin told us, contra Freud, that motivational explanations in psychoanalysis do *not* qualify as a *species* of causal explanations.[30] And he did so by *miscontrasting* motives ("reasons") for action and causes for action by relying on ordinary language usage,[31] which is scientifically inadequate. By means of such question-begging reliance on the parlance of daily life, he believes to have established that "The [purported] success of psychoanalysis . . . should re-emphasize the importance of 'reasons for action' as opposed to causes of action."[32] And, in this way, he believes to have vindicated his initial contention that "troubles arise from thinking of psycho-analysis too much on the analogy of the natural sciences."[33] But, as I have just shown, all of this is wrongheaded qua purported accounts of Freud's conceptualizations.

In his full-length book on Freud, Ricoeur endorses Toulmin's claim that psychoanalytic explanations are *not* causal, just *in virtue* of being motivational.[34] As Ricoeur saw it then, in psychoanalysis "a motive and a cause are completely different," instead of the former being just a *species* of the latter. Hence, one must welcome that, under the influence of the late Boston psychoanalyst Michael Sherwood,[35] Ricoeur did have second thoughts in his later work[36] and, commendably enough, *repudiated* the ordinary language approach to Freudian explanations along with the "dichotomy between motive and cause."

As I have noted, the absolution of psychoanalysis from the validational rigors appropriate to its causal hypotheses can also serve to license or abet epistemological nonaccountability and escapism. It is therefore not surprising that, at a Pittsburgh meeting of the Society for Philosophy and Psychology, Toulmin patronizingly told the eminent American psychoanalyst Benjamin B. Rubinstein not to worry, when Rubinstein publicly expressed his epistemological misgivings about psychoanalysis. The ordinary language construal of psychoanalysis was anathema to Rubinstein. And it was salutary that he emphatically reiterated his evidential qualms in his contribution to a 1983 *Festschrift* for me. There Rubinstein wrote:

> It is the clinical part of psychoanalysis that is really disturbing. It is top-heavy with theory but has only a slim evidential base. I have used the theory of hysteria to illustrate the arbitrariness, because of lack of adequate confirmation, of a great many clinical interpretations. This statement holds also beyond hysteria.[37]

Ricoeur celebrated the failure of Freud's theory to pass muster qua natural science *as a virtue*, and even called for a "counterattack" against philosophers like Ernest Nagel who *deplore* this failure.[38]

Thus, there is a basic divergence between the hermeneuts and myself as to both the source and the import of Freud's theoretical shortcomings. Indeed, I contend that the triumph of the hermeneutic conception of the psychoanalytic enterprise would be a *Pyrrhic* victory by being the *kiss of death for psychoanalysis*. Fortunately, such well-known psychoanalysts as Charles Brenner[39] and Benjamin Rubinstein,[40] no less than Marshall Edelson,[41] have thoroughly rejected the sterile hermeneutic construal of Freudian theory and therapy.

The issues raised in this debate go far beyond psychoanalysis. In my view, the proper resolution of the relation between thematic connections that relate mental states, on the one hand, and causal connections between these states, on the other, not only spells a major general moral for the human sciences, including history, but also has instructive counterparts in biology and even in physics. Let us disregard the hermeneutic polemic for now and examine Freud's own use of meaning connections to *infer* causal connections. That examination will yield an unfavorable verdict on the hermeneuticists's indictment of Freud, but also a critique of Freud *opposite* to theirs.

After I elucidate the concept of "meaning connection," one of the key lessons for which I argue will be essentially the following: meaning connections between the mental states of a given person *by themselves* never attest their causal linkage, even if these thematic connections are very strong. Typically, I will argue, a good deal else is needed to vouch for a *causal* connection. This precept will emerge, I trust, from my analysis of just how Freud failed in his account of the relations between meaning kinships, on the one hand, and causal linkages, on the other. One important corollary of his miscarriage will be my claim that Freud gave *much too much explanatory weight* to meaning affinities, rather than much *too little* weight, as charged by Jaspers and the other hermeneutic critics.

But what are the so-called "meaning connections" in this context? And just what are their relations to *causal* connections? First, I shall consider some *paradigmatic* illustrations of these connections from psychoanalysis. Yet, as I have already explained, I deplore and regret the use of the term *meaning* as a characterization of these connections, because it is ambiguous and lends itself to misleading use. I myself use it here only because the philosophers I cite have employed it.

PARADIGMATIC CASES OF "MEANING"-CONNECTIONS FROM PSYCHOANALYSIS

Let me now mention some paradigmatic cases of "meaning"-connections from psychoanalysis, which Freud himself *linked* to causal connections.

Case 1. In 1893, he wrote:

> Breuer's patient [Anna O.], to whom I have so often referred, offered an example of a disturbance of speech. For a long period of her

illness she spoke only English and could neither speak nor understand German. This symptom was traced back [etiologically] to an event which had happened before the outbreak of her illness. While she was in a state of great anxiety, she had attempted to pray but could find no words. At last a few words of a child's prayer in English occurred to her. When she fell ill later on, only the English language was at her command [footnote omitted].

The determination of the symptom by the psychical trauma is not so transparent in every instance. There is often only what may be described as a 'symbolic' relation between the determining cause and the hysterical symptom. This is especially true of pains. Thus one patient [footnote omitted] suffered from piercing pains between her eyebrows. The reason [cause] was that once when she was a child her grandmother had given her an enquiring, 'piercing' look. The same patient suffered for a time from violent pains in her right heel, for which there was no explanation. These pains, it turned out, were connected [etiologically] with an idea that occurred to the patient when she made her first appearance in society. She was overcome with fear that she might not 'find herself on a right footing.' Symbolizations of this kind were employed by many patients for a whole number of so-called neuralgias and pains. It is as though there were an intention to express the mental state by means of a physical one; and linguistic usage affords a bridge by which this can be effected. *In this case, however, of what are after all the typical symptoms of hysteria —such as hemi-anaesthesia, restriction of the visual field, epileptiform convulsions, etc.—a psychical mechanism of this sort cannot be demonstrated.* On the other hand this can often be done in respect to the hysterogenic zones (S.E., 1893, 3, pp. 33–34; emphasis added).

It will be a corollary of my critical scrutiny later that the thematic affinities adduced here by Freud do not warrant at all the etiologic inferences he drew from them. The less so, since the "symbolic" affinities he marshals as support are grossly far-fetched and very tenuous.

Case 2. In 1896, Freud used the mere thematic kinship between a patient's experience of disgust and her symptoms of supposedly hysterical vomiting to claim the suitability of the given repressed experience as an *explanatory causal determinant* of the pertinent symptom.[42] In particular, he gives the following example:

Let us suppose that the symptom under consideration is hysterical vomiting; in that case we shall feel that we have been able to understand its causation (except for a certain [hereditary] residue) if the analysis traces the symptom back [etiologically] to an experience which *justifiably produced a high amount of disgust*—for instance, the sight of a decomposing dead body [S.E., 1896, 3, pp. 193–194].

Thus, on the strength of mere thematic kinship, Freud *infers* that the repressed disgust was an essential *cause* of the hysterical vomiting in a person made vulnerable by heredity. And, in due course, our problem will be whether such an *etiologic* inference from a thematic ("meaning") kinship is sound.

The theme of aversion is likewise common to another traumatic experience and a subsequent hysterical symptom in the life of Josef Breuer's famous first patient Anna O. As reported in her case history, she had silently endured traumatic disgust on seeing a dog lapping water from a companion's glass (S.E., 1893, 2, pp. 6–7 and 3, pp. 29–30). And later she almost died of thirst because of her phobic aversion for drinking water. In Jasper's parlance, we can say that the shared theme of aversion makes for a "meaning connection" between the original trauma and her later symptom. But I myself speak of such episodes instead as exhibiting "thematic kinship or affinity." And the main question will be what epistemological and ontological relevance, if any, these thematic kinships between mental events have to *causal* linkages between them. It will also be *relevant* that the thematic etiology on which Breuer based his hypnotic therapy of Anna O. was discredited by *therapeutic failure*.

Case 3. Freud's famous 1909 case history of the *Rat Man* Ernst Lanzer provides a cardinal exemplar of his inferential reliance on a *thematic* connection. And this reliance is not lessened, I emphasize, by the fact that Freud supplies *other, temporally intermediate* events between the thematically cognate ones!

During the Rat Man's army service, he had become aware of an Oriental punishment in which rats are allowed to bore their way into the criminal's anus (S.E., 1909, 10, p. 166). And one of the dreadful thoughts he was obsessed with was that just this rat punishment would victimize both the woman whom he eventually married, and his father, whom he loved and who had actually been dead for years by then.

But how does Freud propose to explain those of the patient's obsessions that featured the awful rat theme? As we learn, at the age of three or four, the Rat Man had misbehaved *like a rat* by *biting* someone, presumably his nurse. Just as rats themselves are punished for such behavior, so also the naughty little boy Rat Man had thereupon been soundly beaten for it by his father and had therefore borne him a permanent unconscious hatred ever since. Freud then *explicitly infers* the supposed *cause* of the rat obsession via the *thematic kinship* between the patient's own punishment for biting-*like-a-rat*, on the one hand, and the role of biting rats in the dreaded Oriental anal punishment, which is supposedly going to afflict his father, on the other.

As Freud reasoned, the patient's latent memory of the cruel paternal punishment for biting had produced repressed hostility toward his father. This antagonism, *in turn*, had allegedly generated the unconscious wish—

and, by the defense mechanism of "reaction-formation," the *conscious fear*—
that the father would undergo the *particular* monstrous punishment of anal
penetration by biting rats. The *hypothesized* hostile *wish* that the father would
suffer this punishment had been morally unacceptable to the patient's consciousness. Therefore, he had repressed it, and had then supposedly turned
it into a conscious obsessive *fear* of the father's punitive victimization by rats
via "reaction-formation."

Clearly, without reliance on the *thematic affinity* between the patient's
biting-like-a-rat and the rat obsessions, the boy's unconscious hatred for the
father could *not* give rise to Freud's etiologic scenario for the patient's obsessions. Thus, Freud interprets the rat obsessions etiologically as the patient's
neurotic defense against his own unacceptable wish that his father would
suffer the particular punishment of rat penetration.

Let us assume the actual occurrence of the punitive childhood scenario. Then the important issue of causation posed by Freud's etiologic inference is *not* whether the severe paternal punishment for biting produced
hatred toward the father; instead, the etiologic issue is *whether that particular
presumed hatred then became the pathogen of the patient's obsessive fear of the
father's victimization by the rat punishment.*

Therefore, when I address *that* issue in due course, I have to ask the
following question: granting the existence of a causal link between the punitive childhood experience and hatred toward the father, does it at all support
the *further* major etiologic hypothesis that this hatred, in turn, was the intermediate pathogen of the rat obsessions? My answer will be a clear "No!"

My last psychoanalytic example will now be drawn from *etiologic inferences in the theory of transference.*

Case 4. Inferences from thematic affinity also play a central, though
logically somewhat different role in Freud's theory of the so-called transference neurosis, a theory that is fundamental to the hypothesized dynamics of
psychoanalytic therapy and to Freud's entire theory of psychopathology. These
inferences, I claim, will likewise turn out to be fallacious.[43]

According to this part of psychoanalytic theory, the patient *transfers*
onto his or her psychoanalyst feelings and thoughts that originally pertained
to important figures in the patient's earlier life. In this important sense, the
fantasies woven around the psychoanalyst by the analysand, and quite generally the latter's conduct toward his doctor, are hypothesized to be *thematically recapitulatory* of childhood episodes. And, by thus being recapitulatory,
the patient's behavior during treatment can be said to exhibit a thematic
kinship to such very early episodes. Therefore, when the analyst interprets
these supposed reenactments as recapitulatory, the ensuing interpretations
are called *transference* interpretations. This much involves a retrodictive
inference of *thematic* affinity.

But Freud and his followers have traditionally also drawn the following
highly questionable causal inference: precisely in virtue of being thematically

recapitulated in the patient–doctor interaction, the hypothesized earlier scenario in the patient's life can cogently be held to have *originally* been *a pathogenic factor* in the patient's affliction.

In short, in the case of transference interpretations, the causal inference from thematic affinity takes a somewhat different logical form from the one we encountered in our previous examples. In the earlier examples, such as Anna O.'s hydrophobia, Freud had inferred the existence of a *direct* causal nexus between thematically similar mental events by relying crucially on their thematic similarity. But in the context of his *transference* interpretations, the thematic reenactment is held to show that the early scenario had *originally* been pathogenic. And once this etiologic conclusion has been drawn, the patient's thematic reenactment in the treatment setting is also asserted to be *pathogenically* recapitulatory, rather than only *thematically* recapitulatory! Freud extols this dubious reasoning in his 1914 "History of the Psychoanalytic Movement" (S.E., 1914, 14, p. 12), where he claims that it furnishes the most unshakable proof for his sexual etiology of the neuroses [den *unerschüttterlichsten Beweis* in his German original].

So far, I have outlined representative illustrations of psychoanalytic causal inferences based on thematic or "meaning" kinships.

THEMATIC KINSHIPS VIS-À-VIS CAUSAL CONNECTIONS

Now we can turn to the following pivotal question: To what extent, *if any*, do mere thematic kinships bespeak causal connections? As I will illustrate presently, thematic kinships are not only of various sorts, but are also encountered in varying *degrees*, ranging from very high to very tenuous. Yet it will be crucial to appreciate the following impending moral: even when the thematic kinship is indeed of very high degree, it does *not* itself license the inference of a causal linkage between such thematically kindred events.

Thus, let us now consider just a few examples from some fields of inquiry *outside* psychoanalysis in their bearing on the inferability of causal relatedness among events or states that feature diverse sorts of thematic affinities or isomorphisms. These examples will serve as salutary preparation for appraising Freud's etiologic inferences from thematic affinity as well as of the objections of some of his hermeneutic critics.

1. A tourist looking at an otherwise desolate beach notes that the sand reveals a string of configurations exhibiting *the same shapes* as the left and right shoes worn by humans. In short, the tourist observes a geometric isomorphism—or "thematic affinity" of shape—between the sand configurations and the shoes. He will then draw the causal inference that a person wearing shoes had actually walked on the beach, and had thereby produced the sandy shapes that we call footprints. But just what *licenses* this causal inference?

The lesson of this example, I claim, is as follows: the striking geometric kinship between the two shapes does *not itself* suffice to license the tourist's inference that the foot-*like* configurations were, in fact, caused (or produced) by the impact of human feet on the beach. To draw the inference, the tourist avails himself of a crucial piece of *additional information* that cannot be known a priori from the mere geometrical kinship: foot-like beach formations in the sand never or hardly ever result from the mere collocation of sand particles under the action of air, such as some gust of wind. Indeed, the additional evidence is that, with overwhelming probability, in the class of beaches, the incursion of a pedestrian into the beach *makes the difference* between the absence and presence of the foot-like beach formations.

In short, going *beyond* the mere sameness of shape, the tourist relies on essential empirical evidence for the overwhelming probability that the sameness of shape was *not* a matter of mere chance, when he or she draws the causal inference that the sandy simulacrum of a human foot is, in fact, actually the trace or mark left by a human foot, and thus a bona fide foot-*print*.[44] Let me just remark that one reviewer of my 1984 book *The Foundations of Psychoanalysis: A Philosophical Critique* incomprehendingly ridiculed this telling epistemological point as pedantic talk about the *word* footprint!

2. Two significantly different dreams will now serve to show that reliance on mere thematic connections to draw causal inferences is a snare and a delusion. This moral will, of course, also apply to Freud's particular dream theory as a special case. But for simplicity, I will deliberately *not* make any psychoanalytic assumptions in dealing with my two dream specimens. In the *first*, though *not* in the second, we will indeed have license to draw the causal inference that the manifest dream content was ˙shaped˙ thematically by a salient component of the waking experience on the day before.

But my point in giving this first dream example will be to contrast it with a second, which is of another kind: In the latter, it is demonstrably fallacious to invoke a thematic connection between the waking experience of the previous day and the manifest dream content as a basis for inferring a *causal* linkage between them.

Let me now turn to the first of the two dream examples. Note that this specimen is hypothetical, since I don't know of anyone who actually had the putative dream. I devised this first example because it features a bona fide case of *both* causal relevance *and* thematic affinity. The dreamer is a woman, whom I shall name Agnes. The night after her first visit to Frank Lloyd Wright's famous house "Falling Water" (in Ohiopyle, Pennsylvania), she dreamt about a house *just like it*, down to many of the fine details of its interior appointments. It is important that Agnes had never heard of "Falling Water" until the day of her visit, let alone seen a picture or description of it. It is also crucial that the very first time that Agnes's manifest dream content ever contained such a simulacrum was the night after her daytime visit to that Frank Lloyd Wright house. Without these additional facts, the strong thematic affinity between "Falling Water" and the dream content would *not itself* legitimate the inference that Agnes's visit to "Falling Water" was *causally relevant* to the presence of a simulacrum of that mansion in her dream during the night after the visit. In short, Agnes's visit *made a difference* to her having that dream. And the relation of making a difference is a crucial ingredient of the relation of causal relevance. Thus, in this case of thematic affinity, there is warrant for the causal inference, because of the availability of appropriate additional facts. But now consider a related example of thematic affinity with the *opposite* inferential moral.

3. Assume that last night, my manifest dream content included the image of a house. In my urban life, I routinely see and inhabit houses daily. Thus, my impressions on the day before this dream featured visual and tactile impressions of at least one dwelling. Indeed, over the years, on the day before a dream, my waking experience *always* includes seeing some domicile or other, *regardless of whether the ensuing manifest dream content then features the image of a house or not.* In *this* case, I claim, seeing a house on the day before does *not* make any difference to dreaming about a house the night after, because I see houses during the day before whether I then dream about them *or not.*

Evidently, in the latter dream example, when a house is an element of the manifest dream, the presence of a house theme in the prior day's waking experience does *not* meet the key requirement for being *causally relevant* to the presence of a house-image in the dream. To put it more precisely, my seeing a house on-the-day-before-a-dream does *not* divide the class of my-day's-waking-experiences-on-the-prior-days into two subclasses, such that the *probabilities* (or frequencies) of the appearance of a house in the next dream *differ* as between the two subclasses. On the other hand, in Agnes's life, just such a division into subclasses by the experience of seeing the "Falling Water" house does occur, with ensuing *different* probabilities of dreaming about that house.

We see that there is a *sharp contrast* between my two dream examples: If a house-image occurred in my dream last night, it is a *mistake* to attribute that image *causally* to my having seen one or more houses yesterday, although there is undeniably *thematic* affinity between them. Thus, it is eminently reasonable to conclude that, despite their thematic affinity, the dual presence of the house theme both in yesterday's daytime experience *and* in last night's dream was a happenstance, rather than a case of causal linkage between them.

The major significance of the *second* dream example for *psychoanalytic* causal inferences turns out to lie in the following fact: as illustrated by the rat theme in the case of Freud's Rat Man, in the typical psychoanalytic etiologic inferences, the thematic affinity is *no greater,* and *often even weaker,* than in the second house dream case. In fact, it is fairly easy to weave thematic affinities between almost any two experiences, and the vivid imaginations of psychoanalysts enable them to have a field day with doing so.

My account of the second dream example may be greeted by disbelief, because it might be thought that I have overlooked an important pertinent fact. We might never have dreamt about any house *at all, unless we had seen one at some time or other in our lives.* Far from having overlooked this necessary condition for house-dreams, I will now explain why this *mere* necessary condition is demonstrably *not* tantamount to the *causal relevance* of my house-seeing-experience-on-the-day-before-a-dream to my dreaming-about-a-house-the-night-after.

This lack of causal relevance of a *mere* necessary condition can be seen at once from the following example: breathing is a *necessary condition* for being paranoid, but breathing is *not causally relevant* to being paranoid. If the wife of a paranoiac were to ask a psychiatrist why her husband is paranoid, the doctor would surely *not* answer, "Because he is a breather." Let us see *why* not.

Breathing is a *necessary condition* for being paranoid, because a person has to breathe to be alive, and in turn has to be alive to be paranoid. A dead paranoiac is surely *not* paranoid. What matters is that all living *non*paranoiacs breathe no less than all paranoiacs do! Thus, breathing does not affect the incidence of paranoia within the class of living humans because it does not even divide this class into two subclasses. A fortiori, it does not divide it into two subclasses in which the incidence of paranoia is *different*. Though breathing is thus a necessary condition for paranoia, it is surely *not* causally relevant—within the class of living persons—to becoming paranoid. In other words, although breathing *does* make a difference to *being alive* or dead, it makes *no* difference to being paranoid rather than nonparanoid.

Thus, in the context of dreams as well, a state of type X may be a necessary condition for the occurrence of some other sort of state Y in a given reference class, although X is *not* causally relevant to Y within that reference class. As I have illustrated, if X is to be causally relevant to Y in a reference class C, X must *partition* C into *two* subclasses in which the probabilities or incidences of Y are *different* from one another. But let me add parenthetically for the case of house-dreams: in the different reference class of *all humans*—which includes people who may never get to see a "house"—seeing-a-house *may* indeed be at least *statistically* relevant to dreaming about it. But even that would not necessarily bespeak *causal* relevance.

It is true that, in the case of *the second* house dream now at issue, which was dreamt by me rather than Agnes, the thematic affinity between the-day's-waking-experience-of-some-house and the next dream about-a-house is clearly *much weaker* than in the Agnes and "Falling Water" example. But there is a telling counterexample to the supposition that every case of *high* thematic affinity also turns out to qualify as an instance of causal relevance: Consider a woman who sees her husband every day of their married life, and whose dreams over the years occasionally feature him undistortedly. Then precisely her inseparability from her husband in waking life shows that her having-been-with-him-as-well-on-the-very-days-before-dreaming-about-him is *not causally relevant* to the production of that thematic dream content the night after.

Besides, recall my earlier *caveat* that even in the example of the footprint, which features *very strong* thematic affinity, the mere presence of a very high degree of such kinship was quite insufficient to validate the causal linkage. Hence it would be a momentous error to believe that causal inferability goes hand-in-hand with a very high degree of thematic kinship.

For brevity, I add an instance from evolutionary biology that tells against drawing causal inferences from thematic kinships. As Elliott Sober[45,46] has pointed out: when species match with respect to what are called ancestral characteristics—which is a certain *kind* of thematic affinity—this similarity is *not* cogent evidence for the causal inference that they share a common descent. Yet, in the context of other information, a match in regard to "derived" characteristics—which is another sort of thematic affinity—does qualify as evidence of a shared genealogy.

We are now ready to appraise Freud's own causal inferences from *thematic* connections. As a corollary, we can reach an important verdict on the objections that Freud's hermeneutic critics leveled against him.

FALLACIOUS ETIOLOGIC INFERENCES FROM THEMATIC INFINITY

FALLACIOUS ETIOLOGIC INFERENCES IN THE CASE HISTORIES OF THE RAT MAN AND THE WOLF MAN

As we saw in the case of the Rat Man, Freud appealed to the thematic kinship between the punitive biting episode and the adult rat obsessions as his basis for inferring an *etiologic linkage* between them. But, as is now clear, the thematic connection adduced by Freud does *not* vouch for the *etiologic role* of the paternal punishment in the pathogenesis of the rat obsessions. And Freud simply begs the etiologic question here by trading on thematic affinity. Furthermore, as I have noted elsewhere,[47] in the case of his Wolf Man, Freud appealed to a thematic affinity of upright physical posture as a basis for fallaciously inferring an etiologic connection between an eighteen-month-old child's presumably witnessing *a tergo* intercourse between his parents and his wolf obsessions in adult life.

FALLACIOUS ETIOLOGIC INFERENCES IN THE THEORY OF TRANSFERENCE

An equally unfavorable epistemic judgment applies to the web of causal inferences that were drawn in Freud's theory of transference, which I have articulated. For argument's sake, let us grant the retrodictive inference that the patient's behavior toward the doctor does actually recapitulate *thematically* scenarios from the patient's childhood. Then this thematically recapitulatory behavior toward the psychoanalyst does *not* itself *show* that the behavior is also *pathogenically* recapitulatory, because it does *not* show that the *original* childhood scenario had been *pathogenic* at all in the first place. Yet that is precisely what the psychoanalyst infers. How, for example, does the reenact-ment, during treatment, of a patient's early conflict show that the original conflict had been at all pathogenic in the first place?

So much for my appraisal of Freud's own handling of so-called meaning connections. But what of the *hermeneutist* objection that Freud gave a "*scientistic*" twist to these connections? Let me use my answer to this question to draw a general twofold moral for the human sciences.

CONCLUSIONS

I have argued that it is always fallacious to infer a causal linkage between thematically kindred events from their mere thematic kinship. Yet it *may* happen that *additional* information will sustain such a causal inference in certain cases. Thus, as illustrated by my example of Agnes's dream about the "Falling Water" mansion, the existence of a strong thematic connection between two mental events, or two series of such events, does *not militate* against there *also* being a causal linkage between them. Thus, Freud should surely *not* be faulted for asserting, in principle, that some mental events can be linked *both* thematically *and* causally, though he mistakenly claimed entitlement to *infer* the causal linkage from the thematic one alone.

Yet as I remarked at the outset, the German philosopher and psychia-trist Karl Jaspers chided Freud: "In Freud's work we are dealing in fact with *psychology of meaning*, not *causal explanation* as Freud himself thinks."[48] But since *causal relevance* is entirely *compatible* with *thematic* or so-called meaning *kinship*, Jaspers's objection to Freud here rests on a *pseudo-antithesis* of "either . . . or."[49] Thus, there is no merit in Jaspers's indictment of Freud as having incurred a "confusion of meaningful connexions with causal connexions."[50] Nor is there warrant for his claim that Freud's psychoanalysis is being vitiated by "a misunderstanding of itself,"[51] a patronizing charge echoed later on by Ricoeur and Habermas, as we recall.

As against these philosophers, it emerges precisely from my demonstra-tion of Freud's *inferential failings* that he gave *much too much* explanatory weight to thematic affinities, rather than too little, as they have charged. Indeed, such mere "meaning connections" tell us nothing about the supposed unconscious *motives* or causes for symptom-formation, dream-genesis, and the provenance of Freudian slips. Yet such a motivational account is pre-cisely what psychoanalytic theory claims to offer.

I draw a *twofold moral* for the human sciences from my stated criticisms of Freud and of his hermeneutic critics: (1) Let us indeed be alert to thematic connections, but do beware of their beguiling *causal* pitfalls, a fortiori. (2) Narratives replete with mere hermeneutic elucidations of thematic affinities are explanatorily sterile or bankrupt; at best, they have *literary* and reporto-rial value, which may be useful as such; at worst, they are mere cock-and-bull-stories lacking both etiologic and therapeutic significance.

Patronizing hermeneutic sermons by Jaspers, Habermas, and Ricoeur against alleged "scientistic" misunderstandings of the role of meanings do nothing, in my view, for the fruition of the psychoanalytic enterprise, or for any other *explanatory* theories of human psychology or of history. What they tend to do, however, is foster *ideological hostility* to scientific thought in the social sciences and in psychology. As I have argued elsewhere at length,[52] after a veritable cornucopia of brilliantly articulated thematic connections in Freud's case history of the Rat Man, a validated etiology of the patient's obsessions *remains deeply obscure* to this very day, over eighty years later. Similarly for the Wolf Man.

But that is not all. To my mind, it speaks volumes that those who espouse the hermeneutic reconstruction of psychoanalysis have *not* come up with a single *new* psychoanalytic hypothesis that would demonstrate the fruitfulness of their approach. Theirs is a negativistic ideological battle cry and a blind alley. After a while, it ought to die a well-deserved death from its sheer sterility.

Often, a new interpretation or reconstruction of a theory, or a new style in philosophy —even when flawed by major errors—nonetheless can be illuminating in *some* respects. Hence I regret to say that, as I see it, the dichotomous hermeneutic reconstruction of psychoanalysis and of the human or social sciences generally *has no redeeming features*.

The hermeneutic philosophers have tried to force psychoanalysis onto the Procrustean bed of their preconceived philosophic notions about the human sciences. To implement this program, they begged the epistemological questions by simply downgrading those features of the Freudian corpus that did not fit their prior philosophic doctrines. And, as a normative recipe for the human sciences generally, their program seems to me to darken counsel.

NOTES

1. K. Jaspers. "Causal and 'Meaningful' Connexions Between Life History and Psychosis," in: S. Hirsch and M. Shepard, eds., *Themes and Variations in European Psychiatry* (Charlottesville: University of Virginia Press, 1974), 91.

2. P. Ricoeur, *Freud and Philosophy* (New Haven: Yale University Press, 1970), 359.

3. J. Connolly and T. Keutner, eds., *Hermeneutics Versus Science?* (Notre Dame: University of Notre Dame Press, 1988).

4. R. Sullivan, Book Review of "Hermeneutics Versus Science?," *Philosophy of the Social Sciences 23*, No. 2 (June 1993).

5. J. Phillips, "Hermeneutics in Psychoanalysis," *Psychoanalysis & Contemporary Thought 14* (1991): 382.

6. P. Rubovitz-Seitz, Letter to the editor, *Journal of the American Psychoanalytic Association 42*, No. 4 (1994): 1311.

7. M. Edelson, *Psychoanalysis: A Theory in Crisis* (Chicago: University of Chicago Press, 1988), 246–249, chap. 11.

8. Ibid., 247–248.

9. Ricoeur, *Freud and Philosophy*, 359.

10. S. Freud, "Psychoanalysis: Freudian School," in *Encyclopedia Britannica*, vol.14 (New York, 1929), 673.

11. All citations of Freud's writings in English are from the *Standard Edition of the Complete Psychological Works of Sigmund Freud*, translated by J. Strachey et al. (London: Hogarth Press, 1953–1974), 24 vols. Each reference will use the abbreviation "S.E." followed by the year of first appearance, volume number, and page(s).

12. A. Grünbaum, *Validation in the Clinical Theory of Psychoanalysis: A Study in the Philosophy of Psychoanalysis* (Madison, CT: International Universities Press, 1993), 115.

13. A. Grünbaum, " 'Meaning' Connections and Causal Connections in the Human Sciences: The Poverty of Hermeneutic Philosophy," *Journal of the American Psychoanalytic Association* 38 (1990): 559–577.

14. Grünbaum, *Validation in the Clinical Theory of Psychoanalysis: A Study in the Philosophy of Psychoanalysis*, op. cit., Chap. 4.

15. A. Stephan. *Sinn Als Bedeutung: Bedeutungstheoretische Untersuchungen Zur Psychoanalyse Sigmund Freud's*. (Berlin and New York: Walter de Gruyter, 1989), 144–149.

16. Quotations from Stephan below are my English translations of his German text.

17. Ricoeur, *Freud and Philosophy*, 123.

18. Stephan, *Sinn Als Bedeutung: Bedeutungstheoretische Untersuchungen Zur Psychoanalyse Sigmund Freud's*, 146. item (3).

19. Ibid., 148.

20. Ibid., 148–149.

21. Ibid., 149.

22. F. Brentano, *Psychology from an Empirical Standpoint* (New York: Routledge & Kegan Paul Ltd., 1995).

23. M. Carrier and J. Mittelstrass, *Mind, Brain, Behavior: The Mind-Body Problem and the Philosophy of Psychology* (New York: Walter de Gruyter, 1991), 68.

24. Brentano, *Psychology from an Empirical Standpoint*, 89–91.

25. J. Searle, *Intentionally* (New York: Cambridge University Press, 1990), Chap. 1.

26. Ibid., 2.

27. Ibid., 161–167.

28. Ibid., 175.

29. Ibid., 5, 160, and 177.

30. S. Toulmin, "The Logical Status of Psycho-Analysis," in M. MacDonald, ed., *Philosophy and Analysis* (New York: Philosophical Library, 1954), 138–139. Reprinted from *Analysis* 9(1948).

31. Ibid., 134.

32. Ibid., 139.

33. Ibid., 134.

34. Ricoeur, *Freud and Philosophy*, 359–360.

35. M. Sherwood, *The Logic of Explanation in Psychoanalysis* (New York: Academic Press, 1969).

36. P. Ricoeur, *Hermeneutics and the Human Sciences* (New York: Cambridge University Press, 1981), 262–263.

37. B. Rubinstein, "Freud's Early Theories of Hysteria," in R. S. Cohen and L. Laudan, eds., *Physics, Philosophy and Psychoanalysis: Essays in Honor of Adolf Grünbaum* (Dordrecht and Boston: D. Reidel Publishing Co., 1983; reprinted 1992), 187.

38. Ricoeur, *Freud and Philosophy*, 358.

39. C. Brenner, *The Mind in Conflict* (New York: International Universities Press, 1982), 4.

40. B. Rubinstein, "On the Role of Classifactory Processes in Mental Functioning: Aspects of a Psychoanalytic Theoretical Model," *Psychoanalysis and Contemporary Science* 3 (1975): 104–105.

41. Edelson, *Psychoanalysis: A Theory in Crisis*, 246–251.

42. A. Grünbaum, *The Foundations of Psychoanalysis: A Philosophical Critique* (Berkeley: University of California Press, 1984), 149–150. There are German, Italian, Japanese, and Hungarian translations.

43. Grünbaum, *Validation in the Clinical Theory of Psychoanalysis: A Study in the Philosophy of Psychoanalysis*, 152–158.

44. cf. Grünbaum, *The Foundations of Psychoanalysis: A Philosophical Critique*, 63.

45. E. Sober, "Parsimony, Likelihood, and the Principle of the Common Cause," *Philosophy of Science* 54 (1987): 465–469.

46. E. Sober, "The Principle of the Common Cause," in J. Fetzer, ed., *Probability and Causality* (Dordrecht and Boston: D. Reidel Publishing Co., 1988), 211–228.

47. A. Grünbaum, "The Role of the Case Study Method in the Foundations of Psychoanalysis," *Canadian Journal of Philosophy* 18 (1988): Sec. III, 654–657. Reprinted from *Die Philosophen und Freud*, L. Nagl and H. Vetter, eds. (Vienna, Austria: R. Oldenbourg Verlag, 1988).

48. Jaspers, "Causal and 'Meaningful' Connexions Between Life History and Psychosis," 91.

49. cf. Grünbaum, *The Foundations of Psychoanalysis: A Philosophical Critique*, 69–83.

50. Jaspers, "Causal and 'Meaningful' Connexions Between Life History and Psychosis," 91.

51. Ibid., 80.

52. Grünbaum, *Validation in the Clinical Theory of Psychoanalysis: A Study in the Philosophy of Psychoanalysis*, Chap. 4.

EIGHT

THE POSSIBILITY OF A
SCIENTIFIC PSYCHOANALYSIS

JOSEPH MARGOLIS

I

IT IS, I DARESAY, beyond dispute that Freud and Lacan formulated their theories of the human mind on the basis of an intense and sustained psycho-analytic practice. But what is it that they actually did in doing that, in formulating their picture of the human mind?

We know from Freud's letters to Wilhelm Fliess of his extreme discom-fort regarding the "literary" or "poetic" cast of his early clinical reflections as well as his inability to destroy the actual manuscript of the *Scientific Project* (1895), whose obsessive materialism—which Freud describes as "a kind of economics of nervous force"[1]—utterly failed to stem the profoundly inten-tional and subjective thrust of his own evolving psychological idiom. It gradu-ally dawned on Freud that his "neuronal machinery" was simply unable to provide a description or an explanation of "the property of being conscious or not." He took consciousness to be a "fundamental fact"—an ineliminable posit—in any adequate psychology, a theme he himself noted was disas-trously abandoned by American behaviorism. For reasons of this sort, Freud's conception of scientific discipline clearly departed from the scientism he favored as a medical student.

Of course, there could not fail to be a deep connection between Lacan's theory and practice and Freud's original work: one could hardly have been

161

a psychoanalyst in Lacan's time without submitting to Freud's immense influence. But Lacan is also thought to have been original—even maverick—in a deeper sense than the usual run of the early luminaries of the psychoanalytic world who were personally and professionally associated with Freud; when one asks about the connection between Freud's and Lacan's theory and practice, one asks for word about a significant conceptual departure that begins somehow, as Lacan would say, with a "return to Freud." The fact is, Lacan was expelled, in 1953, under a cloud of professional acrimony, from the International Psychoanalytical Association, which signaled the depth of his departure from any canonical Freud, though he himself viewed the event in terms of a deeper recovery of Freud's most original themes.[2]

What Lacan meant by his "return" involved the recovery of the central role of the unconscious in Freud's psychodynamics and its correction along the lines of his own innovations. Here what may be the best-known of Lacan's explanatory pronouncements runs as follows:

> My doctrine of the signifier is first of all a discipline in which those I train have to familiarize themselves with the different ways in which the signifier effects the advent of the signified, which is the only conceivable way that interpretation can produce anything new.
>
> For interpretation is based on no assumption of divine archetypes, but on the fact that the unconscious is structured in the most radical way like a language, that a material operates in it according to certain laws, which are the same laws as those discovered in the study of actual languages, languages that are or were actually spoken.[3]

Viewed simplistically (though not inaptly), Freud's achievement centers on his having assembled with great force the stunning evidence offered in the interval from *The Interpretation of Dreams* (1900) to the metapsychological papers of 1915 that confirm the ubiquity of the unconscious and a great many of its principal mechanisms—displacement, concatenation, association, substitution, metonymy, symbolism, and the like—by which repressed materials "rise" to consciousness. What Lacan produced, in turn, was a ramified, enormously bold radicalization of Freud's themes cast in terms of an analogue of Saussure's and Lévi-Strauss's structuralist conceptual machinery adjusted in an increasingly ample way in favor of his own psychogenetic themes. In one sense, Lacan converts the verbal process by which the psychoanalytic exchange between analyst and analysand proceeds into the constitutive medium of unconscious processes themselves. But in another sense, he alters, by the first "correction," the very source and nature of unconscious processes. In effect, the unconscious becomes a thoroughly cultural medium for Lacan, whereas it remains essentially biological (or biochemical) for Freud. Here you have, in very general terms, the key to the continuity and discontinuity between Freud and Lacan without regard to their particular theories of such fundamental psychological structures as the Oedipal complex, narcis-sism, ego formation, and the like. The contrast may be the single most important legible distinction between their respective metapsychologies.

If you bear in mind the small passage cited from *Ecrits*, then the fol-lowing passages from the important final chapter of *The Interpretation of Dreams* (ch. 7) help to establish very quickly the principal differences be-tween Freud's and Lacan's orientation regarding the unconscious. Freud, I would say, is incomparably clear in his attempt to explain his notion of the unconscious—an enormously tangled but not conceptually obscure or difficult idea. He offers two insights: the first, to locate the analyst's account in terms of scientific methodology; the second, to give us his best conjecture about the general topology of psychical space in which the unconscious relates, one way or another, to consciousness. You must remember that, in 1896, when, apparently, *Interpretation* was completely drafted (though it was printed in 1899 and released in 1900), Freud had not yet formed a suitably developed account of sexuality (by his own lights); so that he treats the *Interpretation* volume largely in terms of the developing rigor of the strategies of interpre-tation viewed procedurally. In the first passage he says:

> It is true that the physician cannot learn of [say, the] unconscious processes [of a neurotic] until they have produced some effect upon consciousness which can be communicated or observed. But this conscious effect may exhibit a psychical character quite different from that of the unconscious process, so that internal perception cannot possibly regard the one as a substitute for the other. The physician must feel at liberty to proceed by *inference* from the con-scious effect to the unconscious psychical process. He thus learns that the conscious effect is only a remote psychical result of the unconscious process and that the latter has not become conscious as such; and moreover that the latter was present and operative even without betraying its existence in any way to consciousness.[4]

The second passage collects the decisive theme of the psychical "topology" informing his "dynamics":

> The new discovery that we have been taught by the analysis of psycho-pathological structures and of the first member of that class— the dream—lies in the fact that the unconscious (that is, the psy-chical) is found as a function of two separate systems and that this is the case in normal as well as in pathological life. Thus there are two kinds of unconscious, which have not yet been distinguished by psychologists. Both of them are unconscious in the sense used by psychology; but in our sense one of them, which we term the *Ucs.*, is also *inadmissable to consciousness*, while we term the other the *Pcs.*

because its excitations—after observing certain rules, it is true, and perhaps only after passing a fresh censorship, though nonetheless without regard to the Ucs.—are able to reach consciousness.[5]

Freud, we may say, biologizes the Ucs.: its relation to consciousness and the Pcs. is purely theoretical—it is completely inaccessible to inspection; hence, the "logic" of its processes are assigned only inferentially. But it must (according to Freud) be in place in some primal sense that is modularly sealed off from any perceptual or cognitive processes. That is, of course, the conceptual link with the theory of the *Scientific Project*, whose language still colors the theoretical parts of the *Interpretation* essay, possibly the whole of Freud's psychoanalytic output. Consciousness (Cs.) is analogized by Freud to the part played by "a sense organ for the perception of psychical qualities" (including "pleasure–unpleasure"); it has, as such, no memory of its own but requires (to account for its own recovery, against repression) a connection with deeper structures that sense our mnemic powers, which are themselves open to being directly affected by the dynamic interaction between Cs. and Ucs. through Pcs.[6]

Lacan essentially makes the Ucs. a culturally formed structure: because, first of all, the unconscious obeys the laws of naturally acquired languages (according to the structuralists' account) and, second, we are said to *know* how it actually is structured, even if we must puzzle out the meaning of its material expression on particular occasions. Lacan hardly follows Freud here.

If we view matters in terms of this fundamental contrast, some forceful findings will seem surprisingly straightforward. First, Freud makes instantly legible the fact *that* unconscious processes *are* at work in dreams, jokes, the parapraxes, literature and art, hysteria, and neurotic behavior; and, second, *that* we can formulate reasonably strong, reasonably confirmable interpretive conjectures about repressed materials drawn from the Pcs. *and* (relative to the validity of our theories about the Ucs. and its relation to the Pcs.) conjectures about the deeper Ucs. Here Freud's principal contribution as a scientific psychoanalyst and theorist of psychoanalysis lies with his making the case he does for the actual existence of the unconscious and its characteristic mode of functioning—on inferential grounds that rely on there not being (otherwise) a convincing way to explain a very large run of familiar manifestations in conscious life. That is, Freud has definitely enlarged our spontaneous run of descriptive and explanatory factors in what may be called our "folk-psychological" idiom.[7] Even nonprofessional observers have enlarged their descriptive and explanatory resources conformably and fluently.

The point is: Freud's theory of the unconscious does not depend on his discoveries of the Oedipal complex, neurosis, narcissism, and the like; on the contrary, *those* discoveries invoke the processes of unconscious life itself. The analyst is always subject to his or her own reactive transference, but there is no question (for Freud) that he can, in principle, provide an objective account of his analysand's unconscious processes. There is a sense, in Lacan, that this is *never* true in the analytic context; yet, of course, if it is offered, it must be true that *someone* can confirm the fact! Lacan acknowledges this implicitly but never quite provides for its systematic admission. It would force an adjustment in his theory. He assigns the dynamics of psychical life largely to the unconscious, but he is remarkably frugal regarding the psychology of objective confirmation.

It is true that this entire idiom (Freud's, paradigmatically) has been challenged (not always explicitly) as profoundly mistaken.[8] It remains something of an unresolved question philosophically, but then, subject to its resolution (which is hardly pending, unless the evidence may already be taken to go against eliminativism), Freud has plainly strengthened the "folk-sciences" (in effect, the "human sciences" as distinct from the "physical sciences"), has added considerably to their resources and scope and sense of rigor, and has surely strengthened our appreciation of the full import of the contest between the "scientific" and "folk" conceptions of our mental life. That is, I take it to be decisive that the phenomena regarding the unconscious, which Freud isolates both descriptively and explanatorily, have been spontaneously coopted at the folk-theoretical level as a natural extension or enrichment of our common idiom of description and explanation.

Freud's explanatory mechanisms, whether in terms of the logic of dream construction (say) or in terms of the theory of dreams as forms of wish fulfillment or of the dynamics of the Oedipal complex, are certainly open to challenge. But they enjoy (and are entitled to claim) a prima-facie plausibility comparable in all regards to older parts of our folk account. Put another way: assuming, for the sake of argument, that eliminativism and materialist reduction remain unconfirmed—my own conviction, frankly, is that they are less than promising—then a viable theory of science will have to come to terms with our "folk-theoretic" descriptions and explanations wherever (as in the human sciences) we cannot yet invoke any radically physicalistic account of the entire human world.

Lacan's innovations, read as possible adjustments or enlargements of Freud's collection of psychic mechanisms, would, of course, enjoy the same methodological tolerance. The trouble is, Lacan would not be willing to subordinate his "linguistic" or artifactual account of the unconscious to the biologized convention Freud favors. The reason, as we will see, is bound up with a fundamental paradox at the basis of Lacan's theory of the unconscious: to have subscribed to Freud's model would have restricted in a fundamental way the scope of Lacan's conception of the unconscious.

To return to the deeper philosophical question: I don't believe we have any clear-cut canon of scientific procedure that would permit us to pronounce with assurance on the difference between science and nonscience or on the application or violation of any would-be canon of scientific rigor. I have always been impressed, for instance, by the fact that Galileo's splendid conjecture about imperceptible motion—for which he did not have the slight-est empirical evidence, according to the best views of scientific rigor favored in his day—implicates an improvisational element in the practice of science itself, an element that cannot be captured by any fixed or determinate canon. Certainly, there is no settled "inductive" or "falsificationist" rule or procedure that anyone could seriously advance.[9] It is in fact much too easy to disqualify unfavorable data in any science (but particularly the human sciences) as failing to measure up to the supposed mark of what a "science" should be, by simply stonewalling on what a science rightly demands or sanctions.

Here, for instance, is a fashionable view that, taken seriously, would rule out of bounds at a single stroke the entire psychoanalytic undertaking—the author is Daniel Dennett:

> The Behaviorists [Dennett says] were meticulous about avoiding speculation about what was going on in my mind or your mind or his or her or its mind. In effect, they championed the third-person perspective, in which only facts garnered "from the outside" count as data. . . . The idea at its simplest was that since you can never "see directly" into people's minds, but have to take their word for it, any such facts as there are about mental events are not among the data of science, since they can never be properly verified by objec-tive methods. This methodological scruple . . . is the ruling prin-ciple of all experimental psychology and neuroscience today (not just "behaviorist" research). . . . [A]ll science is constructed from [the third-person point of view].[10]

I'm afraid Dennett must believe that saying all this emphatically makes it so. But any careful review of the history of the philosophy of science would make it more than clear that we simply lack a compelling philosophical ruling on the matter: not the least evidence for which being that we do have good reason to believe, as a result of the work of the tradition that runs from Kant to Hegel, that there is no coherent, no defensible way to segregate the analysis of the objective world and the analysis of the epistemic conditions on which we claim to know the way the world is; hence, no way to segregate the would-be cognitive resources of the first- and third-person points of view. That is a most strategically placed verdict. But of course, if the objection were allowed (against Dennett and against others—Adolf Grünbaum, say), then it would be reasonable to suppose that the differences in the properties of the physical and human worlds oblige us to consider the methodological difference in the respective sciences that address their characteristic data.

You must see that there cannot be any scientific psychoanalysis of Freud's or Lacan's sort if there is no ground for admitting first-person avowals, reports, confessions, conjectures that *are not* invariantly matched, though they *are* (certainly) reliably linked and (often) detectable from the "third-person" vantage. If you consider such puzzles as those regarding the visually "apparent" size and distance of the moon under what are generally admitted to be experimental conditions, Goethe's and Helmholz's conjectures about the perceptual hue of a curl of cigar smoke, the alterability of the apparent relative size and distance of the Müller-Lyer lines vis-à-vis one another, the reliable correlation between the interoceptive discrimination of the placement of the limbs and bodily conditions and the results of "external" perception, diplopia, and related perceptual disorders plainly open to medical explanation and treatment, the discrimination of pain (as in dental and chiropractic cases) as bridging the difference between bare sensations and perceptual modalities, color blindness and the very perception of hues as such, the methodology for discerning the difference between perceptual hallucination and actual sensory perception, you begin to see the impoverishment (and even the incoherence) that result from disjoining first- and third-person "points of view" in any viable account of scientific practice.

Add to this the familiar puzzles regarding personal intentions and intentional distinctions and you will have begun to lay the ground for the impossibility of disallowing the scientific status of psychoanalysis itself. The decisive lesson is that the scientific standing of psychoanalysis *cannot* be settled by reference to the criterial conditions of objectivity that belong to the very conception of a science. There are no prior findings to draw on.

II

If the history of the theory of science has taught us anything, it is surely that science has no strict canons or methods, must be open-ended, and must remain profoundly improvisational. The same is true, of course, of "induction" and "confirmation" and "falsification." Also, any talk of the exceptionless adequacy of materialism or extensionalism or behaviorism or computationalism or anything of the kind is completely utopian when matched with the actual work of practicing "scientists."[11]

It's in this spirit, in any case, that I suggest that the contribution of Freud and Lacan to the theory of the mind cannot be defeated or demeaned by whatever may be their own limitations and mistakes regarding the empirical import of what they have produced. Put another way: if Freud and Lacan have contributed to our understanding of the human mind, then what we should count as a relevant psychological "science" will have to accommodate whatever they have in that regard disclosed—at whatever level of reflection invites the question of the scientific standing of psychoanalysis itself. We cannot really pretend to judge (with Dennett, say) whether *their* would-be contributions are valid, on the grounds that they have or have not met the established canons of scientifically acceptable work. I am not objecting to rigor as such, of course, but rigor is wherever it is actually found—in accord with a proper grasp of what is possible and what has been convincingly established. There is no principled disjunction or hierarchical ordering between first-order and second-order inquiry: every would-be empirical discovery challenges the closure and adequacy of whatever methodological canons are thought to be in force *ante*. The guardians of science are whistling in the wind, and we would be fools to admit their authority.

Since Freud thinks of the libidinal dispositions of the inaccessibly unconscious *id* as biologically given—apparently autonomous, possibly even innate in a genetic sense—he needs a strong conception of the reality and the reality-testing of the psychodynamics of repressed materials generated from painful experiences in the real world and relieved through therapy. He cannot, on his own theory, derive a "reality principle" from the id directly. So he opts for an ontogenesis of ego and superego from the sources of the id. The theory of the id (as distinct but not separable from the theory of the existence of the unconscious) presupposes his account of infantile sexuality and so is absent in the *Scientific Project*.

We find there, however, an anticipation, along materialist lines, of the need to discharge cathexis—quantities of a putative biochemical source—that takes two forms, an unimpeded flow of Q through a network of neurones and a relatively static buildup of Q within particular neurones. The organism needs to be "defended" against a buildup of Q, which suggests the unconscious teleology that finds relief in psychical processes for discharging cathexis (in effect, the buildup of Q), where Q itself, being material, comes from real sources.[12]

Freud abandons the *Project's* theory, though not its materialism and not his conviction about recovering a scientific psychology. But once launched on his psychoanalytic practice, he does not regard his older loyalties as disallowing the postulation of consciousness and the unconscious; gradually, his sense of scientific rigor accommodates the interpretive turn that proves irresistible once the clinical importance of "the dream" becomes clear. One can also find a certain figurative use of the quantitative idiom that Freud developed in the *Project* applied to the generally qualitative, intentional idiom of his mature psychoanalysis. It needs to be said that Freud is at his most scrupulous in explaining his scientific conjectures—where, for instance, he has no supporting evidence about this or that supposed neuronal functioning or where he is frankly making an educated guess (the salient experiences of infantile sexuality, say).

The main impression of his theorizing lies with his good sense, his avoidance of arbitrariness, his economy, and his generally conservative inventions in an area that might easily call for wild conjectures. The theory of infantile sexuality is, of course, his most radical innovation: there, one must admit, the question of "scientific validity" is at its most extreme—*not* by any means wild but certainly bold and iconoclastic. Without it, the entire theory would be hopeless. Hence, all the more reason for remarking the plausibility and empirical scruple of Freud's conjectures. Needless to say, it is here, as also in developmental hypotheses about narcissism, the Oedipal situation, the significance of the phallus, and the like, that Freud and *all* his most important disciples, opponents, and successors are bound to diverge. Just think of Melanie Klein's particular form of daring, for instance, and you begin to see the point and possibility of Lacan's departures (which are altogether different and more radical, of course). But these are comparatively ordinary, garden-variety empirical questions.

Freud's account of the distinction between the unconscious and the conscious changes decisively with the penetration of his studies of repression (as in hysteria) and the elaboration of the nature of the id and ego in the context of his account of the instincts and the psychic development of the human organism. Here, his principal essay is *The Ego and the Id* (1923), which rounds out his original speculation. The key theme is, of course, the replacement of a simple bifurcation between the conscious and the unconscious by a psychical evolution of the ego (as well as the superego) from the id. Freud is at his clearest and most explicit here; he is always aware of further possible complications, but he minimizes his didactic account to emphasize the most salient and familiar complications. The result is that his theorizing is always linked to commonplace and indisputable experiences acknowledged at the "folk-theoretic" level. The only place in *The Ego and the Id* where this is not quite true concerns the instantiation of the so-called death drive, which Freud is unwilling to relinquish; but he is entirely open about the fact.[13] I think this accounts in good measure for the enormous plausibility of Freud's metapsychology and the ease with which ordinary untrained observers find it relatively easy to fall in with Freud's analytic orientation. (I mention the fact, because, of course, Lacan affords an entirely different—even opposed—impression.) One usually enters Lacan's speculations at the level of professional analysis: Lacan's metapsychological conjectures are always paradoxical and difficult to admit in their sweeping generality—for instance, in the thesis that the real is impossible.

In any case, Freud's master innovation comes to this: that the unconscious (both the *Ucs.* and the *Pcs.*) are present in the ego, which doctrine might well have been judged to be self-contradictory. Freud offers the following extreme simplification:

> the ego is that part of the id which has been modified by the direct influence of the external world through the medium of the *Pcpt.-Cs.* [i.e., the "perception" of the sensory world as well as of thought-processes, memory, emotions, the affects of repression and censorship and the like]; in a sense, it is the extension of the surface-differentiation. Moreover, the ego seeks to bring the influence of the external world to bear upon the id and its tendencies, and endeavors to substitute the reality principle for the pleasure principle which reigns unrestrictedly in the id. For the ego, perception

plays the part which in the id falls to instinct. The ego represents what may be called reason and common sense, in contrast to the id, which contains the passions.[14]

The "reality principle" is entirely straightforward (quite apart from the rather different question of the various equivocations between dreams and reality). The reason seems to be due to Freud's general biological view of psychical life: even the function of the id (now impossible to equate in any simple way with the unconscious) has its assignable function within the larger life of the human organism.

III

Lacan is at once at a simpler and at a more complex stage of speculation. Because *his* conception of the unconscious entails—as far as I can see—an inextricable linkage between certain significative (or semiotic) structures involving "primary process" operations that are themselves "modeled" on language, possibly even constituted by processes of (semiotic) "condensation" and "displacement" that underlie both linguistic and analogous nonlinguistic structures; whereas Freud reserves the mixing of related semiotic processing (if, following Lacan, we read *The Interpretation of Dreams* conformably, though anachronistically) only for the *Pcs.*, *not the Ucs.*

This single postulate marks the essential difference between Freud and Lacan, as far as the theory of the unconscious is concerned. In the Freudian account, we cannot directly address the instinctual drives of the id (or the *Ucs.*) at all; we can address only its theoretically posited effects *in* the observable linkage between the *Pcs.* and the *Cs.*, as in overt behavior and speech. In the Lacanian account, even the putatively real self, the Freudian ego, is not the actual (or any actual) speaker or agent *whose* instinctual drives are thwarted, displaced, sublimated, or fulfilled: the ego and its "others" are themselves constructs of a prior underlying autonomous (or language-like) process (the unconscious) that, proceeding by metaphoric and metonymic devices according to the laws of a structuralist semiotic (which Lacan invents), replaces the theory of instinctual drives.[15]

In this sense, Lacan's psychoanalysis is an analysis of discourse—or of its true "subject" and the "Other" it addresses (in discourse), the entire field of the unconscious, the agency of all symbolic or semiotic process—in which (more narrowly) psychoanalysis attends to the explication of a range of inevitable disorders that result from the false self-identities generated (at different stages of would-be conscious "development") among communicating *human subjects* (the would-be "subjects" and their "others": in particular, the analysand and his or her analyst).

All the paradoxes of Lacanian analysis—they seem ubiquitous—rest on the "mistaken" identity of the communicants of discourse: analogously, the communicants of unconscious process. The "true" subject and its communicating "other"—paradigmatically, in the psychoanalytic episode—is not the "actual" analysand and his or her "actual" analyst but the unconscious "subject" of "each," who are "themselves" variants of one and the same unconscious bifurcating "signifier"; or, better, the "self"-communicating, relationally divided "subject" and its "other"—functioning symbiotically at the unconscious level and affirming their linked identity in the psychoanalytically defined episode in which an ordinary human subject apparently begins to realize (speaking to his analyst, say) that *he* does not really understand the meaning of what he himself is saying![16] This accounts for the topsy-turvy impression, in Lacan, that the "real" is really "impossible" (inaccessible) in terms of unconscious process, that what "human" subjects appear to offer is "imaginary" or "symbolic" (substituted or displaced) from what is going on at the unconscious level.[17]

It would be entirely reasonable to suggest—reading Lacan as sympathetically as possible, as intending to "return to Freud"—that, although he obviously does not hold to Freud's sense of the "reality principle," which engages (and, in effect, accounts for the emergence of) the ego, he must have been struck by the pivotal importance of Freud's summary of the linkage between the *Pcpt.* and the *Cs.*: as in remarks like this: "In essence a word is after all the mnemic residue of a word that has been heard."[18] This suggests the plausibility of conjecturing that Freud "really" meant to say that, as in dreams and in the analysand's free associations, *it is the unconscious that speaks or thinks.* But that is precisely what Freud *did not mean:* in the double sense that the analysis of unconscious meaning must (for Freud) be the analysis of what (say) the analysand consciously volunteers, which fixes the fact of *what is really said* (thereby inviting interpretation); *and* that it *makes no sense to affirm the reality of speech without affirming the existence of an actual speaking agent,* where, that is, the unconscious is itself posited as the theoretical source of perceivable *effects.*[19]

It is here that one is said to find an affinity between Lacan and Heidegger on the matter of language.[20] But it is really Lévi-Strauss's gloss on Saussure that emboldened Lacan to interpret Freud as he does. Thus, following Lévi-Strauss, he declares:

> Before strictly human relations are established, certain relations have already been determined [regarding a natural semiotic system]. They are taken from whatever nature may offer as supports, supports that are arranged in themes of opposition. Nature provides—I must use the word—signifiers, and these signifiers organize human relations in a creative way, providing them with structures and shaping them. . . . In our time, in the historical period that has seen the formation of a science that may be termed human, but which must be distinguished from any kind of psychosociology, namely linguistics, whose model is

the combinatory operation, functioning spontaneously, of itself, in a presubjective way—it is this linguistic structure that gives its status to the unconscious. It is this structure, in any case, that assures us that there is, beneath the term unconscious, something definable, acceptable and objectifiable. . . . The unconscious, the Freudian concept, is something [altogether] different [from all this].[21]

At one level of analysis, adopting such a conception precludes the Freudian idea of a conflict between adhering to the "pleasure principle" and adhering to the "reality principle." At a deeper level, the counterpart thesis (whether Lévi-Strauss's or Lacan's) risks incoherence, since it would signify that the unconscious speaks more or less in the same way that you and I ("seem to") speak! Otherwise, the extreme notion that language speaks through us—the Heideggerean formula—would inform the structuralist account of discourse in a way (I might add) that could be called Cartesian (if the Cartesian subject could also be manifested as the structuralist "subject" of discourse).[22] The underlying intuition seems to be this: (1) that the "real" structure of language and discourse is an analogue of the unconscious—being both prior to it and providing the ground on which it first arises and is formed; and (2) that the "agents" of discourse are doubtful artifacts of autonomous pragmatic processes, as are the human subjects of psychoanalysis.

Here, I plead insuperable—but not fatal—paradox. I have no competence to judge the fruitfulness of Lacan's schematism for interpreting psychoanalytic material. It evidently permits Lacan to reverse our usual associations in surprising (possibly productive) ways—particularly in ways that deny the literal sense and reference of anything we say. So that (by his own appropriation of Roman Jakobson's distinction between metonymy and metaphor)[23] any utterance or text can be instantly drawn into the intricacies of unconscious processes.[24]

What I must emphasize is that Lacan obviously avails himself of the *realist discourse of ordinary science and practical exchange* to affirm the validity of his psychoanalytic practice and theory; but, unlike Freud, *his* theory appears to afford no legible space for the very conditions (whatever they may be) under which the theory of the unconscious *is* valid. The trouble is that to make the correction—if a correction is really needed, as I believe it is—is inevitably to alter the theory of the "subject" *who* speaks and acts: in such a way that Lacan's account and practice are put at insuperable risk. For, the appeal to "scientific objectivity" requires criterial considerations that override the apparent agencies of the unconscious and make provision for admitting the unconscious process in the first place. Nevertheless, I can see how all this could be tolerated within the terms of an actual psychoanalytic practice. What I cannot see (or cannot yet see) is how the practice yields a coherent metapsychology that could (in its own terms) be an alternative to Freud's. I see how it could be "corrected"; but I cannot see how a correction could actually support Lacan's account of the unconscious subject. Here, I can do no more than locate Lacan's paradox; I have just cited one telltale passage: Before strictly human relations are established, certain relations *have already been determined*. Strictly speaking, this means that "human relations" are made intelligible within and only within the terms of the structured processes of the unconscious; but it also means that the validity of Lacan's "discovery" *of* the modes of unconscious functioning is not always relevantly subject to the dynamics of the unconscious itself. Otherwise, the theory would risk incoherence. It seems an obvious point. But I see no way of accommodating it without altering fundamentally Lacan's own theory of the human subject.[25] Of course, the paradox, if it is a genuine paradox, is precisely the same puzzle that confronts the whole of post-Saussurean structuralism—without yet insisting on the essential fixity of the human subject.

NOTES

1. Sigmund Freud, "Project for a Scientific Psychology," *The Standard Edition of the Complete Psychological Works of Sigmund Freud*, vol. 1, James Strachey et al., trans. (London: The Hogarth Press and the Institute of Psycho-Analysis, 1966); the remark is cited on p. 283 (from Letter 24: May 25, 1895).

2. See Malcolm Bowie, *Freud, Proust and Lacan: Theory as Fiction* (Cambridge: Cambridge University Press, 1987), ch. 4, and *Lacan* (Cambridge: Harvard University Press, 1991).

3. Jacques Lacan, "The direction of the treatment and the principles of its power," *Ecrits: A Selection*, Alan Sheridan, trans. (New York: W. W. Norton, 1977), 233–234.

4. Sigmund Freud, *The Interpretation of Dreams*, *The Standard Edition of the Complete Psychological Works of Sigmund Freud*, vol. 5, James Strachey et al., trans. (London: The Hogarth Press and the Institute of Psycho-Analysis, 1958), 612.

5. Ibid., 614–615.

6. Ibid., 615–616.

7. The term has been made a term of art by Paul M. Churchland, in *A Neurocomputational Perspective: The Nature of Mind and the Structure of Science* (Cambridge: MIT Press, 1989). Churchland's thesis is that the "folk-psychological" theory is irretrievably false and will and must be replaced. I suggest, in opposing Churchland, that the materials of the folk-psychological account are not "theoretical" in the usual way or are largely not; and that all theories that can be effectively contested implicate our reliance, one way or another, on certain core conceptual regularities of the folk-psychological vision.

8. See, for additional specimen views, Wilfrid Sellars, *Science, Perception and Reality* (London: Routledge and Kegan Paul, 1963), and D. C. Dennett, *Content and Consciousness* (London: Routledge and Kegan Paul, 1969).

9. This goes very much against the well-known claims of Adolf Grünbaum, *The Foundations of Psychoanalysis* (Berkeley: University of California Press, 1984) and *Validation in the Clinical Theory of Psychoanalysis: A Study in the Philosophy of Psychoanalysis* (Madison: International Universities Press, 1993).

10. Daniel C. Dennett, *Consciousness Explained* (Boston: Little, Brown, 1991), 70–71; see also Daniel C. Dennett, *Darwin's Dangerous Idea: Evolution and the Meaning of Life* (New York: Simon & Schuster, 1995).

11. For a particularly egregious pronouncement on the "canon" of contemporary science, see Henry Plotkin, *Evolution in Mind. An Introduction to Evolutionary Psychology* (Cambridge: Harvard University Press, 1998), 88.

12. Freud, *Project for a Scientific Psychology*, Part I. Compare *The Interpretation of Dreams*, ch. 7, sec. E.

13. See Sigmund Freud, *The Ego and the Id, The Standard Edition of the Complete Psychological Works of Sigmund Freud*, vol. 19, James Strachey et al., trans. (London: The Hogarth Press and the Institute of Psycho-Analysis, 1961), ch. 4.

14. Freud, "The Ego and the Id," 25.

15. See, for instance, Jacques Lacan, "The function and field of speech and language in psychoanalysis," *Ecrits: A Selection*, Alan Sheridan, trans. (New York: W. W. Norton, 1977), for example, Lacan's summary remarks: "What we teach the subject to recognize as his unconscious is his history"; "every fixation at a so-called instinctual stage is above all a historical scar"; "the instinctual stages, when they are being lived, are already organized in subjectivity" (p. 52).

16. I have found extremely helpful the overview of Lacan's psychoanalytic theory offered in Juan-David Nasio, *Five Lessons on the Psychoanalytic Theory of Jacques Lacan*, David Pettigrew and François Raffoul, trans. (Albany: State University of New York Press, 1998). Nasio is not entirely in accord with Lacan. But I cannot see any more perspicuous way of reading Lacan than along the general lines Nasio lays out. In particular, Nasio makes very plausible the idea that the identity of the unconscious subject belongs to the "in-between" (in Heidegger's sense) in the communicative process. All the otherwise perplexing puzzles of Lacan's metapsychology become strangely legible. But then *that* idea itself generates the ultimate paradox of Lacan's entire formulation. For we are to suppose that the doctrine *has* scientific status, which is to say some cognizing subject (outside the space of unconscious thought) construes the processes of the unconscious correctly.

17. See, for example, Nasio, *Five Lessons on the Psychoanalytic Theory of Jacques Lacan*, 45–47, 73–80.

18. Freud, *The Ego and the Id*, 21.

19. For a compelling analysis of this aspect of Lacan's thought, see Antoine Vergote, "From Freud's 'Other Scene' to Lacan's 'Other,'" in Joseph H. Smith and William Kerrigan, eds., *Interpreting Lacan* (New Haven: Yale University Press, 1983).

20. But see Lacan's own comment: Jacques Lacan, "The Freudian Unconscious and Ours," *The Four Fundamental Concepts of Psycho-Analysis*, Alan Sheridan, trans. (New York: W. W. Norton, 1981), p. 18.

21. Lacan, "The Freudian Unconscious and Ours," 20–21.

22. See, for instance, William J. Richardson, "Lacan and the Subject of Psychoanalysis," in Joseph H. Smith and William Kerrigan, eds., *Interpreting Lacan* (New Haven: Yale University Press, 1983).

23. See Roman Jakobson and Morris Halle, *Fundamentals of Language* (The Hague: Mouton, 1956).

24. See, for example, Jacques Lacan, "The Freudian Thing, or the Meaning of the Return to Freud in Psychoanalysis," *Ecrits: A Selection*, Alan Sheridan, trans. (New York: W. W. Norton, 1977), particularly 139–142. Compare Slavoj Žižek,

"Beyond Discourse-Analysis," in Ernesto Laclau, *New Reflections on the Revolution of Our Times* (London: Verso, 1990) for an example of how to apply the Lacanian schema to the analysis of political life.

25. The most sustained attempt at analyzing Lacan's paradoxes that I know of can be found in François Roustang, *The Lacanian Delusion*, Greg Sims, trans. (New York: Oxford University Press, 1990), ch. 2. Roustang's challenges are carefully presented and need to be answered.

NINE

INCOMPLETENESS AND EXPERIMENTAL UNTESTABILITY IN PSYCHOANALYSIS

Donald Levy

Nebuchadnezzar, the king had dreams that left his mind no peace and deprived him of sleep. So he had the magicians enchanters, sorcerers, and Chaldeans summoned, that they might tell him what he had dreamed. When they came and presented themselves before the king, he said to them, "I had a dream that will leave my mind no peace until I know what it is . . . tell me the dream, that I may be sure that you can also give its interpretation." The Chaldeans answered the king . . . "What the king is asking is so difficult that no one but divine beings can reveal it to him, and their abode is not among mortal men."

—*The Book of Daniel*

If God had looked into our minds he would not have been able to see there whom we were speaking of.

—Wittgenstein

MANY INTELLIGENT, serious people come away from an examination of Freud's thought with the firm impression that "a complete interdisciplinary science of mind"[1] was what he had hoped to achieve, and thought he had succeeded in producing. On that reading, the founder of psychoanalysis can even be seen as a rival to Plato insofar as both, it is supposed, created incompatible theories of human nature,[2] including equally incompatible,

177

"grand, coherent . . . theories of love."[3] Probably, there is much in the words and deeds of Freud and his followers that has given rise to such an impression, and much also in the response to psychoanalysis, both popular and learned, that has nurtured it. But however much there may be to support that way of understanding Freud, there is much more to be said for the opposing view, which emphasizes the numerous kinds of *incompleteness* or limitations self-consciously built into the structure of psychoanalysis by Freud himself. Thus, Freud emphasized that "Psychoanalysis has never claimed to provide a complete theory of human mentality in general, but only expected that what it offered should be applied to supplement and correct the knowledge acquired by other means."[4]

Later, he expanded on the same point—

> If we accept the distinction which I have recently proposed of dividing the mental apparatus into an ego, turned towards the external world and equipped with consciousness, and an unconscious id, dominated by its instinctual needs, then psycho-analysis is to be described as a psychology of the id (and of its influence upon the ego). In each field of knowledge, therefore, it can make only *contributions*, which require to be completed from the psychology of the ego. If these contributions often contain the essence of the facts, this only corresponds to the important part which, it may be claimed, is played in our lives by the mental unconscious that has so long remained unknown.[5]

In a footnote[6] James Strachey exclaims, "Freud seems, in this passage to be imposing unusual restrictions on the scope of psycho-analysis," without any further explanation about why he finds Freud's restrictions unusual. As Robert Waelder (whose remarks on this topic I am partly retracing) observes, concerning Freud's estimate of the range of psychoanalysis,

> Its fundamental conservatism was reinforced by a personal factor, viz., Freud's dislike for sweeping generalizations and for system building. Once, probably towards the end of 1926, the late Dr. Schilder presented a paper on characterology in which he outlined a multidimensional system of classifying character. Freud said in his reply that he felt like someone who had hugged the coast all his life and who now watched others sailing out into the open ocean. He wished them well but could not take part in their ventures: "I am an old hand in the coastal run and I will keep faith with my blue inlets."[7]

But the dislike for sweeping generalizations Waelder refers to was not the only basis for Freud's self-imposed restriction of scope; there are, in addition, individuals about whom analytic efforts are necessarily limited in ways that do not apply to others. "Before the problem of the creative artist analysis must, alas, lay down its arms,"[8] Freud wrote. What he was thinking of comes out in his preface to a book by a psychoanalyst on Edgar Allan Poe:

> In this volume my friend and pupil, Marie Bonaparte, has directed the light of psycho-analysis upon the life and work of a great writer of a pathological type. Thanks to her interpretative efforts, we can now understand how much of the characteristics of his work were determined by their author's special nature; but we also learn that this was itself the precipitate of powerful emotional ties and painful experiences in his early youth. Investigations of this kind are not intended to explain an author's genius, but they show what motive forces aroused it and what material was offered to him by destiny.[9]

The implicit contrast here between the productions of the creative artist and, say, the dreamer, seems clear; in the case of the latter, psycho-analysis has more to offer than merely an accounting of materials and motive forces, since free association can help to unravel the "dream-work," that is, the operations by which the motives and materials of the dream are transformed into its manifest content, an interpretive effort to which nothing in psychoanalysis corresponds concerning the creative artist, Freud thought.

Finally, without implying that this short list is at all complete, an entirely different sort of self-imposed limitation should be noted in Freud's thinking about the unconscious, one whose implications need to be worked out in full. The importance of this limitation derives from its relevance, I shall argue, to the single most important criticism of psychoanalysis—namely, the charge that psychoanalytic claims consistently fail when subjected to experimental testing, and that this failure properly discredits them. It is this criticism and what I take to be the best answer to it that will occupy me in the rest of this chapter. The self-imposed limitation I have in mind is a distinction Freud made in the way he conceived of the contents of the unconscious. Briefly, the unconscious contents psychoanalysis is concerned with are unconscious *ideas and wishes* (including the unrepressed "[w]ishful impulses which have never passed beyond the id,"[10] according to Freud's metapsychology), in contrast with the unconscious contents cognitive science focuses on. What is unconscious, for Freud, or, less broadly, what gets repressed, are ideas and wishes, and the repression process itself (which is also unconscious), consists in a certain kind of wish, that is, the wish to forget. Thus, Freud writes: "In our discussion so far we have dealt with the repression of an instinctual representative, and by the latter we have understood an idea or group of ideas."[11] He goes on specifically to rule out the complete legitimacy of speaking of "unconscious instinctual impulses, emotions and feelings,"[12] after having written: "the essence of the process of repression lies, not in putting an end to, in annihilating, the idea which represents an instinct, but in preventing it from becoming conscious."[13] Concerning repression, Freud, and Breuer had earlier written of "things which the patient wished to forget, and therefore intentionally repressed from his conscious thought and inhibited and suppressed."[14]

WISHES AND DESIRES, IDEAS AND BELIEFS

To see what Freud's choice of words implies, we need to remind ourselves that wishes and ideas in nonpsychoanalytic discourse share peculiarities setting them apart from desires and beliefs. Thus, according to Aristotle, "wish can be for the impossible, e.g., immortality,"[15] whereas it would be strange to say of someone that he wanted or desired what he knew (or believed) to be impossible. The reason for this is that desires and beliefs are rather tightly tied to action, whereas ideas and wishes are not. Roughly, if one believes something is possible to achieve, and if one desires it, other things being equal, one can be expected to choose actions one believes are suited to produce the desired thing. So a large class of beliefs and desires can be inferred from nonverbal action and patterns of action, other things being equal. Hence, if someone knows or believes that bodily immortality is impossible, that person cannot try to get it for herself under any circumstances, and so she cannot be said to *desire* it. This aspect of "folk," or "commonsense" psychology explains Bolingbroke's choice of words toward the end of Shakespeare's *Richard the Second*; having forced King Richard to surrender the crown, Bolingbroke, the new king, says in the presence of Exton, "Have I no friend will rid me of this living fear?"[16] In the play, after Exton murders Richard on the assumption that that was what the new king wanted of him, Bolingbroke rebukes Exton, saying, "though I did wish him dead, I hate the murderer, love him murdered."[17] Bolingbroke cannot simply order Richard's execution without a trial, or legitimately seek his death, however much he might fear that the deposed and imprisoned Richard remains a threat.[18]

The distinction between wishes and desires illustrated here is mirrored in an analogous distinction between ideas and beliefs. Just as there are 'idle' wishes, which cannot be assumed to issue in action, precisely because the thing wished for is not really desired at all, there are also idle thoughts or ideas that we do not believe to be true, and so we cannot be made to act in pursuit of a desired thing on their basis. One clear example of such a combination of ideas and wishes can be found in the common experience of dreaming, but there are many others. Such phenomena have been of interest to philosophers for as long as philosophy has existed, and certainly for much longer than psychoanalysis has; thus Plato has Socrates, just before he dies, remind his friends of the phenomenon of recollection, which he uses to argue for the soul's immortality, by giving such examples of recollection as (1) seeing a musical instrument played in the past by a loved one and being reminded of the player; (2) seeing one member of a loving couple and being reminded of the other member; (3) seeing a picture of a person or thing and being reminded of what is depicted.[19] In each of these cases, the occurrence of some idea is causally explained by reference to something perceived; variants of this pattern would be cases in which the thought of one thing triggers the thought of another, and the thought or perception of one thing triggers the forgetting of another thing.

Wittgenstein discusses the following cases, which, like Plato's, are illustrations from ordinary language—

> "What is in my mind when I say so and so?" I write a sentence. One word isn't the one I need. I find the right word. "What is it I want to say? Oh yes, that is what I wanted." The answer in these cases is the one that satisfies you, e.g. someone says (as we often say in philosophy): I will tell you what is at the back of your mind: . . ."
> "Oh yes, quite so."
> The criterion for it being the one that was in your mind is that when I tell you, you agree.[20]

There are in addition a large number of different cases also suggested here; we can distinguish, for a start, (1) explaining what one is referring to in saying or thinking something, where one spoke ambiguously, or obscurely, or was misunderstood; (2) remembering with ease what one was going to say, and also trying to remember what one was going to say, and then remembering; (3) trying to decide which of several possible words best conveys what one wants to say, and not being able to think of any words to convey what one wants to say, and then thinking of one; (4) indicating what one intends or intended to do, or what one intends or intended in doing something. Wittgenstein's point about his earlier example, that the criterion for what "was in your mind is that when I tell you, you agree," can often be applied to the other cases, too, if we think of "agreement" as also including "self-ascription," and it also applies to Plato's examples as well; why this should be, and what it implies about psychoanalytic cases, remains to be seen.[21]

THE EXTENSION RELATION

There are no patterns of nonverbal action indicative of wishes and ideas (either individually or in combination), whereas there are such patterns for many desire-and-belief combinations. For this reason, there is a criterion problem concerning ideas and wishes, one mostly absent in the case of desires and beliefs; we cannot usually "read off" the ideas and wishes of others based on their nonverbal behavior alone, although there is a large class of desires and beliefs where this is possible. Our criterion for ascribing ideas and wishes to others seems to be twofold : (1) there is, first, the *self-ascription* of such mental states by subjects, as well as their *assent* to such ascriptions by others to themselves;[22] (2) However, the truth of such an assent or self-ascription can be defeated in a number of ways. At very least these include: (a) if such assent or self-ascription is shown to be a lie; (b) if the speaker shows defective or incomplete grasp of the specific words used, as in young children and nonnative speakers (who may, for example, show that the names of colors they use to describe items in reports of dreams are wrong by mis-naming the colors of objects while awake); or importantly, for our purposes, (c) if the speaker does not have the ability to ascribe desires and beliefs based on action correctly. None of these defeating conditions involves abandoning assent and self-ascription as criterion conditions, however. Rather, they tell us when we cannot tell what ideas or wishes the speaker refers to, precisely because, in those cases, the assent and self-ascription criterion can appear to be fulfilled, but are not really. In other words, (a), (b), and (c) do not involve introducing alternative criteria to (1); rather, they are situations in which the assent criterion is presupposed.

So there appears to be a hierarchy here of psychological and linguistic skills; only if one is able to ascribe desires and beliefs, on the basis of action (as well as on the basis of self- ascription and assent to such ascriptions), to others, as well as to oneself can one normally make credible ascriptions of ideas and wishes. A person who made plausible-seeming ascriptions of ideas and wishes, but whose ascriptions of desires and beliefs were all completely inept, would also be hard to credit in ascribing ideas and wishes. Such a person would be like someone out of whose mouth came words expressive of Goldbach's conjecture, say, but who could not count, add, subtract, or divide. We would know what the words he uttered meant, but we would not know what they meant *to him*. Indeed, we would not know how those words could mean anything at all to him.[23] For the same reason, we would not credit a person's self-ascriptions of ideas and wishes in the absence of any ability on their part to ascribe desires and beliefs to others or to themselves since there are no patterns of action by which to determine that the self-ascriptions of ideas and wishes are correct.

The hierarchy here is defined by an asymmetrical relation between two kinds of discourse; it rests on the fact that (1) it is possible for someone to have the ability to describe the beliefs and desires of themselves and others (where overt, i.e., nonverbal, actions are often dispositive), but not have the ability to describe their own and others' ideas and wishes; and (2) it is not possible for someone to possess the ability to ascribe ideas and wishes to themselves and others but be unable to name their own and others' beliefs and desires. More precisely, what strains credibility is that *we* could have a reason to credit the self-ascriptions of ideas and wishes by such a person.

Given these two conditions, the second kind of discourse can be thought of as an *extension* of the first, because of the dependence of the second on the first. The point of saying this is not to deny the logical possibility of someone able to say true things about the wishes and ideas of others, but who is unable, quite generally, given their actions, to name their own and others' desires and beliefs. However, it is doubtful that we would know what to make of such a person, and highly implausible that we would believe such a person's self-ascriptions of ideas and wishes were true.

EXPERIMENTAL UNTESTABILITY

If assent and self-ascription are the criterion condition for ascriptions of ideas and wishes, then a problem arises in trying to test such ascriptions experimentally. Experimentation, after all, introduces a new criterion of truth; for of course, if assent and self-ascription are retained as the criterion conditions for any claim to truth, then the experimental results—that is, whatever this new criterion indicates—can be trumped by what is assented to. Then not only is there no practical reason to conduct the experiment, but, more important, a genuine experiment is impossible. After all, a real experiment is one whose expected outcome can fail to be observed. So the task of proving that some claims in "commonsense psychology," that is, self-ascriptions of ideas and wishes, are experimentally untestable is, for our purposes, equivalent to the task of showing that the assent (and self-ascription) criterion for their truth is *inescapable*. A formal proof of this is not easily imagined, nor is there a way to tell if one is even possible; however, an examination of typical examples drawn from the ones already mentioned, in which the implications of each are worked out, can help to answer the question: is a genuine case possible in which the assent criterion has been abandoned, that is, is it ever possible to abandon the assent criterion for ascribing ideas and wishes without producing absurdity? Only if such a case can be found will we conclude that ideas and wishes can be determined to be present in a subject by experimental testing.

Dream reports are a good place to begin, although they have the complication, irrelevant for our purposes, that they necessarily involve memory. We are never in a position to compare dream reports with the dream itself, if there even is such a thing, unlike waking memories where objective evidence of what is remembered is possible, in principle. Suppose a dreamer writes down an account of a dream immediately on awaking, and then later that day narrates the dream to someone else. If the later version differs from the written one, which one is the "correct" version? Of course, neither report can be *mistaken* about what its version consists of, that is, as a report in the present of what the memory is; and if the two versions differ merely in that one, the earlier one, say, is fuller, more detailed, than the later one, the natural response is likely to be that that is the way dreams are—unstable, shifting things.[24] Such a case does not cast the assent criterion into doubt. However, our question is, could anything show that neither version is correct? That is, could anything show that the dream was really about completely different objects, actions, emotions, and persons than appear in any of the dreamer's (presumably truthful) dream reports? Could an experiment establish that our dreams, quite generally, are really about completely different things from what we dreamers think they are about, so that we are all always in error about the content of our dreams, and all of our dream reports are therefore always completely wrong? Such a possibility has to be taken seriously, if the assent criterion is to be replaced.

It is tempting to think that in principle, at least, brain physiology might advance to the point where dream contents could be "read" directly from observation of the brain. Our problem is, would assent then cease to be the criterion condition for the correctness of dream reports? And are the obstacles to developing such a technology entirely practical ones? If it were merely a practical problem, there are possible circumstances in which people would come to accept the new brain evidence and regard it as revealing their real dreams. This would be plausible if the brain evidence provided, from the dreamer's point of view, a much fuller version of the dream than even one the dreamer writes down and is initially satisfied with on awaking. In other words, if the brain research version is recognizably a "better," more interesting version of the same dream, the dreamer might come to welcome and value it. But this seems a not very relevant case, for, in it, the dreamer must assent to the interest of the brain version and must also assent to its being (a version of) the same dream. After all, a dreamer might regard the brain version as merely similar to, but different from what he continues to regard as his real dream, that is, the one he wrote down, or later recounted; all the brain version's additional detail, for example, might seem completely tacked on, alien to him. So, in such a case, assent as criterion of correctness for dream reports would not have been undone after all.

Perhaps what would be needed to illustrate genuine escape from the assent criterion would be a case in which people accepted the brain versions of other people's dreams as revealing the real dream, even when these did not seem to the dreamers themselves to be versions of the same dreams as the ones they remembered, and did not seem to them to be more interesting, or to cast any light at all on their own remembered dreams. But then what attitude could someone who sees other people's brain versions of dreams as those people's real dreams take toward her own dreams, and what attitude could such a person expect those others to take toward her dreams? Indeed, all meaningful connection between the remembered dream (even if reported in several versions) and the brain version would have been severed, so it is would be puzzling for dreamers even to accept the brain version as at all relevant to their remembered dreams. The case now appears to be indistinguishable from one in which a simple malfunction in the technology designed to enable direct "reading" of dreams from the brain has occurred. After all, something has to serve to indicate that the equipment is misreading a dream. If this doesn't indicate it, what does?

There are further changes that could be rung on this piece of science fiction; for example, suppose the brain version seems to the dreamer to have little relevance to the remembered *dream*, but rather seems to dreamers themselves to provide deep insight into their own *lives*. The brain version could not then be dismissed as merely the result of equipment failure, but might instead attain the status of a kind of religious revelation; even so, its relation to the dreamer's *dream* would still be obscure—why call that revelatory brain version a version of the subject's dream, at all? Once again, it seems, we have failed to produce a scenario illustrative of escape from the assent criterion, for of course it is still true here that the person whose brain it is assents to the revelatory quality of what the brain report tells. Without that assent, the case becomes indistinguishable from that of equipment failure.

There are two lessons to be drawn from this sequence of thought-experiments: first of all, it is clearly much harder to escape from the assent criterion for ideas and wishes than might at first have appeared; indeed, it seems to be impossible to do so in the case of dreams. Second, it looks as though the obstacle to experimental testing of the *general* correctness of dream reports is not a purely practical one, since it seems that nothing could reveal that such reports are generally erroneous.[25] There is, after all, no possibility of testing a statement *experimentally* if it is known to be incapable of being false before the experiment is even designed (perhaps such a statement can be tested, but not tested experimentally; we will have more to say about this later). Since it is impossible, apparently, for the reliability of dream reports quite generally to be subverted, experiments to determine whether reliance on such reports is warranted would not only be idle, they would be incoherent.

Analogous arguments are possible for the same sort of conclusion concerning other examples already mentioned; for example, in Plato's recollection cases, if we try to imagine experimental testing of the claim that people quite generally are right when they say that one thing, seen/heard/tasted etc. (label it X), reminded them of something else (Y), or that the thought of one thing made them think of another. For the proposal that in all such cases, it was really the perception or thought of something else entirely (W) that caused them to think of the second thing (Y) or that the perception of the first thing (X) really reminded them of something else entirely (Z) lead to similar absurdities as in the dream report cases, precisely because they involve suspension of the assent criterion. I do not mean to deny the possibility that, within the framework of the assent criterion, cases are possible in which people revise their belief that the thought or perception of one thing caused them to think of another. Such cases might be compared with the case mentioned earlier, in which the same dream is reported in different (remembered) versions.

However, if, instead of questioning whether the thing responsible for the resultant thought was the thought or perception of X (as claimed by the thinker), we raise the possibility, based on experiments, that the real cause might, in all cases, have been a brain process, we are back on terrain familiar from the preceding thought-experiments concerning dream reports, and analogous arguments can be applied. In this new case, how the brain process supposedly producing the resultant thought is to be identified as its real cause is crucial; if it is identified by way of the idea of X, that is, if it is assumed that the real cause will be whatever brain process coincides with (or immediately precedes) the occurrence of the thought or perception of X, the assent criterion seems still to be in place. For a case in which the assent criterion is genuinely suspended, we need one in which a brain process corresponding to the perception or thought of W (or to no perception or thought at all) is claimed to be the real cause of the thought of Y, even though the person whose brain it is claims that the perception or thought of X (not of W) caused the thought of Y (not of Z). Here, indeed, the assent criterion would have been set aside, but again, as in the dream cases, the relevance of such a brain process to the instance of being reminded of something is now problematic. What principle could have led to the selection of W as the correct brain process to be the cause of the thought of X, and how does such a case differ from one in which the technology for identifying brain processes as causes of thoughts has broken down?[26]

If we turn to Wittgenstein's example and the others suggested by it, the point seems even clearer. In saying (a) what word I need to express my thought, or (b) explaining what I am referring to in saying something, or (c) what I was going to say before I was interrupted, or before I forgot it, assent is normally the criterion, and supposing it suspended, as experimental testing of such claims requires, leads to ultra-paradoxical conclusions. That is, if such claims are to be tested experimentally, it must be possible to imagine that some or all people are generally wrong when they say these things, where the source of the "error" is not for example, defective grasp of language, as in children or non-native speakers. However, the supposition that in (b) we are all mistaken about what we are referring to when we say or think things, or that I am always so mistaken, leads to the self-destroying conclusion that I also do not know what I am referring to in proposing an *experiment* to *test* whether I do; referring has ceased to be a thing I am capable of doing. It will not do here to bring in philosophical disputes about what these things "really" consist in (or what *reference* itself really consists in), for such disputes operate within tightly constrained norms that allow only a few possible alternatives, where we are assumed to know what we are referring to, for example, but not to know what referring essentially consist in. Thus, "this grapefruit" is not a possible answer to the question, "what am I really referring to when I refer to an experiment, or to a test, or to myself?" (I ignore here the possibility of stipulating, as in a code, that that is what I am referring to.) Language itself becomes unworkable and thought becomes impossible if the assent criterion is bypassed in this way, as experimental testing would require.

Compound examples of (c) illustrate the point just as well as simple ones; thus, if I say in the midst of a conversation, "I suddenly realized where she must have hidden the long-sought document, and that made me forget what I was about to say," how might the separate claims involved here be tested experimentally? Such claims as (C_1) "the document I am referring to is the one we have all been looking for for the last three years"; (C_2), "just now, thinking of where the document must be has caused me to forget what I was about to say"; and (C_3), "what I was about to say before I was distracted was that I had realized only this morning her real reason for hiding it," are all instances of statement-types for which assent is the criterion, and which for that reason alone are incapable of being tested experimentally. Although it is possible to challenge or question such claims as implausible in various ways, or as lies, such challenges are not genuine suspensions of the assent criterion, since, when they are challenged, assent to some other claim by the person challenged is precisely what is sought; in any case, such assent is never irrelevant. (Comparable claims apply to cases of asserting what one intends to do, or what one intends in doing something.)

PSYCHOANALYTIC CASES

When we turn at last to the problem of psychoanalytic interpretation, it is pretty clear that we can directly apply to it the lessons already learned. First, if psychoanalytic interpretations are understood to be ascriptions of unconscious ideas and wishes, it is evident that, as such, they constitute an *extension* of that part of commonsense psychology in which ascriptions of conscious ideas and wishes occur; just as the latter comprises an extension, in commonsense psychology, of our language of desires and beliefs, psychoanalysis is, on this view, essentially an extension of the ascription of conscious ideas and wishes in the same sense, for precisely the same relationships between the two kinds of discourse are to be found. That is, a subject can have the ability to make ascriptions of conscious ideas and wishes while lacking the ability to ascribe unconscious ones, but could not intelligibly have the ability to ascribe unconscious ones while lacking the ability to ascribe conscious ones. As before, we would not know what self-ascriptions of unconscious ideas and wishes would mean to someone who lacked all ability to self-ascribe conscious ideas and wishes; we would not know what such ascriptions would mean to him, or even if they meant anything at all *to him*. Such inability to self-ascribe conscious ideas and wishes would be manifest if, for example, a person could not self-ascribe desires and beliefs in credible ways, or if their self-ascriptions of ideas and wishes were systematically internally inconsistent or incoherent or implausible.

It would be natural to infer, by analogy, that the assent criterion is also inescapable here, too; if the arguments presented above show that it is not possible to produce a genuine case in which conscious ideas and wishes can be ascribed without reference to the assent of the subject of the ascription, it is surely natural to suppose that the same is true in the case of ascriptions of unconscious ideas and wishes. In both cases, it should be emphasized, there are conditions or qualifications without which the claim that the assent criterion is inescapable becomes absurd. First, there are conditions under which assent can seem to be satisfied, but not really be satisfied, as in the case of the child and nonnative speaker. Then, too, we are not counting cases in which subjects change their accounts (as when multiple, successive dream-reports are given, in which one account is more detailed than another), as exceptions to the inescapability thesis. Last, especially in the case of psychoanalytic interpretations (but not only there), challenges based on the implausibility or inconsistency of what the subject has assented to may be made, without escaping, or even trying to escape, from the bounds of discourse created by the assent criterion. Such cases cannot be treated as exceptions to the universality of the assent criterion for ascriptions of ideas and wishes (conscious and unconscious) because all such cases presuppose that criterion's applicability.

But is there anything more than the analogy to support the claim that the assent criterion is inescapable for attributions of unconscious ideas and wishes? Isn't it conceivable that that criterion should be inescapable for attributions of conscious ideas and wishes, but be escapable for attributions of unconscious ones? Why should we assume that unconscious ideas and wishes are modeled on conscious ones in *this* regard, even if ascription of the former is an extension (in the sense defined) of ascription of the latter? These questions are not idle ones, since not many commentators have agreed that assent is the criterion for psychoanalytic interpretations; indeed, the dominant view among philosophers today is that *therapeutic success*, not assent, is the criterion Freud explicitly accepted,[27] and several have agreed to the rightness of that criterion, presumably because therapeutic success can plausibly be viewed as experimentally testable. Nevertheless, several of the arguments already presented for the claim that assent is the criterion for ascriptions of conscious ideas and wishes seem to be adaptable to the case of unconscious ideas and wishes.

Thus, suppose the assent criterion to be suspended so that people come to accept some new brain evidence, say, as revealing their own "real" unconscious ideas and wishes, ones utterly different from those they continue to ascribe to themselves, and *instead* of the unconscious ideas and wishes they continue to ascribe to themselves independent of such evidence. As before, their acceptance seems crucial, for without it, the supposedly real unconscious ideas and wishes have no claim to be labeled *their* ideas and wishes at all; even if they seem to shed more light on the lives of those whose ideas and wishes they are supposed to be than the ideas and wishes they ascribe to themselves, unless they are accepted as such by them, they cannot be ascribed to them. So then the assent criterion has not been suspended after all. Nor indeed, does there even seem to be any reason to label them "ideas" and "wishes" when not accepted as such by those to whom experimentation ascribes them. After all, there is plenty of light to be shed on human behavior from an experimental viewpoint, where the assent criterion has no force, but where the results of such experimentation are not thought of as revealing unconscious ideas and wishes of those experimented on. As before, it is unclear how the case in which such supposed unconscious ideas and wishes are ascribed to subjects who do not assent to them at all can be distinguished from the case in which the technology has failed, and the wrong unconscious ideas and wishes are ascribed to subjects.

After all, our starting point was that ideas and wishes lack regular behavior patterns connected to them in the way that desires and beliefs (in combination) have them; there are no truths of commonsense psychology or of psychoanalysis, to the effect, for example., that the presence of idea (I) and of wish (W) in someone can be expected to result in action (A), other things being equal. This is so whether conscious or unconscious ideas and wishes are considered. So it is prima facie difficult to see what experimental testing of ascriptions of (unconscious) ideas and wishes could even be about. Perhaps, it might be suggested, rather than some action resulting from the unconscious (I) and (W), certain conscious ideas and wishes might be expected to result; but then the criterion for the presence of those resulting ideas and wishes would be assent and self-ascription, as before.

FREUD AND THE CRITERION PROBLEM

As already noted, that assent is the criterion in attributions of unconscious ideas and wishes (i.e., in psychoanalytic interpretations) has been disputed; what Freud thought, and what he should have thought on this point, are both controversial matters. The evidence for seeing Freud as committed to criteria other than the assent criterion, for example, to the criterion of therapeutic success, consists in passages whose meaning does not really support that view, as I have explained elsewhere.[28] One passage recently enlisted in support of ascribing the success criterion to Freud[29] nicely illustrates the difficulties; Freud writes, in justifying the concept of the unconscious: "When . . . it turns out that the assumption of there being an unconscious enables us to construct a successful procedure by which we can exert an effective influence upon the course of conscious processes, this success will have given us an incontrovertible proof of the existence of what we have assumed."[30] However, the success referred to here cannot be assumed to be therapeutic success; it is more likely a reference to success in constructing a procedure by which conscious processes can be unconsciously influenced, as in posthypnotic suggestion, which Freud had explicitly relied on earlier to prove the existence of unconscious mental processes.[31] But there is no necessity that posthypnotic suggestion will be used for therapeutic purposes, or that, if so used, it will succeed, as Freud well knew. The "we" he refers to in the quoted passage should not be assumed to be psychoanalysts, but merely those interested in whether the concept of the unconscious can be justified, which includes many nonpsychoanalysts.

Freud's most extensive discussion of the criterion problem is his paper, "Constructions in Analysis,"[32] in which the lack of interest in therapeutic success as the criterion of interpretive truth is very evident. His acceptance of the assent criterion, however, is complex and nuanced; thus, he emphasizes that assent by the patient is not, by itself, enough for confirmation of an interpretation, or "construction;" it "has no value unless it is followed by indirect confirmations . . . which complete and extend the construction."[33] Indeed, Freud even considers the possibility that in some patients, the sign of a correct construction might be that "he [the patient] reacts to it with an unmistakable aggravation of his symptoms and of his general condition."[34] Further evidence there against ascribing acceptance of the therapeutic success criterion to Freud emerges in his remarks concerning the relation between delusion and historical truths; Freud writes:

> Often enough, when a neurotic is led by an anxiety-state to expect the occurrence of some terrible event, he is in fact merely under the influence of a repressed memory . . . that something which was at that time terrifying did really happen. I believe that we should gain a great deal of valuable knowledge from work of this kind upon psychotics even if it led to no therapeutic success.[35]

Perhaps the most obvious evidence of Freud's views on the question of the criterion is the overarching analogy on which much of "Constructions in Analysis" is based, namely, the comparison between the efforts of the psychoanalyst and those of the archaeologist,[36] where the analyst's efforts to reconstruct the psychic past "ought to end in the patient's recollection."[37] For the criterion of recollection is assent, however much that assent may be hedged round with qualifying conditions of plausibility; and of course, archaeology is not an experimental scientific inquiry at all, however much it may draw on experimental results from other disciplines.

In support of Freud on this point, it should be noted that the assent criterion, unlike the reliance on therapeutic success, makes it possible for interpretations to be true within the therapeutic context even when no therapeutic success is expected or is the result; and the assent criterion also makes it possible to search for examples of unconscious ideas and wishes outside the therapeutic context, which the success criterion does not seem to allow. Besides, examples relatively free of the suspicion of suggestion and placebo effects can more easily be found when no therapeutic outcome is even intended. Looked at in the framework of Freud's comparison between psychoanalysis and archeology, we might say that psychoanalytic interpretations are testable, that is, in ways similar to the ways in which archaeological and historical claims, quite generally, are tested. They can be shown to be true, that is they can be tested, but not experimentally tested. This is due, in part, to the fact that historical events are unique and not repeatable—we cannot repeat the deposition of Richard II, or the battle of Iwo Jima, so we cannot perform experiments on them. Even considered as members of classes (political/military insurrections, marine invasions), when non-experimental testing is possible on different members of such classes, the participants are biologically (e.g., genetically) unique entities—so it is not obfuscation to insist that unique aspects can be expected to set *this* insurrection, *that* invasion apart from all others. As Alan Greenspan once remarked, "Every business cycle is the same with the exception of some fundamental difference that characterizes that particular cycle and rarely, if ever, is in evidence in other cycles."[38] This is bound to be even more pertinently true when our inquiry concerns what someone's joke, dream, slip or symptom, for example, meant to that individual. When we want to know what it was like for this person on that occasion to do or say, or think or feel something, our inquiry can be expected to involve conscious and unconscious ideas and wishes, whatever else may need to be discussed.[39]

CRITIQUE OF THE EXTENSION RELATION

The theme of this chapter thus far has been the fundamental continuity between the psychology of ordinary life and that of psychoanalysis—it is that continuity that the extension theory with its emphasis on the basic symmetry between conscious and unconscious ideas and wishes was designed to reinforce and bring to the fore. From the viewpoint of that theory, the source of the difficulty about psychoanalytic interpretations is not, as has been widely supposed, that such interpretations ascribe *unconscious* mental processes to subjects; rather, the trouble arises from neglect of the "grammar" of ideas and wishes already to be found in the commonsense psychology of ordinary life, on which psychoanalysis depends for its sense—in particular, from neglect of the asymmetry in commonsense psychology between desires and beliefs, on the one hand, and ideas and wishes, on the other. That symmetry between conscious and unconscious ideas and wishes, and that asymmetry between desires and beliefs on the one hand, and ideas and wishes on the other, underlie and support the extension theory's claim to continuity between commonsense psychology and psychoanalysis, as well as the implication that I have drawn from it: namely, that psychoanalytic interpretations, when seen to be ascriptions of unconscious ideas and wishes, are not experimentally testable. In this regard, psychoanalysis can be seen as an extension of that part of commonsense psychology which is already not experimentally testable. Possibly, it is this important fact about commonsense psychology, namely, that many statement-types occurring naturally in it are

not experimentally testable, that has been crucially overlooked by critics of
the extension theory when they try to bring out a discontinuity between
commonsense psychology and psychoanalysis; since they tend not to devote
much attention to commonsense psychology as a subject of intrinsic interest,
such an oversight would not be surprising.

From the viewpoint argued for here, the "failure"of psychoanalytic
interpretations when experimental testing of them is attempted, that is, their
failure to be shown to be true by those means, is not at all what it appears
to be; rather, what is revealed by that failure is the inapplicability of experimental testing, with its intrinsic denial of the assent criterion, to the statements in question. Another way to bring this out would be to examine the
most fully developed critique to date of the extension theory—Edward Erwin's
rejection of it in *A Final Accounting*. It is important for Erwin to refute the
extension theory, since if it were to succeed, the failure of psychoanalytic
claims to gain support through experimental testing (which Erwin is confident
of having shown)[40] would not by itself warrant his negative final verdict on
psychoanalysis; there would still remain the possibility that psychoanalytic
claims are warranted in the same way, that is, without experimentation in
any scientific sense, as are our everyday psychological explanations, which
Erwin accepts.

Now Erwin holds that psychoanalytic interpretations are experimentally testable, and he also claims that many statements in commonsense
psychology are known to be true without having to be tested experimentally;
for example, in a case Erwin provides, we normally infer the desire for a
drink as the cause of someone's intentionally reaching a glass toward a tap.[41]
Here, according to Erwin, the "background information"[42] everyday life provides,[43] for example, "what people tell us about their intention, observations
of their subsequent behavior,"[44] makes this inference legitimate.

However, when Erwin agrees that [A] those explanations of
commonsense psychology are legitimately supported without experimental
testing, there is an ambiguity needing to be untangled. That agreement [A]
could mean that (1) although experimental testing is not needed, insofar as
the background information, empirical details, surrounding those claims allow the often obvious inference that the claims are true, nevertheless, such
claims *could* be tested experimentally, if necessary. But [A] could also mean
that (2) experimental testing of such claims is not only not needed, in
reality, such experimental testing is impossible. The difference between
(1) and (2) appears to arise from the way in which the background information is regarded. In (1) that information is conceived merely as a *proxy* for
experimental testing, if and when such testing is required, it replaces that
background information as the warrant. In (2), that background information
is not proxy for anything else, as is, that background information justifies the
claim independent of experimental testing, which, anyhow, (2) says is impossible. Obviously, (1) and (2) are contradictory claims, although they agree

that warranted inferences in commonsense psychology are not, in fact experimentally tested, and do not need to be; they only disagree about whether such claims are *capable* of being tested experimentally. The puzzle Erwin leaves unresolved, is whether he accepts (1) or (2). It is a remarkable fact about Erwin's book that although he treats psychoanalytic interpretations as both capable of being tested experimentally (since he assumes they have been so tested), and needing to be tested experimentally before they are warranted, he leaves the question undiscussed whether the comparable claims of commonsense psychology are *capable* of such testing, even though he is emphatic that those commonsense claims do not need experimental testing for them to be warranted.

If we suppose that Erwin subscribes to (1), that is, to the view that the main part of this chapter has been designed to refute, it is enough to refer to the arguments already provided above against it, and to note the curious absence of any discussion of the question in Erwin's book.[45] Considering how crucial to his critique of the extension theory the contrast is between commonsense psychology and psychoanalysis, neglecting even to see the need to argue in support of (1) seems careless, to say the least. In order for Erwin's project to succeed, (1) would seem to be a vital premise in need of proof.

If, instead, we suppose Erwin accepts (2), the result is equally troubling, since (2) is constitutive of the extension theory as presented here, a type of theory Erwin criticizes at length. It would be very strange for Erwin to adopt (2), since granting that claims in commonsense psychology can be warranted without even the possibility of their being tested experimentally should support the claim that psychoanalytic interpretations might also be free of defect even if they were to turn out to be incapable of being tested experimentally, as has already been argued here. The mere fact of being untestable experimentally, in itself, would then cease to be a defect. So if Erwin accepted (2), his whole argument against psychoanalysis and the extension theory would collapse.

Therefore, there is a dilemma here for Erwin's critique of the extension theory: neither (1) nor (2) are satisfactory choices—and there is no third choice. For without the assent criterion for distinguishing claims that are experimentally testable from those that are not, one is necessarily also without a criterion for distinguishing when a hypothesis has "failed" its experimental testing, that is, has been proved false by experimental testing, and when it is experimentally untestable. Erwin's dilemma is a sign of the conceptual vacuum created by the absence of the assent criterion—a vacuum in which one cannot tell the difference between real and apparent experiments and between the failure of an experimentally testable hypothesis, that is, its experimentally proven falsehood, and the experimental untestability of a hypothesis, which encompasses truths as well as falsehoods. Abandoning the assent criterion for ascriptions of ideas and wishes, in commonsense psychology as well as in psychoanalytic interpretations, has the consequence that when this is done, it is then in principle impossible to distinguish [T] experimentally testable propositions that are false, from [U] propositions that are experimentally untestable, whether true or false. Without the assent criterion, supporters of experimental testing for such propositions face a conceptual problem, that is, not one merely about the correct *application* of a non-problematic concept of the sort involved, for example, in classifying whales as fish. The point is that supporters of experimental testing for ascriptions of ideas and wishes face an apparently insoluble problem—how, apart from the assent criterion, to distinguish [T] from [U]? And, of course, if [T] and [U] are not distinguishable from one another without the assent criterion, within [U], the true and the false will also not be distinguishable. So the dismal score psychoanalytic interpretations have to report when (supposedly) subjected to experimental testing is not properly viewed as proof of their falsehood—after all, the same would then have to be said about the comparable experimentally unestable truths of commonsense psychology. Rather, that low score should be seen as good evidence in their case for the ultimate inescapability of the assent criterion.

NOTES

1. P. Kitcher, *Freud's Dream: A Complete Interdisciplinary Science of Mind* (Cambridge: MIT Press, 1992).

2. L. Stevenson, *Seven Theories of Human Nature*, 2nd ed. (New York: Oxford University Press, 1987). chap. 6.

3. G. Santas, *Plato and Freud: Two Theories of Human Nature* (London: Blackwell, 1988), ix.

4. "On the History of the Psycho-Analytic Movement," *Standard Edition*, vol. 14, 50.

5. "A Short Account of Psycho-Analysis," *Standard Edition*, vol. 19, 209.

6. Ibid.

7. R. Waelder, *Basic Theory of Psychoanalysis* (New York: Schocken Books, 1964), 56.

8. "Dostoevsky and Parricide," *Standard Edition*, vol. 21, 177.

9. "Preface to Marie Bonaparte's *The Life and Works of Edgar Allan Poe: A Psycho-Analytic Interpretation*," *Standard Edition*, vol. 22, 254.

10. *Standard Edition*, vol. 22, 74.

11. "Repression," *Standard Edition*, vol. 14, 152.

12. "The Unconscious," *Standard Edition*, vol. 14, 177.

13. Ibid., p. 166.

14. *Studies on Hysteria, Standard Edition*, vol. 2, 10. For the evidence in support of the claim that repression is itself an unconscious process, see the editor's footnote, ibid. On repressed wishes, see also pp. 302–304. On the meaning and evolution of the repression concept in Freud's thought, see M. H. Erdelyi, *Psychoanalysis: Freud's Cognitive Psychology* (New York: W. H. Freeman and Company, 1985), chap. 5.

15. *Nicomachean Ethics*, book 3, chapter 2, 1111b23.

16. Act V: scene 4.

17. Act V: scene 6.

18. Perhaps Shakespeare means to show Bolingbroke duping Exton into committing the murder without himself having to take responsibility for ordering the deed. However, even if that is what Shakespeare meant to suggest, the point about "wishing" remains intact; compare *Richard the Third*, Act IV: scene 2.

19. *Phaedo*, 73d2–74a1.

20. Wittgenstein, *Lectures and Conversations*, 18. In a note, Rush Rhees reports, as a variant reading of the first quoted sentence, "What people really want to say is so and so." Wittgenstein's response to psychoanalysis, on which much of this chapter is based, is examined in chapter one of D. Levy, *Freud Among the Philosophers: The Psychoanalytic Unconscious and Its Philosophical Critics* (New Haven: Yale University Press, 1996).

21. For the purposes of this chapter, several of Wittgenstein's ideas have been drawn together in a way he never did; so it would be a mistake to treat this discussion as a guide to Wittgenstein's thinking, although it also does not distort it, as far as I am aware. See *Philosophical Investigations*, I, 633–693, and N. Malcolm, "Knowledge of Other Minds," in Malcolm, *Knowledge and Certainty* (Englewood Cliffs, NJ: Prentice-Hall, 1963), 130–140.

22. From now on, "assent criterion," or some near relative of that locution, will mean both assent and self-ascription criterion whenever convenient.

23. We would, of course, also not know how he could have acquired the ability to perform as he does.

24. We will save for later the kind of case exemplified by the quote from *The Book of Daniel* at the start of this chapter, in which the king has forgotten his dream and demands to be told what it was before he will trust the interpreter's account of its meaning.

25. Asserting that dream reports are in general inerrant is consistent with, e.g., dreamers changing their minds about which version of a dream is the best one, since assent remains the criterion; for "general inerrancy " to be false, the assent criterion would have to be displaced.

26. Nothing said here rules out the possibility that some brain process, one corresponding to no thought or perception, causes the thought or perception of X to remind one of Y. Such a claim does not involve replacing the assent criterion. The point here is not to discredit brain research, but to ascertain the role of the assent criterion in it.

27. The most important statement of this view can be found in A. Grunbaum's *The Foundations of Psychoanalysis: A Philosophical Critique* (Berkeley: University of California Press, 1984); I have discussed and criticized his view in *Freud Among the Philosophers*. Support for Grunbaum's view can also be found in E. Erwin, *A Final Accounting: Philosophical and Empirical Issues in Freudian Psychology* (Cambridge: MIT Press, 1996), and in G. Rey, "Unconscious Mental States," *Routledge Encyclopedia of Philosophy*, general editor, E. Craig (London: Routledge, 1998), vol. 9, 523. I have reviewed Erwin's book in *Mind*, vol. 110, No. 439 (July 2001), 740–746.

28. See D. Levy, *Freud Among the Philosophers*, chapter 4, and the Afterword and Appendix.

29. By G. Rey, "Unconscious Mental States," 523.

30. "The Unconscious," *Standard Edition*, vol. 14, 167.

31. "A Note on the Unconscious in Psycho-Analysis," *Standard Edition*, vol. 12, 255–266. I have questioned the success of Freud's proof in *Freud Among the Philosophers*, chap. 2.

32. *Standard Edition*, vol. 23, 255–269.

33. Ibid., 262.

34. Ibid., 265.

35. Ibid., 268.

36. Ibid., 258–260.

37. Ibid., 265.

38. *Newsweek*, November 22, 2000: 59.

39. Cross-cultural studies in anthropology of aspects of psychoanalytic theory (e.g., of the Oedipus complex, by J. W. M. Whiting, R. Kluckhohn and A. Anthony, "The Function of Male Initiation Ceremonies at Puberty," in E. E. Maccoby, T. Newcomb, and E. A. Hartley, eds., *Readings in Social Psychology* (New York: Holt, 1958); W. N. Stephens, *The Oedipus Complex* (New York: Free Press of Glencoe, 1962); and M. E. Spiro, *Oedipus in the Trobriands* (Chicago: University of Chicago Press, 1982) should not be assumed to be equivalent to the experimental testing of a psychoanalytic interpretation. Only if a society were an individual or exactly like one, would that equivalence succeed. But there is nothing that can easily be identified as a society's wishes and ideas, and *assent* and *therapeutic success* are hard (though not impossible) to apply to a society. Relating such cross-cultural studies to psychoanalytic interpretations, without assimilating the two, is a task awaiting completion.

40. E. Erwin, *A Final Accounting*, 296.

41. Ibid., 28.

42. Ibid., 26–27.

43. That is, "empirical evidence of a nonexperimental kind," ibid., 28; cf. 107.

44. Ibid., 28.

45. Erwin discusses extension theories on pages 106–124; cf. 27–28.

CONTRIBUTORS

MARCIA CAVELL is Visiting Professor in philosophy at the University of California, Berkeley. She is a training candidate at the San Francisco Psychoanalytic Institute, and a former graduate of the Research Program at the Columbia Psychoanalytic Institute for Training and Research. She is an editorial consultant for *The International Journal of Psycho-Analysis*, and an academic associate of the American Psychoanalytic Association. She is the author of numerous publications on psychoanalysis and philosophy including, *The Psychoanalytic Mind: From Freud to Philosophy*. She received her doctorate in philosophy from Harvard University.

JAMES C. EDWARDS is Professor of Philosophy at Furman University. He earned his B.A. in English and religion from Furman, his M.A. in philosophy from the University of Chicago, and his Ph.D. from the University of North Carolina, Chapel Hill. Professor Edwards continued postdoctoral training at Cornell, Princeton, and Berkeley, was a visiting scholar at the C. G. Jung Institute in Zurich, and a Fellow of the American Council of Learned Societies in Vienna. He has published extensively in many areas of analytic philosophy and ethics. His most recent book, *The Plain Sense of Things: The Fate of Religion in an Age of Normal Nihilism*, won the John Findlay Prize awarded by the Metaphysical Society of America.

ROGER FRIE is Adjunct Professor of clinical psychiatry at St. Luke's-Roosevelt Hospital Center, Columbia University College of Physicians and Surgeons, and a Clinic Fellow at the William Alanson White Institute of Psychiatry, Psychoanalysis, and Psychology in New York. He received his Ph.D. in phenomenological psychology, psychoanalytic theory, and philosophy from Trinity College, Cambridge University, and his Psy.D. in clinical psychology from George Washington University. He has taught in the fields of psychology, psychoanalysis, and philosophy at The New School, Harvard, and Northeastern Universities. He has written widely about the interface between psychology, psychoanalysis, and philosophy and is author of *Subjectivity and Intersubjectivity in Modern Philosophy and Psychoanalysis* and editor of *Understanding Experience: Psychotherapy and Postmodernism*.

ADOLF GRÜNBAUM is the Andrew Mellon Professor of Philosophy of Science, Research Professor of Psychiatry, and Chairman of the Center for Philosophy of Science at the University of Pittsburgh. As one of the most internationally recognized philosophers of psychoanalysis, Professor Grünbaum has published several books including *The Foundations of Psychoanalysis: A Philosophical Critique*, and *Validation in the Clinical Theory of Psychoanalysis: A Study in the Philosophy of Psychoanalysis*. Among his many accomplishments, he was president of the American Philosophical Association and the Philosophy of Science Association, and delivered the Gifford Lectures in Scotland. He is the recipient of the Senior U.S. Scientist Humboldt Prize, and of Italy's Fregene Prize for science.

DONALD LEVY is Professor of Philosophy at Brooklyn College, City University of New York. He earned his B.A. and Ph.D. in philosophy from Cornell University. Professor Levy has published widely in the areas of analytic philosophy and psychoanalysis and is the author of *Freud Among the Philosophers: The Psychoanalytic Unconscious and Its Philosophical Critics*.

JOSEPH MARGOLIS is Laura H. Carnell Professor of Philosophy at Temple University. Earning his Ph.D. in philosophy from Columbia University, Professor Margolis is also the recipient of an honorary doctorate from the University of Helsinki. He has written extensively on the philosophy of psychology, medicine, and psychiatry and is the author of thirty books including *Psychotherapy and Morality*, *Values and Conduct*, *Knowledge and Existence*, *Persons and Minds*, and the *Philosophy of Psychology*. For several years he was Senior Research Associate in Psychiatry at the University of Cincinnati, and served as Special Fellow for the National Institute of Mental Health. Among his many research and teaching awards including grants from the Rockefeller Foundation and the Fulbright Commission. He also serves as a consultant on multiple editor boards including *The Monist*, *American Philosophical Quarterly*, *Philosophy, Psychiatry, and Psychology*, *International Journal of Applied Philosophy*, *Metaphilosophy*, and the *Journal of Value Inquiry*.

JON MILLS is a psychologist and philosopher in private practice in Ajax, Ontario. He received his Ph.D. in philosophy from Vanderbilt University, his Psy.D. in clinical psychology from the Illinois School of Professional Psychology, Chicago, and was a Fulbright scholar of philosophy at the University of Toronto and York University. He is currently Chairperson of the Section on

Psychoanalysis of the Canadian Psychological Association and on Senior Faculty at the Adler School of Professional Psychology in Toronto. He is also Editor of Contemporary Psychoanalytic Studies and the Value Inquiry Book Series in Philosophy and Psychology, and is on the Editorial Board of the journal *Psychoanalytic Psychology*. He is the author and/or editor of six books including most recently *The Unconscious Abyss: Hegel's Anticipation of Psychoanalysis*, and *When God Wept*, an existential novel.

DAVID LIVINGSTONE SMITH received his Ph.D. from the University of London. For many years he directed the graduate program in Psychotherapy and Counselling at Regent's College, London where he was also interim Academic Dean. Dr. Smith is the author of *Freud's Philosophy of the Unconscious*, *Approaching Psychoanalysis*, and *Hidden Conversations*, as well as many book chapters and articles on psychoanalysis, psychotherapy, the philosophy of mind, and evolutionary psychology. In addition to his academic activities, Dr. Smith is also a qualified psychotherapist. He is presently Professor in the Department of Social and Behavioral Sciences and Director of the New England Institute for Cognitive Science, Evolutionary Psychology, and Psychotherapy at the University of New England. His current research focus is on the evolution of unconscious social cognition and communication, the history of psychology, and Freud's philosophy of mind.

M. GUY THOMPSON is founder and Director of Free Association, Inc., in San Francisco, and is on the faculties of the California School of Professional Psychology, Berkeley, and the Psychoanalytic Institute of Northern California, San Francisco. He received his Ph.D. in clinical psychology from the Wright Institute, Berkeley, and his psychoanalytic training at the Philadelphia Association in London. Dr. Thompson is on the editorial boards of *Psychoanalytic Psychology* and the *Journal of Phenomenological Psychology*, and is past president of the International Federation for Psychoanalytic Education. Among his numerous publications on psychoanalysis, phenomenology, and schizophrenia include *The Death of Desire: A Study in Psychopathology*, *The Truth About Freud's Technique: The Encounter with the Real*, and *The Ethic of Honesty: The Fundamental Rule of Psychoanalysis*.

INDEX